TOBY SANDERS

Compleat Clown

Illustrated by David Schure
and the author

15173

STEIN AND DAY/*Publishers*/New York

First published in 1978
Copyright © 1978 by Toby Sanders
All rights reserved
Designed by Ed Kaplin
Printed in the United States of America
Stein and Day/*Publishers*/Scarborough House,
Briarcliff Manor, N.Y. 10510

Library of Congress Cataloging in Publication Data

Sanders, Toby.
    How to be a compleat clown.

  Bibliography: p. 259
  Index: p. 267
  1. Clowns.   1. Title.
GV1828.S36   791.3′3   78-7520
ISBN 0-8128-2508-X

To Anna, who never saw me clown,
and
Sunnee, who put up with all this
nonsense

ACKNOWLEDGMENTS

I would like to thank the following people for their invaluable assistance in collecting and preparing the material for this book:

Marvin Kaye, for his advice on preparing the manuscript; Tom Ogden, for permitting the use of his treatise on audiences; Ron Edenfield, for assisting with the research; Burt Sikorsky, for helping to locate sources of information; Circus World, for their gracious cooperation; Alan Klem, for his assistance in planning the illustrations; Derren Getz, for devising an alternative paper tear for the chapter on magic; Charlotte Grim, Saralee Kaye, Betsy Hollinger, Elaine Douthett, and the other typists, who worked their fingers to the bone; and Kitty Lawerance, for helping me become a starving young writer in New York City. If anyone was forgotten, I offer my deepest apologies.

Contents

x · CONTENTS

Preface

A book about clowns must be a strange amalgam because clowns themselves happen to be unlikely blends of many diverse elements. A single clown *is* Everyman in that he reflects the failings and foibles of every one of us. He is also Parzival in that he *is* the eternal fool. He possesses the innocence that all of us wish we had. He is a child. He is a state of mind.

To capture the essence of the clown, the feeling of fun, this book was written in the voice of a clown describing his craft. Therefore, it contains a number of grammatical anomalies.

1. Occasionally, a word is misspelled to heighten a pun that might be missed in print or to set up a play on words.

2. Miscoined words are used to bring the reader back to earth after a fanciful flight through necessary passages dealing with the philosophy of performing.

3. A number of compound and hyphenated words have been separated to stress their individual meanings and sometimes play off a previous word or phrase.

4. A few trite phrases and clichés have been hyphenated or compounded so that they appear foolish visibly.

5. Most of the text has been punctuated as if it were a script to establish the tone and rhythm of presentation.

6. Words and phrases that might seem non sequitur have been included to lure the reader into thinking like a clown and make sure that he never takes any of this too seriously.

7. Grammar is occasionally bent to fit the clown's peculiar way of looking at the world.

In short, this book intentionally avoids a few conventions in order to avoid becoming another pretentious volume on humor, comedy, and everything else that makes people laugh. As a result, it should be read with a broad sense of humor. The reader will find some passages funny and others silly, but he should always remember that the quips *he* laughs about might not even amuse his neighbors. Humor is funny like that.

For the rest, my only advice is to think like a clown.

Toby Sanders
New York, 1978

How to Be a Compleat Clown

Introduction

Tent 327, the Camel Lodge of the Loyal Mahars of Eliazar, has decided to include a clown in the entertainment at its Annual Combined Lay Them Low Charity Bazaar, Barbecue, and Family Field Trip. Since the treasurer has reported that the coffers of the lodge have been all but depleted by last year's Christmas party, the thirty-five-dollar fee asked by the professional clown they have already contacted is out of the question. Therefore, the High Gen declares that the clown should come from its own ranks. Joe Jones, a new member who is out of town on a business trip, is unanimously elected. When he returns, he is informed of his singular honor.

What should he do?

First, he knows that every clown wears colorful makeup, so he destroys his wife's vanity drawer looking for makeup to use. He ends up with a small plastic container of blue eye shadow and some red lipstick. He finds nothing that will make his face white in the manner of clowns he has seen at the circus.

Next, he trundles off to the attic to find a costume. All clowns wear funny clothes, and the costume he put together last Halloween was a riot. After two hours of digging through trunks, he assembles a pair of white ice cream pants, an orange and puce sports jacket his kids got him for Christmas three years before, and a very wide tie. The tie is handpainted with a hula girl who has the words "Atlantic City '58" embroidered around her navel.

Now that he has a costume and some makeup, he is still in a quandary. He has no idea how to entertain the people at the get-together. Clowns tell jokes, and everybody seemed to enjoy the ones he told at the New Year's party, but clowns do other things, too. He slumps into a chair and pages through a newspaper while he thinks. At page 37, he freezes. There, near the edge at the top, is a one-inch advertisement that reads:

Gag yourself to popularity
Hrafnkel's Joke and Novelty Shop

Jumping into his car, he drives twenty miles to visit Hrafnkel and pick up a few laugh getters. His trip nets him a dozen plastic ice cubes containing one fly each, several pounds of presliced rubber cheese to slip into sandwiches, a bag of balloons, a few packs of spiced gum, three whoopee cushions (that Hrafnkel threw in on the side), and a sundry collection of other horrors.

He was prepared.

How did his performance go over?

Next year, the lodge made sure to schedule the annual function during Joe's summer vacation. Then, with their coffers as low as the year before, they called back the professional clown they had originally contacted and offered him fifty dollars to do the show.

I accepted.

What did Joe do right?

He picked up the newspaper and bought a bag of balloons.

Had Joe thought for a moment, he would have junked his purchased jokes in favor of the newspaper. It would have provided him not only with a ready source of humor but also with material to construct better gags than Hrafnkel could ever sell him. More people are offended by practical jokes than pleased with them. However, to be honest, he did not need to joke around at all. The balloons would have been an ample source of amusement for the entire length of his performance.

His costume might have been passable, with the exception of the tie, but his choice of makeup could cause him no end of trouble. Lipstick stains the skin, and so does some eye shadow. Joe would have to spend a week or more after his performance waiting for the shadowy shape of a foolish grin to wear off his face. His only failing as a clown was that he did not know the range of materials, equipment, and skills available to him.

Most people are like Joe. They believe that all one must do to become a clown is splash some colorful grease paint on the face and put on some old clothes. They have no notion of the centuries of development that have refined the art of the clown.

The clown is not simply a painted face and a colorful costume that moves clumsily in parody of the human being. He is a mirror that reflects the faults and foibles of the world around him. Yet most of the literature on the subject deals only with the superficial, outward manifestations of the clown and not with the manner in which these characteristics are attained.

How to Be a Compleat Clown attempts to rectify this situation. It describes the physical skills and abilities necessary to the work of the clown and suggests how these may be used effectively. It is aimed at all jesters, amateur and professional. Makeup, costuming, acrobatics, puppetry, ventriloquism, balloon sculpture, juggling, slapstick, working with animals, music, drama, and magic are all arts in themselves, but when a clown uses them, they become part of his higher art.

The art of the clown comprises a diversity of elements. The clown must be a dramatist, a musician, a dancer, an acrobat, a juggler, and a wit. He must be adept at using the skills of makeup and costuming to caricature or parody. He must have imagination, an understanding of human nature, and a sense of both comedy and tragedy. He must be able to use surprise, anticipation, and pathos tempered with timing to make his slapstick work. Unfortunately, the modern clown often neglects the skills that would permit him to make a meaningful humorous statement about his condition in relation to his world. He needs all of these skills and abilities simply to cope with life and make people laugh.

Laughter is a necessity. It is a tool to cope with existence. It temporarily transports the audience away from the problems of daily life. The futility of a clown attempting to douse a fire with a bucket full of holes is laugh provoking because everyone watching has faced problems with which they were ill equipped to cope. In laughing at the predicaments of the clown, audiences laugh at the difficulties they have faced again and again. Like Atlas, the clown carries the burdens of the world on his shoulders—but makes them light with laughter.

1

The Clown Through History

"Quit clowning around."
"Don't talk to him, he's a clown."
"Ah, don't worry, they're just clowns."
"You're a real clown."

Nobody likes to be called a clown because it is a word usually associated with fools. In fact, the first clown *was* a fool, but that does not mean that he was foolish. On the contrary, he generally possessed rare intelligence, and his humor was directed at royalty.

The fool or jester served as a conscience to the king. Jibing, cajoling, and sometimes berating the king, the jester used humor as a leveling force to give perspective to all the king's decisions. Shakespeare presents an excellent example of the jester's craft in *King Lear*. King Lear has just divided his kingdom between two of his daughters and banished the third. When he is alone, his fool engages him in conversation;

FOOL: Sirrah, I'll teach thee a speech.
LEAR: Do.
FOOL: Markit, nuncle.

> Have more than thou showest,
> Speak less than thou knowest,
> Lend less than thou owest,
> Ride more than thou goest,
> Learn more than thou trowest,
> Leave thy drink and thy whore,
> And keep in-a-door,

And thou shalt have more
Than two tens to a score.

The Fool describes the philosophy that has made him a skillful jester and counsels King Lear to embrace that philosophy. He tells Lear to his face that nothing is ever gained by stopping an endeavor too soon right after Lear has quit being king. This is wise advice from a man supposed a fool to a fool supposed a sage.

FOOL: ... Can you make use of nothing, nuncle?

LEAR: Why, no, boy. Nothing can be made of nothing.

FOOL (to Kent): Prithee tell him, so much the rent of his land comes to; he will not believe a fool.

LEAR: A bitter fool.

FOOL: Dost thou know the difference, my boy, between a bitter fool and a sweet one?

LEAR: No, lad; teach me.

FOOL: That lord that counselled thee
        to give away thy land,
    Come place him here by me—
        Do thou for him stand.
    The sweet and bitter fool
        will presently appear;
    The one in motley here,
        The other found out there.

LEAR: Dost thou call me a fool, boy?

FOOL: All thy other titles thou hast given away: that thou wast born with.

Openly, the Fool equates Lear with himself, and the king does nothing in retribution.

The Fool walks away unpunished after criticizing a man who has banished his own daughter for the same criticism. Lear ignored his fool's advice.

Unlike Lear, other rulers attended their fools and used them as sounding boards of the surrounding court. The political tenor of any situation in the court or the outside world could be reflected in a subtle wisecrack or a well-placed pun. Posing as an idiot (protected by God), the fool or jester was given full reign to speak his mind on subjects of foreign policy, the political maneuvering of ambitious courtesans, and the king's shortcomings. Such topics would have spelled death to anyone foolish enough to discuss them within earshot of an intemperate ruler. Lear's fool calls Lear a fool, yet Lear takes no action. There is no need since Lear's detractor is only a fool: a mere clown.

The clown remained a fool until the sixteenth century and the rise of the Italian street theater, the *commedia dell'arte*. The *commedia dell'arte* was a popular form of entertainment that utilized stock comedic characters and improvisatorial scenarios. It changed the clown's form from that of a bungler to that of a trickster. One *commedia* character was a clown in his own right: his popularity spread all over Europe: his name was Harlequin.

Harlequin was a clown quite different from the jester. He was invested with a few magical properties. He was invisible to everyone, but his sweetheart, Columbine. Columbine, in turn, was invisible to everyone but Harlequin. Their love affair was constantly punctuated with lighthearted pranks that continually landed Harlequin in trouble. Harlequin's main purpose in life was to cause the pranks of other clowns to fail. Dressed in a colorful checked costume with a white ruff and wearing a black mask, Harlequin entertained his audiences with his audacious, wasteful use of power. He was as indefatigable as Puck. His fanciful nature is best depicted in this scene in which he explains to a doctor how he came to go to the moon:

THE DOCTOR: How did you manage to reach the moon?

HARLEQUIN: Well, it was like this. I had arranged with three friends to go to Vaugirard to eat a goose. I was deputed to buy the goose. I went to the valley of misery, made my purchase, and set out for the place of our rendezvous. When I had arrived in the plain of Vaugirard six famished vultures appeared, seized my goose, and tried to make off with it. But I held on to its neck for dear life, and the vultures carried us both away. When we had gone rather high a new regiment of vultures came to help the others. They threw themselves upon us, and in a moment neither the goose nor I could see the peaks of the highest mountains. . . . I fell into a lake. Fortunately some fishermen had stretched their nets there, and I fell into them. The fishermen pulled me out of the water, and, taking me for a fish of some consequence, loaded me on to their shoulders and carried me as a present to the Emperor.

During this passage, Harlequin goes to extraordinary lengths to explain physically what is being described in words. He struggles to carry the heavy goose to Vaugirard. He rises on his toes when the vultures grab the goose and carry it skyward. He creates the physical illusion of flight. Unswervingly, he weaves a web that leads the other characters in the play inevitably toward a prank or pun.

Harlequin was established as the epitome of the prankster and as such became popular all over Europe and dominated the Christmas pantomimes in England and France. None of the other characters who grew from Harlequin's exuberant personality ever lived up to the original. Such *commedia* figures as Truffaldino, Gauzzeto, Zaccagnino, and Bagatino drifted into obscurity, but Harlequin survived and became identified with the clown.

But there were other characters of the *commedia dell'arte* who contributed significantly to the evolving image of the clown. For instance, Brighella, *commedia dell'arte's* answer to gallows humor, was a despicable character typified by an olive-colored mask. He was comic only because his atrocities were always overblown. He would not kill a single man—if he could kill a married one.

More important than Brighella was Pantaloon, the old fool. He watched his wallet carefully and gladly lived in poverty to guard his wealth from being spent. His baggy pants and brilliant illogic can be seen in the costumes and characters of the clowns of today. He became the prototype for a number of characters in the comedies of Molière, especially *The Miser*.

Pedrolino, the sensitive youth, gave way to Pierrot. Originally a creation of Debrau, a highly respected comedian during the time of Baudelaire, Pierrot could play a variety of roles. Pierrot was very close to the modern conception of the clown. He was the first clown to wear makeup. His garb, consisting of a baggy shirt and pants and sporting oversized buttons, resembled the clown costumes of modern times. Also, Pierrot was represented as crying on the inside while laughing on the outside. Pierrot, in later years, was the prototype for the broken-hearted clown of the opera *I Pagliacci*.

The most influential single figure in the *commedia dell'arte* pertaining to the clown is that of Pulcinella. Pulcinella (a quick, fawning, witty, silly, impertinent, timid, ironical, self-sufficient, cruel, and boastful fellow) gave birth to Punch of Punch and Judy and an autonomous character usually referred to as Clown. Clown was initially a minor character who acted as a foil for Harlequin. He was generally portrayed as a country rustic possessing a great amount of naïveté. He had red hair and a ruddy face and wore the clothes of a servant. In 1802, his costume changed. Charles Dibdin the Younger constructed a number of extravagant costumes for the two clowns performing at Sadler's Wells. One of the clowns was a young man by the name of Joseph Grimaldi. Using the costumes as a starting point, Grimaldi developed the character of Clown until he dominated the stage, eclipsing even Harlequin. Joseph Grimaldi was so successful in establishing the character of Clown that even today circus clowns are referred to as Joeys in his honor.

The makeup and costume of Clown became increasingly fantastic after Grimaldi's time as other clowns improved and refined the absurd character. Eventually, three distinct types of clowns evolved: the Auguste, the Grotesque, and the Character. Each of these three has a character and a specific function.

The Auguste clown deals mainly in slapstick humor. His white face is painted with bright colors, usually red and blue. He wears no specific costume and can appear in anything from a one-piece outfit to an exaggerated suit of tails. The function of the Auguste clown is similar to that of Harlequin. The Auguste usually springs on other clowns and hits them over the head with a slapstick or other noisemaking objects. His intent is not to destroy the prank of another clown but to demonstrate that the one he hits is nothing more than a clown. He adds a touch of harsh reality to the bumblings of the other pranksters. Yet he is not cruel when he hits them. He does not intend to hurt. He simply wants to topple the foolishness of his fellows.

The Grotesque clown is pompous, foolish, and, at times, at a loss to cope with the world. His makeup is typified by a large red mouth and a bulbous rubber nose. His clothing is outlandish. Usually, he pads his stomach to appear grotesquely fat. He carries grotesquely large objects like huge lollipops or oversized cigars. He is a buffoon and the brunt of the Auguste's slapstick. Everything he attempts to do ends in futility. Therefore, he is always grotesque.

The Character clown is a modern innovation, typified by the tramp clown. The clothes the Character wears are contemporary but ill fitting and tattered. His face sports a painted beard and is traditionally sad. He is a born loser. When anything goes right for him, he looks for the black lining in the silver cloud. He knows before he even attempts to accomplish some action that his efforts are doomed to failure.

The Character has also been used as a catchall category for women clowns, who are usually of two types: Sadie Hawkins and Exaggerated. The Sadie Hawkins clown is a hillbilly with freckles, braided hair, and an old-fashioned gingham dress. She resembles the clown of Joseph Grimaldi's time. The Exaggerated female is a cruel parody of womanly endowments: exaggerated breasts and buttocks combined with a grotesque wiggle. Neither of these characters are very endearing creatures, but they epitomize the treatment of womankind in the history of the clown.

During the time that the clown was evolving, women played a very minor role. Some clowns, like Harlequin and Pierrot, had sweethearts, but they were treated as mere conveniences by their male counterparts. Women did not actually participate in the clowning art until 1858. That year, Nixon and Kemp Circus took on Amelia Butler as a clown. A newspaper reporter records her performance with a show of what he must have considered an open-minded attitude: "She takes well and tumbles about as much as if she was a bona fide." Why the reporter did not consider her fully "bona fide" is anyone's guess. If she could "take" and "tumble," she was in better shape than most contemporary male clowns, who can do neither of these well.

The reporter's attitude is still rampant in contemporary circus circles. Annie Fratellini, the twenty-fifth member of her family to don the white face and motley and the only professional female clown in Europe, found a rather cool reception when she followed her father's footsteps. "Circus people didn't believe that a woman could take pratfalls, get slapped and kicked, and be ridiculous." This is a surprising attitude because the long-held chauvinistic view of womankind has been that women are "ridiculous," flighty creatures who should be "slapped and kicked" if they move out of their predestined domain, the kitchen.

The only understandable part of the disbelief expressed by Miss Fratellini's peers is that a woman can take pratfalls. Western women have always been taught that they must be graceful. If they fall, they must fall daintily. This extends to every movement the woman is expected to make. Hence, in sports, running like a woman, tossing a ball like a woman, and falling like a woman have all come to represent the wrong way to run, toss a ball, or fall. In fact, if a tumbler were to consistently fall like a woman, that tumbler should expect a long career of sprains and breaks because the way a woman is expected to fall is the most dangerous way to fall. It is considered dainty only because the movements involved possess a milquetoast, insipid quality. No wonder Miss Fratellini's circus people viewed her with disbelief. She fell correctly.

In America, this attitude is as prevalent as it is in Europe. Women clowns are usually cast strictly in feminine roles. They are given far less latitude in playing different characters than men. Ringling Brothers and Barnum & Bailey Circus trains many women at their clown college in Florida, yet they carry only a token number of women on their show. None of these female clowns have ever been given a featured spot.

To be fair to Ringling Brothers, this can also be said of many of the men trained at their school. William Ballantine, dean of the clown college, has gone on record that this show hires Americans to serve as clowns and show girls only so they can import major acts from foreign countries. Allen J. Bloom, senior vice president and director of promotion and sales for the Ringling Corporation, refused to make any comment about the clown school or the percentage of graduates hired by that circus.

The clowns who graduate from the college are generally well versed in a number of circus techniques: juggling, unicycle riding and the like. This enables them to function in the ring with versatility. They are being trained to be competent performers.

Gale Lajoye, director of clowns at Circus World in Haines City, Florida, and a former instructor at the clown college, states that focusing the instruction of the clown on these techniques and skills permits him to perform to the full extent of his abilities. This attitude is shared by Paul Binder, director of the New York School for Circus Arts. According to Mr. Binder, "Our concept of the clown is that after intensive circus training and after working twelve hours a day and sleeping with the angels at night, you might learn to become a clown." To this, Mr. Lajoye would add experience in arts and skills outside the circus field. With such a potential outlet for American talent, one wonders why Ringling bothers to scour Europe for future acts. Their own school could provide them with acts tailor-made to fit their show. Perhaps they think ability is less important than a foreign-sounding name.

Nevertheless, the waiting list of applicants for the Ringling clown college is very long. So the modern American clown is fortunate that instruction is available from other schools. As a symbol of Everyman, the clown has sparked a number of universities to offer courses in this art. New York University and the State University of New York have been the most active schools in offering the clown as a course of study. The contemporary clown is no longer merely the conscience of a king but has become the conscience of a whole society.

Humor

The clown is not just another comedian. Throughout his performances, he should endeavor to transport his audiences through a host of emotions that include sadness as well as joy. Laughter, for the clown, is only a cathartic device that can be used to bring his audiences back to reality after he has led them to the realization of some truth or brought them to an understanding of themselves. Nevertheless, critics insist on viewing the clown exclusively as a figure of comedy.

These same critics, however, shy away from defining comedy itself. They insist that if a joke is taken apart for analysis, its humor is lost. This is true, but only if the joke remains dissembled. Once put back together, the joke should be as funny as it was before. If it is not, then it most probably was a bad joke. Scholars, after carefully analyzing historical references and translating syntax, would be unable to find a single comedy in the literature of ancient Greece if this were not so. Yet the student can occasionally find his professor chuckling over a centuries old punch line while rereading Aristophanes. What the critics seem to forget is that humor is predicated on understanding. This knowledge sparked Freud to refer to humor as rebellious because understanding is always at odds with the dictatorial and the bigoted. People who refuse to understand never laugh. They prefer to remain self-satisfied with their own misconception and are angered by any attempt to illuminate their folly. Their self-satisfaction is probably what started the rumor that ignorance is bliss.

The rebelliousness to which Freud refers is part and parcel of the clown because to the Merry Andrew nothing is sacred. He looks at his world through glasses of crystal clarity and reflects what he sees through a distorted mirror. His audiences are made to understand the absurdity of their condition and accept it because the clown has made it funny.

What, then, is funny?

Anything that makes people laugh.

And what makes people laugh?

This question has plagued psychologists for years. According to Freud, man laughs when he is released from his inhibitions. For Y. C. Gregory, laughter is an expression of superiority. Henri Bergson believed that people laugh at the dichotomy inherent between the machine of the body and the spirit of the mind. To Max Eastman, a person laughs when in a state of "fun" to deal with the brutality of existence. And Abraham Maslow considers laughter the result of a primary psychological process. Each new thinker on the subject advocates the validity of his own pet theory to the exclusion of all others. Of the above thinkers, the only exception to this rule is Freud, who had the good fortune to die before this controversy started.

Do any of these theories come close to defining humor?

Yes. All of them. An inhibited id will cause laughter just as easily as a man slipping on a banana peel.

Each theorist has latched on to one single aspect of the laughable and refuses to let go. Something as complex as laughter cannot be restricted to one cause. After all, laughter itself, although one word, does not represent one effect. Laughter can be kindly or cruel or joyful or relieved. It is used to signal discovery as well as diversion. To restrict it to a single cause is to ignore its many effects.

In *Insight and Outlook* and, again, in *The Act of Creation*, Arthur Koestler develops a theory of creativity that seems capable of including all of the variant ideas expounded by the many psychologists and philosophers who have tried to define the subject of laughter. Besides including humor in the creative process, Koestler's theory could be a practical device to be used by the clown to understand the lighter side of his art. He hypothesizes two unrelated fields of thought that bisociate or intersect spontaneously. The diverse ideas that come together at the point of intersection can be the basis of invention, art, or laughter. When laughter is produced, it will arise no matter if the fields are brought together by any of the prevailing theories mentioned above. Bypassing the factor of spontaneity, the clown should be able to use this concept to establish his own intersecting fields of thought and create his own comedy. To check the validity of this theory, the clown only has to apply it to the forms of comedy available to him and discover how well it works with each form.

Robert Orben in *Comedy Technique* lists 28 forms of comedy, by far the longest list of any writer on the subject. Therefore, these are the forms discussed below. Two changes have been made to update Orben's list. "Mispronunciation" has been replaced by "Misuse of Language," and "Super Comedy" by "Heckler Stoppers," which should never be used on an audience by any performer because they alienate the audience more than they create laughter. Even comedians like the master of venom, Don Rickles, do not use heckler stoppers. They heckle the audience instead.

COMIC FORMS

Ad-libs The art of speaking off the top of one's head has been popularized by such contemporary performers as Steve Allen, Carl Reiner, and Mel Brooks. However, ad-libs have always been with the clown. Jesters such as Triboulet, Will Somers, and Richard Tarleton used extemporaneous humor to bedevil and thwart their detractors and rivals at court. Dan Rice, an early American clown who was the forerunner of Will Rogers, was infamous for his caustic, irreverent wit. The secret behind this kind of comedy is in being able to make quick connections between something said or done and an inappropriate or unexpected response. In this case, the action that sparks the ad-lib is represented by one bisociative field, and the response comes from the intersection of this field by another. To facilitate this process, many contemporary clowns keep joke files, or collections of gags. These are memorized so that when a situation arises, the clown can respond to it with an appropriate remark. However, most audiences can distinguish between a true ad-lib and a piece of material pulled from a dusty file. Collecting humor is no substitute for rich experience. The well-read clown will always be better off then the collector.

Catch Phrases Certain words and phrases have an effect on an audience all their own. When placed into a routine, they can help to hold an audience's attention or punch up the comedy. Most modern catch phrases are taken from commercials. For example, in "Swallowing the Balloon," which is described later in the book, the clown apparently swallows a long, thin, inflated balloon. When he has finished his rubbery meal, the announcer can come in with, "I don't believe he ate the whole thing." In this case, the announcer is giving voice to what the audience is thinking, but he is taking his words from a source totally unrelated to the event that has taken place. The resulting bisociation links the unexpected commercial tag line to the actions of the clown. The clown will also find that catch phrases will arise from the character he uses in performance. Jack Benny could bring down a house just by saying, "Well!" Jimmy Walker accomplishes the same thing today with his, "Dyn-o-mite!" And television audiences wait patiently for Arnold Horshack on "Welcome Back Kotter" to break into his characteristic laugh. When character catch phrases are used, the bisociative fields come from what the audience expects the performer to do and the performer giving it to them unexpectedly.

Characterization The character of the clown will be discussed in greater detail in the next chapter. However, here it should be noted that comedy derived from the character can be a devastating and very original. The way the clown uses the objects around him and deals with his *compadres* in comedy are derived completely from his character. The original Fratellini brothers capitalized on this aspect of the clown in their act. Paul Fratellini portrays a seedy bourgeois character, François was the man-about-town, and Albert was the innocent dope. The characters of these clowns supplied the various fields that would intersect when two or more of the characters were brought together.

Comic Quirks The humor of this form always lies in the ability of the performer to do something uniquely his own: a noise, a face, or unconscious automatic movement. The quirk is funny only if it is inappropriate to a situation; otherwise, it is just annoying. Therefore, if the clown possesses a natural quirk he must be able to control it. For this form, the quirk is one field and the situation the other. When brought together in the person of someone like Don Knotts, whose erratic nervousness always seems to keep him in trouble, an audience cannot help but laugh. In his best-known sketch, the infamous clown John Ducrow, dines with two horses bedecked in wigs and napkins. Mr. Ducrow cracked his jokes amidst this bizarre scene while stirring his tea inappropriately with his big toe.

Definitions The twisted definition produces laughter due completely to the unexpected transfer of an audience's attention from one field of thought to another. The second field must always be noticeably derived from the first, and, above all, the definition must work. If the audience does not see the connection between the definition and the word defined, they will remain silent.

Dialogue Humor An example used by Freud in his *Jokes and Their Relation to the Unconscious* readily illustrates this form:

At a spa, a man was going to the bathhouse to relax. Just outside, he met a friend who was leaving the building.

> MAN: Ah, I see you've taken a bath.
> FRIEND: (*Bewildered*) No. Is there one missing?

Here the fields are derived from the point of view of the characters involved. The man in the joke is operating on one train of thought while his friend operates on another. The lack of communication that takes place when these trains collide produces the comedy. Another classic example of this form can be found in Abbott and Costello's "Who's on First." Poor Costello is unable to get away from the definition of "who" as a pronoun. Abbott, on the other hand, knows exactly what he is talking about when he refers to the baseball player Who. Even after these two divergent definitions collide, Abbott remains unable to explain who Who might be and Costello never finds out who is Who.

Impressions A distinction should be made here between mimics and impressionists. A mimic like Rich Little imitates the voice and movement of a personality. The impressionist latches on to one quality and caricatures a personality. For example, Chevy Chase on "Saturday Night Live" gave an impression of ex-President Gerald Ford by falling over. He capitalized on the clumsiness of the personality, which was overblown by the newspapers. An audience laughs at this because they have a mental conception of the personality. The performer prepares them for the impression by telling them who he will caricature to give them time to visualize the person in their minds. Then he wrecks the audience's conception by giving them the personality's least-common characteristic. Thus, he establishes two fields, one for the audience and one for himself.

Interruptions This clown will find this form of comedy suitable when he wages a running war with the announcer. Unexpectedly, he runs in and fires a line at the announcer, who answers or questions the clown, only to be hit with a bit of absurdity.

Walk-around bits like "The Baby Rattler" or "Chicken Dinner" can be used for this. The announcer helps the clown set up a train of thought in the audience that is exploded when the clown reveals his alternate point of view. Thups, two fields are established with the help of the announcer and intersected by the clown.

Lectures This is a dying form of the clown's art, but it need not be. The fields involved are simple to establish. Every audience member has had to sit through a lecture, so when they are informed that a lecture will take place, they will automatically remember the lectures of days gone by. The comparison of this remembrance with the actual lecture they receive produces their laughter. Such is the case in "The Safety Lecture":

The clown enters, carrying an inflatable floatation device. This can be either a life jacket like those on some cruise ships or a full-size life raft. For the purposes of this script, the life raft will be used.

ANNOUNCER: Ladies and Gentlemen, as most of you know, it is raining outside. The management is, therefore, required by law to acquaint you with the safety devices available for your use should the building sink. I will be assisted in this lecture by (name of clown). *(The clown waves at the audience. He is proud to serve.)* First, a floatation device is located at intervals under the seats. *(A few dummies will actually look.)* They look like the one in front of (name of clown). *(The clown points to the bundle before him.)* These are self inflating and are automatically filled by pulling the red string. *(The clown pulls the red string. This will have to be attached by the performer and is there so the audience can see the activating mechanism.)* But it should not be pulled until the device is thrown over the side.

(The clown realizes his error and, in an effort to save the day, tries to pick up the inflating raft and carry it to the exit. He fails and ends up under the filled device in exhaustion.)

Letters An almost outmoded form of comedy, the letter can still be used to good effect by the clown in a running battle with the announcer. The clown runs in with a piece of mail from a friend and proceeds to bedevil the announcer with a gossipy spoof on some city or resort. A review by a local newspaper praising the announcer in a left-hand manner may also be used. The difference, again, between what the audience expects and what they get are where the fields of humor lie.

Limericks   A traditional piece of comic fun, the limerick, like the poem discussed later on, uses the meter and rhyme of the form to establish a field of thought in the audience. This is exploded by the ringing in of a totally different field at the last moment with the last line. Limericks can be used by the clown as snappy retorts or in a battle with the announcer. The clown should be careful, however, never to use a limerick with risqué intent. The popular conception of the clown is that of a good-natured, wholesome fool. Any deviation from this conception might cause an audience to balk in horror. This goes to show that when two fields intersect, laughter is not the only thing that can be produced. The clown must be aware of this and construct his comedy with taste.

Misuse of Language   The day of the malapropism and mispronouncing buffoon are long gone. Even spoonerisms are only tolerated if made accidentally. However, the clown can still misuse language to his heart's content. Edwin Newman has shown the way. In his book *Strictly Speaking* and later in *A Civil Tongue,* he capably illustrates how the modern bureacracy has distorted and complicated the language used by modern man. Every member of the clown's audience accepts this misuse, and so one field is established. When the clown points out the misuse to them by the overuse of such verbiage, he establishes a second field to bisociate with the first.

One Liners   This form of comedy is really a very short joke. In one sentence, the clown sets up a field of thought in his audience and causes it to explode by ringing in another. It is the type of comedy used by Henny Youngman and Bob Hope. Unlike his stand-up counterparts, the clown relates each one liner to the action he is performing or the object he is handling. The form is a way for him to comment on his world. Each one liner is delivered as if he were talking to himself. One great clown, W. C. Fields, used this method constantly to the delight of his audiences, and the clown may duplicate this success every time, whether he assumes the role of policeman, dentist, or magician.

Pantomime   Unlike the mime, the pantomimist uses objects in his performance. He also eschews stylized movements in favor of exaggerated realistic ones. The result is a dumb show that requires the audience to think. The clown leads them on with movement alone until they think they know what he is getting at. In effect, they try to guess what field the clown is creating. The clown then shatters their guesswork by revealing the real field.

Parodies Any takeoff that pokes fun at a sacred cow is a parody. Fortunately for the clown, contemporary society is so full of sacred cows that no single performer could hope to milk them all. The audience's field in this case is already set. Each member should be familiar with the sacred cow displayed. The clown need only bring in his distorted version to reveal the second field and produce the laughter. In short, he offers his audience sacred sirloin but gives them sacred chuck.

Poems Like the limerick, the poem leads the audience through a field of thought with rhyme and rhythm only to mislead them in the end with an alternate field. Unlike the limerick, however, poems tend to be long. This would seem to make their use difficult for the clown since few contemporary audiences will sit still for a recitation. The clown may get around this by having himself and a partner trapped by the meter and rhyme and unable to stop the flow of the poem. In other words, they can't stop rhyming. This happens occasionally in real life and lends an air of spontaneity to the clown show if handled well.

Puns Basically, a field is established by the common definition of a word that contains an alternate field or definition. The audience recognizes one definition and is immediately hit with the other.

Record Acts A clown may choose to use either a group of his fellows or members of his audience to perform this act. The only two pieces of equipment that are required are a record player and a record. When the record is played, each member of the group moves his lips to match the recorded words. The incongruity produced by intersecting the appearance of the person moving his lips and the sound on the record provide fields that produce the laughter.

Running Gags Many performers harbor the misconception that the running gag is merely a repetition of a funny bit. This is not so. Once a joke has been told, only a bore would repeat the punch line over and over. The running gag is set up by establishing a field in one particular circumstance and then intersecting it with a number of various other fields, one at a time. With each new intersection, a new piece of comedy is produced. The humor is derived from recognition of the first field when applied to a new one. Repetition has nothing to do with it.

Situation Comedy This form establishes a familiar situation easily identified by the audience and adds the clown whose distinctive character makes him inappropriate to the set of circumstances. The clown's actions are determined by the small line of intersection created by these two fields. Like the trains of thought referred to earlier, the clown and situation meet head on.

Slapstick By far the hardest form of comedy to carry off, slapstick relies on the subtlety of fields of movement. For example, in *One Good Turn* Laurel and Hardy sit down for a well-earned meal. Ollie asks Stan, who is reading a paper, to pour him a cup of coffee. At that point, his cup sits directly in front of him. He then initiates a field of movememt by picking up his cup and holding it toward Stan. At the same moment, Stan has begun a field of movement only appropriate if the cup had remained where it was. The cup and coffeepot pass each other over the center of the table, and the coffee is poured. Since the cup is no longer there, the coffee lands in Hardy's lap. If the timing is right and the movements natural, the audience will not see what is coming until it is too late.

Song Titles Playing on the audience's familiarity with popular songs, the clown makes unexpected alterations in the title of a song. When he presents this to the audience, he substitutes a new field for the expected one to fool the audience. Song titles can be an invaluable tool to comment on the actions of a fellow clown. In a few words, the clown is able to suggest whole ideas and attitudes to his audience.

Statistics Newspapers are full of statistics, and as with most abstractions, these statistics can be made to prove anything. Most members of the audience, however, have to be taught to respect these abstractions. This respect establishes a field that can be used by the clown when he offers statistics from his point of view. Thus, the audience reacts to the equation 3×3 within the framework of their learned field of experience. They can only laugh when the clown introduces a field in which $3 \times 3 = 10$ or 11. (See "plates" in Chapter 8.)

Stories The storyteller combines a series of fields that run between reality and fantasy to produce smiles and laughter. Harlequin's description of his trip to the moon in Chapter 1 is an excellent example of this. Throughout his tale, he leads his audience to believe that he is in one field when he actually is in another.

In using this form, the clown should be wary not to commit the faults often stumbled over by amateur storytellers. He should always be sure of the end of his tale; otherwise, the story will be pointless and far from funny. All of the facts of the story should be firmly in his mind so that he need not correct himself continually as he works his way along. If the story does not need an introduction, the clown should not give it one, or he will sacrifice the force of the story by dragging it out. Never should the clown ask, "Have you heard this before?" If the clown does his job properly, he will get a laugh whether the story has been heard or not. Finally, every story should be presented in its logical sequence. The logic or illogic of a story is usually what makes it funny. To wreck the logic is to blow the joke.

Super Comedy Like the ad-lib, this form relies on the clown's being able to think on his feet. This time, however, the clown's work is done for him. Two fields bisociate by themselves to produce laughter. This cannot be planned—it just happens. When it does, the clown should have the presence of mind to go along with it. Some performers ruin the moment by becoming angry that the act is not going as written. This is a foolish attitude since one job of the clown is to create humor. Felix Adler once had no choice in going along with such an incident. Playing the big bad wolf, he delighted his audiences by being chased by three trained pigs. During one performance he was knocked unconscious. The pigs, disturbed by the break in routine, began to nudge Adler's inert body. The illusion presented to the audience was one of the pigs eating the wolf. They howled with laughter, but Adler was never able to duplicate the stunt.

Time Gags This form transverses the boundaries of the other forms and refers to the amount of time an audience takes to perceive a joke. The fields that intersect are so closely related that the audience has to consider for a moment whether a joke was made at all.

Tongue Twister These tangled monstrosities can provide the clown with a good alliterative punch line and, as such, are produced when two fields combine, a field of situation and the field of language. A situation builds to a breaking point and is resolved when the tongue-tied clown twists out the impossible punch, making the provoking prankster's practiced prattle a punny portion of prodigious pastiche.

Topical Lines This form seems related to the ad-lib, but the relation stops at the point of preparation. Topical lines can be written ahead of time and bear a closer relationship to the one liner. The intersecting fields are formulated in the same manner. What distinguishes this form from the others is the type of material used. It uses only current material and is therefore a short-lived form.

These 28 forms of comedy should give the clown some idea of the range of material available to him. All he need do is choose a form and write down whatever comes to mind.

ON WRITING COMEDY

When writing comedy, the clown must begin by choosing a topic. To this subject, he will apply the elements of comedy either singly or in pairs. These elements are the unexpected, the irrelevant, the anachronistic, the ambiguous, and the incongruous. If several topics are used, he can create laughter using the elements of juxtaposition and contradiction.

But how is the clown to decide on a topic?

That depends on how ambitious he is because any topic is potentially humorous. The better topics are ones that the audience will find interesting. This will vary from audience to audience. Taking a look at a local paper will give the clown some idea of the type of material to use. The immediacy of the topic also plays a part in the eventual choice. Few audiences like to hear old news. For example, these days Watergate jokes are out; jokes about the current president are in.

Three criteria that will aid the clown to judge the potential of his material are originality, relevance, and economy. Originality in this case refers to the unexpectedness of his material. If his audience can see the direction he is heading, they will arrive before he does, and he will lose a laugh.

Relevance refers to the ease with which the audience can identify with or even recognize the subject matter. If the audience is unfamiliar with the references made in the joke, they will not laugh. A clown who takes jabs at a current president will receive more laughs than one who spoofs Warren Harding. Likewise, if the audience does not identify with the material or identifies with it too closely, the clown will play to a silent house. Ethnic jokes receive little response from an unbiased child, and if the clown tells a Polish joke to a Pole, that is what he might be sitting on.

The last criterion of humor is economy. When asked to construct a comedy sketch, most people do not know when to stop. The clown must be careful not to say too much, for the greater part of laughter comes from the audience's ability to fill in the unstated portions of the joke. In effect, the clown is helping his audience arrive at his comedic view of a situation or state. He cannot do this by flatly telling his audience his intention. Instead, he must lead them along and allow them to arrive on their own. Thus, the audience is as important to the success of the clown's comedy as is the clown himself.

Once a topic has been chosen and a particular comic element applied to it, the clown can pick a form to fit in. And yet he may still not have a piece of comedy. To get the joke across, he may need to establish a conflict or, if more than one clown is used, orchestrate the dialogue and movement. The transition from one field to the other must be strengthened and the timing and rhythm of the presentation honed to a fine edge.

If the clown finds all of this beyond him, then he should stick with stock pieces. At no time should he steal the routine of another clown or comedian. If he borrows an idea and is able to make it his own, that is one thing. But too many amateur clowns lift material verbatim from professional acts and present it as their own. This does neither the professional or amateur any good. The lifted material is usually presented poorly and serves only to give away the punch line or blow off.

LOGIC

Fallacy is the logic of comedy. The clown's reasoning always seems impeccable until the last moment, when he tumbles the structure of his thought. Therefore, familiarity with the 13 fallacies of relevance and 5 fallacies of ambiguity should help the clown both to construct his comedy and to think quickly—to ad-lib.

Appeal to Force "Might makes right" is a fallacy that has plagued mankind throughout history. It is used by the bullying egotist to assert his authority over his fellow clowns until his weak position is toppled and he is cut down to size.

Appeal through Abuse An outright attack on a man's character is never proof that what he says is right or wrong. A statement may be true even if the speaker is a mere dolt of a clown.

Appeal to Circumstances   If the clown has gotten his costume dirty, he should not stand in the shower fully clothed simply because the running water will wash his suit. His circumstances do not validate the action. The classic example of this is the hunter who justifies his sport because the farmer who criticizes him is guilty of butchering harmless cattle.

Argument from Ignorance   "Ghosts do exist because no one can prove that they don't." This bit of illogic is tailor-made for the clown because it will always take the audience a moment to realize that the reasoning used is false. This fallacy is valid in one special instance: a man is innocent until proven guilty.

Appeal to Pity   In this case, pity is used inappropriately to force the acceptance of some conclusion. It is illustrated by the case of a boy arrested for the crime of murdering both of his parents with an axe. He asked the court for mercy because he was an orphan.

Appeal to the People   This is rabble-rousing at its best. To prove a point to his fellow performers, the clown blatantly whips the audience into a fervor to agree with him, thereby proving his case. This is used by one clown to prove his honesty in the "Boxing" sketch later in the book.

Appeal to Authority   Illustrations of this fallacy can be found by turning on a television and looking at a few commercials. It capitalizes on the respect shown to the famous. By its use, the clown dentist can persuade all his clients to permit him to remove every one of their teeth on the grounds that George Washington wore wooden ones.

Accident   What is generally true might not be true in a particular case. For example, in the three plate routine described later, three multiplied by three equals nine unless the circumstance set up by the clown exists. Then it equals 10 or 11.

Hasty Generalization   Many people make this fallacy when they take twice the amount of a prescribed medication because they believe it will help them to get well twice as fast. Not so for them but maybe for a clown.

False Cause   This fallacy assumes that one thing caused another simply because it happened first. Such is the case in the use of the radio utilized in Chapter 8.

Begging the Question   In this case, the premise is the same as the conclusion. A clown holding a skunk keeps telling his audience that he knows the difference between a cat and a skunk because he knows what a skunk looks like. He has in effect said the same thing twice.

Complex Question   "Have you stopped beating your wife?" Need more be said?

Irrelevant Conclusion   Clown work is rife with this last fallacy of relevance. Simply, it entails reaching a conclusion by arriving at a different conclusion. This is done by Bulwinkle on "The Rocky and Bulwinkle Show" when he says he likes violence because they smell so nice. By confusing one single word, he has confused the conclusion.

Equivocation   The first fallacy of ambiguity involves using or misusing the literal meaning of words. This also can involve punning. It is best expressed when the clown constructs the following syllogism:

> Some times are good.
> I'm having a good time.
> Therefore, I'm having *some* time.

Amphiboly   The Delphic oracle would be hard pressed for prediction if this fallacy did not exist. It is ambiguity plain and simple. A contemporary version of this fallacy can be found in the conservation posters of World War II that urged people to "Save Soap and Waste Paper." The clown uses this fallacy when he drags out walk-around bits like "The Baby Rattler," The Best Seat in the House," and "The Chicken Dinner."

Accent   The innovative clown can construct a comedy routine by simply buying a newspaper. Real headlines can sometimes be deceiving and never fail to grab everyone's attention. Newsmen occasionally stress some words and de-emphasize others. Take, for example, the efforts of the editor of a small-town paper when he tacked the following headline to an article about the appearance of a comedian. In bold letters, he wrote:

THOUSANDS DIE

Beneath this, in very small type, he amended:

laughing!

Composition   This fallacy can best be used by the clown who is moving. He chooses the pieces of property he packs with care and places all of the lightweight pieces in the same trunk. When he is ready to leave, he discovers that he cannot lift the trunk. He cannot understand this. After all, he put only light objects in it. What he fails to realize is that the combined weight of the light objects is close to a ton. He has reasoned incorrectly from particular premises to reach the wrong generality. This fallacy is also useful in dealing with abstract concepts because it encompasses the confusion of using general terms. Thus, although a business insists that its 250 employees can take only one paid vacation a year, it can be said that its employees take 250 paid vacations a year.

Division Reverse the fallacy of composition and there is the fallacy of division. It is arguing from a general premise to reach the wrong specific conclusion. For example, take the following syllogism:

Hawks are an endangered species.
That senator is a hawk.
Therefore, that senator is an endangered species.

Thus armed with comic forms, comic elements, and comic logic, the clown is ready to create some comedy. But being so armed will not help him unless he has a way to present the comedy. That is what the clown's character provides.

3

Character

The consensus among professional comedians seems to be that character is important; and for the clown, it is especially important. In fact, it is very nearly the whole ball of wax. The clown's character is his central core. Without it, he has no basis for movement, appearance, speech, reaction, or emotion. Also, his audiences will have a difficult time relating to him and the things he does, for the character acts as a focus for the audience's attention. They must be able to identify with the figure in front of them and can do so only by recognizing the weaknesses and failings they see in him.

A good number of clowns, amateur and professional, have neglected this aspect. These performers seem to believe that as clowns they need not act any differently than they normally act. One such performer sports exceptional makeup and an excellent costume. He looks every inch a clown. However, when confronting an audience, he is at a loss. He says little. With no character, he has nothing to say and no way to relate to his audience. He is rarely funny. The use of any character could help this clown funnel his energies toward a goal and give him something to say. Without it, he is like a rowboat cut adrift. He can only float along hoping that something funny will happen to him.

How does a clown establish a character?

The clown's character is his nature: those essential qualities that make up the clown's personal pattern of behavior. To find these qualities, the clown must cut through the artificial characteristics imposed on him by society. Otherwise, he will merely imitate the qualities of society reflected in him and so be reflecting a reflection. The clown must look into himself. There he will find the necessary qualities to develop a character uniquely his own. He chooses any personal frailty or weakness with which he feels comfortable and at which he can laugh.

Only one or two of these shortcomings are required to establish the character of the clown. This will allow him to adapt easily to any situation. He need simply apply his character trait to a given situation to arrive at the reaction appropriate to his character. Since he does not have to concern himself with a number of interwoven traits, he will easily be able to perceive the reaction suitable to himself.

Unlike his audience, the clown does not draw his responses from the full range of emotions but from a selection of one or two.

This narrowness of character gives him a cartoonlike quality and prevents him from coping with any given situation. Thus, he is supplied with a built-in conflict that can be used whenever he desires. A look at a few character types will point this up clearly.

CHARACTER TYPES

Bureaucrat Definitely a company person, this clown's view of the world is restricted to the unspoken rules and regulations that crop up in any society. By confining himself to this narrow point of view, this clown exempts himself from thought or feeling. He does not have to consider how his actions affect his fellows because he always acts "properly." The blind spots that are established by this character serve only to point up the absurdity of his position.

The bureaucrat was ably portrayed by Footit in the "Railroad" sketch that he and his partner Chocolat made popular. Footit, the conductor, passes a number of passengers onto the train. To the first-class ticket holder, he shows great respect. The second-class passenger, however, gets bullied to his seat. Only Chocolat remains outside the train with a third-class ticket, uncertain what will happen when the conductor returns. The conductor discovers that the unfortunate Chocolat holds a third-class pass and kicks him and beats him to a seat. The conductor is angered because, besides being black, Chocolat is a third-class passenger and therefore dirt. In the prejudices of that society at that time, being third class was worse than being black. By combining the two, the absurdity of either being inferior was revealed. Footit, trapped in societal restrictions, could never see this.

Demagogue The ill-tempered official has been used in clown

Figure 1

work to poke fun at everything from kings to policemen. The figure of unbridled authority operates on his own set of rules with a narrow-mindedness that excludes variant opinions completely. Oftentimes, jesters such as Triboulet were able to temper the temper of their sovereigns by boldly imitating the royal intemperance of their masters. Unfortunately, contemporary monarchs are not as solidly seated on their thrones as kings of old. They become skittish when mocked, leaving the clown only minor officials and occasional intemperate citizens to pester.

Dummy An extention of the contre-Auguste character developed by Albert Fratellini and the Toby character who gained popularity in America, this character is not really dumb. He is just overly logical. When another clown gives him a job to do, he does it to the letter. If asked to shake, as the clowns are asked in the "Boxing" sketch, the dummy does shake. However, he shakes all over. He is so literal minded that the other clowns must take care in what they say when he is around, or they will find their very words turned against them. The dummy seems dumb through all of the insanity he creates because he cannot understand why everything is going awry.

Egotist This clown is always right, whether he is or not. He pushes the other clowns about to fit his own conception of the way things should be and is always ready to take credit where none is due. Such a clown is the whip cracker described later in the book. The audience can readily identify with this type if they know someone like him—so when the egotist gets slapped down, they enjoy seeing this type of character getting his for a change.

Narcissist Filled with a sense of his own beauty, this character is always a trifle removed from the situation because his attention is centered on himself. Like the egotist, he has little of which to be proud. His appearance belies his belief in his supposed superior looks. A tramp clown is a superb candidate for this character flaw.

By continually checking his appearance, the absurdity of his pride is continually pointed out.

Poor Soul The luck of this character always seems to run against him. That he actually is the author of a major portion of his own misfortune never seems to occur to him. He remains constantly resigned to what he believes is his inevitable fate. Jackie Gleason used this character very successfully on his show. Its popularity comes from the sympathy that it generates in the audience.

Timid Soul This character would be afraid to ask for water even if he were dying of thirst. His insecurity is painfully evident to the audience. The least boisterous of all the clowns, he is often the butt of the pranks of his fellows. But, like the fool, he seems protected by God, for he always seems to come out on top. Through his shyness and uncertainty, he manages to turn the tables on his detractors.

Tippler The word "drunk" is not used to describe this character because the clown should never attempt the portrayal of a chronic drinker. Such a character may be made use of by a comedian like Foster Brooks, but the clown's motley and makeup make him unsuited for the role. The clown uses the character to poke fun at overindulgence, and his performance should be closer to that of Stan Laurel in *The Bohemian girl* than Mr. Brooks. W. C. Fields made lighthearted use of the tippler throughout most of his moves and even took the character to the level of high drama in *David Copperfield*.

In making use of these character types and others, the clown will discover that each one dictates certain movements and manners of speech to the clown. The bureaucrat, for example, uses clipped movements and a terse mode of speech. With broad movements and brassy voice, the egotist cows the other clowns. And, withdrawn and quiet, the timid soul hopes only to make it through the day.

The clown will also find that the harshness of each stock characterization will be tempered by the inner qualities he chooses to exploit from his own personality. These qualities add width to the clown's performance and are part of his psychological makeup. They combine with the stock character that dictates the social function of the clown, giving height to the characterization. Finally the psychological and social qualities together dictate the physiological features of the character and produce depth.

Character can also produce conflict by combining the clown's character with an inappropriate stock type, as is the case in "The Date." In this act the poor soul turns egotist to win the woman of his dreams:

A woman clown enters dressed in a parody of the coquettish socialite. As she sweeps across the performing area, she passes the poor soul, who is immediately smitten by her. Removing a flower from his lapel, he sidles up to her in an attempt to give her the blossom as a gift, but he cannot seem to make her notice his existence. Whenever he gets close to being within her field of vision, she turns in the other direction. She doesn't even know he is there.

As he is about to give up, another clown of obvious sophistication comes in and with great self-assurance presents the woman with a flower of his own. The poor soul, seeing this, begins to believe there is hope for him, after all. He builds himself up and in imitation of the sophisticate he pretends to be, approaches the woman. This time, she notices him and accepts the flower, but now he is faced with another problem. He does not know how to react next. Taking a stab at thinking for himself, he offers her his arm. She accepts it, and he leads her to a table already set for dinner with a candle in the center. They sit down and a clown waiter enters and begins to serve them.

At this point, the poor soul notices that the candle on the table is not lit. In a masterful move of romantic fervor, the clown prepares to light the candle himself. He takes out a pack of matches, and his luck runs out. The poor soul is more "deboner" than "debonair."

On the first match, the clown does not use the proper side of the packet for a striking surface. Realizing his error, he laughs and reverses the packet. This time, the match strikes, but he loses his hold on it, and it sails across the room. On his next try, he manages to get the match to the candle, where it goes out. He moves the candle closer to the edge of the table and on the fourth try lights it.

Delighted at his success, he and the woman kiss. As they do, the clown drops his hand to the table and knocks the candle into the woman's lap. She begins to smolder. When he realizes his love is on fire, he grabs the nearest object—a turkey that a passing waiter is carrying on a tray—and tries to beat out his flaming companion. When this fails, he picks up a pitcher of water and douses her with it. In a huff, his date gets up, tosses the flower into his face, and drips off. He sadly watches her go and then replaces the flower in his lapel. Defeated, he leaves, vowing never to pretend to be more than he is.

ETHNIC TYPES

In America, the successful clown has always been white, Anglo-Saxon, and male or a WASM. This is a pity but true. One reason for this is that most ethnic performers who take on the motley deny their backgrounds to assume the stereotyped view of the clown: white faced, tramp, or partial faced. Women are as guilty of this as are the ethnic men and so are included with them in this lapse.

No clowns readily come to mind who acknowledge their heritage through their use of makeup, costume, and character, but some do exist and the numbers are growing. Few contemporary black clowns use white face or any other kind of makeup. Instead, they choose the historic Auguste form, which uses no makeup at all. This frees them from the stereotypical characters often associated with the clown so that they can develop characterizations uniquely their own.

Other ethnic clowns have begun to use their backgrounds to create clown characters. These clowns do not ridicule their heritages but hold them up with pride to demonstrate comedically that everything isn't superior in this country. Their pride is always reflected in the quality of their performances.

Figure 2

The only group that has avoided voicing pride in their condition is that of womankind. Women clowns have managed to remain silent on their state in society. They don the exact same makeup and costumes of their male counterparts and only assume roles that are blatantly chauvinistic. Perhaps someday they will break out of this mold. If they do, they will probably soar higher than their male counterparts in creating new comedy.

A NOTE ON ACCENTS

Too often the novice clown is tempted to speak in a high, mealy-mouthed, nasal tone that is usually used by adults when speaking to one-year-old infants. With the diversity of tones and patterns the human voice is capable of producing, there is no reason, except sheer laziness, for a clown to lower himself by jabbering baby fashion. No law states that a clown cannot use a Southern drawl, a New England dialect, or the accent he possessed in the first place when he creates his comedy. However, whatever accent the clown decides to use, he must remember to fit it to his character.

Whatever accent is used, the clown should not require a great deal of concentration when he speaks. His accent must appear natural, as if it were his normal manner of speech. If the tone of voice is strained so that the clown obviously is using a voice not his own, it will grate on the audience's ears. They will know that this is a man assuming a character and not a clown.

CHARACTER AND ROLE

Although the clown has only one character, he will find that he can assume a vast number of roles. A role is a part, a set of circumstances applied to a character. In "The Date," the poor soul assumes the role of the sophisticate, and conflict is created by the assumption of an inappropriate role. By taking the part of a policeman, fireman, or Indian chief, the clown uses the role assumed to point out the absurdities of his character. The clown's character is the central core of the clown's existence. The role is mere assumption.

The character, then, is the primary concern of the clown. His makeup, costume, and movement all depend on this one aspect. Minus character, he cannot take up a role and becomes another part of his chaotic environment. The clown *must* be the author of his own order, but he cannot be an author without a character.

Makeup

The painted face and silly grin that many people associate with the clown had its beginnings in the theater. Before stages were lighted by electricity, thespians, directors, and entrepreneurs were stuck with the flickering illumination of candles and kerosene lamps. To ensure that the audiences of those dim days could see the faces of their favorite prima donnas, actors were forced to use thick makeup which was little more than pigmented painted. The stiff look that this early makeup gaves to the faces of performers was made even more bizarre because the actors, in an effort to make their painted faces seem more natural, painted on shadows as well as character lines. This made the actor's appearance, both on and off the stage, a trifle grotesque. Therefore, the clown of that time was left with very few options as to how his makeup would develop. As today, clowns then played exaggerated human beings and had to appear more grotesque than the actors who played wholely human parts. The result was an exaggeration of an exaggeration. The clown's face became a parody, a caricature.

Before makeup became the vogue on stage, the clown either wore a mask or nothing at all on his face. Instead, he used contortion, twisting his face into a screwed-up parody of humanity. He needed little more, for the audiences he played to were close to his performance. Later, covered by makeup, the clown's face became immobile under the masklike pastes and rouges he was required to use. His character thus became set. To change his character, he would have had to remove one conglomerate of features and paint on another. Little wonder many clowns returned to the simpler use of a plain face when the *commedia dell'arte* began to decline. Even today, in Western Europe and Russia, a good number of clowns use only a touch of makeup and reserve the stiff white face for the mime. Only in America are clowns exclusively associated with the mask of clown white and grotesque multicolored features. The only exemption to this is the tramp clown, whose face, for the most part, is covered with black.

As in the days of the *commedia dell'arte,* the features of the contemporary white-faced clown are painted on to exaggerate or obscure the features already there. The clown chooses the features he wishes to enhance always with an eye toward his character. Since the set of his face will be frozen by the grease paint he uses, he must be certain that his looks mirror his actions and vice versa.

The mask of makeup that the clown is expected to wear is so effective in concealing his real features that the majority of modern merrymakers copyright their faces to ensure that no one else can take their places. Two completely divergent physical types. when painted with identical faces and wearing similar clothes, will look like twins. Few television viewers realize that the Bozos haunting the airwaves are pale parodies of the clown they appear to be. Likewise, Ronald McDonald would have a hard time indeed getting from one hamburger stand to the next if he were merely one person.

This is not to suggest that the clown's features cannot move to express emotion. The advantage of makeup as opposed to a mask is that it is painted directly on the skin. As a result, it moves when the contours of the face shift to smile, frown, or grimace. Its thickness, however, combined with the exaggerated features, prohibit it from ever being as expressive as the unadorned human face. With a made-up face, the clown will find his character set for the world to see. Whenever he changes roles, the new role will automatically be tempered by the character painted between his ears.

MAKEUP KITS

A fair number of makeup kits are available through various cosmetic firms. For the most part, these kits are designed exclusively for use by actors. They therefore contain a number of items that the clown will find unusable and omit a greater number of items that the well-stocked clown should have on hand. An ideal makeup kit for the clown would contain the following items:

Clown White This can be purchased in a variety of forms. It comes in pancake, tubes, and tins. The pancake version is the least effective because it is difficult to apply in a smooth, even coat. Clowns who use it usually have streaked faces and look made up. It is generally chosen because it is less messy to apply than the other two forms.

The advantage of the tube of clown white is that it comes in a tightly sealed container that prevents the rest of the makeup in the kit from accidentally mixing with it and leaving the clown with a gray or pink face instead of the wanted white. The clown can buy either grease paint or water-soluble paint in tubes. One company even advertises a hypoallergenic clown white for clowns with sensitive skin, but the effectiveness of the product is questionable.

The preferable form is the tin that comes in a variety of sizes and is less expensive in the long run than the other two. Also, the makeup in the tin usually produces better results since it is a paste and not a thick paint.

Black Grease Paint Packaged in a tube, black grease paint, when applied with a thin brush, produces an excellent line for highlighting whatever colors the clown may use.

Assorted Colors These can be purchased in either tube or stick form. They are coordinated on the face to enhance the features of the clown.

Black Eyebrow Pencil This can be used to highlight the features if the clown does not like the mess caused by the black grease paint or is in a hurry. Less expensive is a black china-marking pencil, but this is harder to use than the other two.

Baby Powder Once the makeup is on the face, it will appear pasty unless "set." Although a wide variety of colored facial powders are on the market, baby powder is the better buy. It is low in cost and does a better job than its competitors. Putting the powder in a white cotton sock tied at the ankle is less wasteful than using a powder puff. A different sock should be used for each color.

Brush Makeup brushes are available at most drug stores or comestic counters but are not the best product for the clown to use. They are small, designed for touch-up jobs and not the full-face brushing the clown will need to remove excess powder once his makeup is set. Shaving brushes or soft-bristle three-inch paint brushes are better buys.

Mirror At times, the clown will have to put on his makeup in the field (literally more often than figuratively). A mirror will help him see what he is doing.

Baby Oil Less expensive and more efficient than cold cream for removing makeup, baby oil or mineral oil should be in every clown's kit.

Paper Towels   In the long run, using disposable paper towels is less costly for removing makeup than ruining their terry-cloth counterpart, which will hold the grease paint in its fibers. However, the clown may want to carry a cloth towel with him to protect his costume when he sets his face.

Head Band or Makeup Hat   This will keep the clown's hair off his forehead and out of his makeup before he has a chance to let it set.

Rubber Nose   A variety of noses is available through various novelty firms, and the clown may wish to own several. Felix Adler had a collection of noses tipped with the appropriate stone for each month. The nose is best held in place with toupee tape.

Toupee Tape   See above.

Paint Brushes and Cotton Swabs   These are used to apply the makeup.

APPLYING MAKEUP

The basic procedure is to start with the foundation color and then add the other features. Starting with the mouth, the clown works his way up to his forehead, setting each color to fix it in place. Finally, he adds character lines and outlines each colored feature with a black or dark line to separate them from the white background. This last is important, or his colors will appear washed out.

Foundation   Depending on the type of clown desired, this may be clown white, black grease paint, flesh-toned grease paint, or nothing at all. The white-faced clown receives a foundation of clown white. Tramp clowns use black grease paint, sometimes in combination with flesh tones. And Auguste clowns use clown white with flesh tones, just flesh tones, or skip the whole thing.

To apply clown white, the clown should cover his finger tips with the paint and dot the paint onto the face. The first temptation of the novice is to smear the makeup on in gobs. If this is done, the white and the colors painted on it will begin to flake off as soon as the face is set. Not much makeup is required, and the important thing is to make sure that it is smooth, not heavy. After the face is well dotted, the clown smears the daubs of makeup

Figure 3

together so that the face is covered. At this point, he should not worry about the smeared appearance of his face. By using the fingertips of the hand that applied the makeup to pat the face, he will find that the foundation will become smooth and evenly distributed. The face is then hit with the sock full of powder to set the clown white. When the excess powder is brushed away, the clown can start on the first feature.

The tramp clown receives a beard of black grease paint. Black grease paint is applied in the same manner as the clown white. If the tramp uses flesh tones also on his face, he may wish to blend the paint of the beard into the other tone to achieve a realistic set of whiskers. This can be accomplished by brushing the face with the finger tips in short brushing strokes at the areas where the two colors meet. This is called feathering and will require some practice. Once done, the face is set and brushed.

Many Augustes forego the use of flesh tones and simply exaggerate their features. Flesh tones are applied in the same way as clown white.

Mouth The mouth of the clown can be made large or small. It can enhance the lower lip, upper lip, jaw, and cheeks. A few examples of the types of mouths a clown can use are found in Figure 4.

To apply the mouth, the clown may use either a brush, a cotton swab, or a finger. The swab is prepared by rolling it in the grease paint until it absorbs the color. Then it is used like a crayon. All are more than adequate for the job. After it is applied, the color should be set and brushed. This will keep it from turning a pasty color and smudging when the clown runs on to the nose.

Nose A painted nose can be chosen from one of the designs above and applied with the brush, swab, or finger. However, if a rubber nose is used, the clown must scrap off makeup rather than putting it on. Fitting the rubber appendage in place, the clown

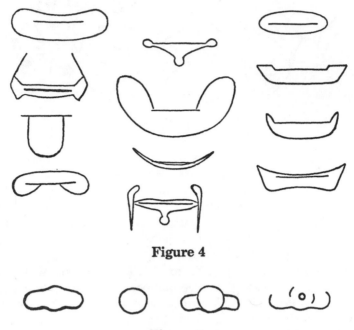

Figure 4

Figure 5

draws a line around its edge. When the makeup below the line is scraped away, the nose will fit flush against the foundation color. In the case of a putty nose, the nose should be attached before any makeup is applied. Of these three types, the painted nose is the nose of preference. Although the rubber and putty noses achieve a greater degree of exaggeration, they can also cause no end of problems. Whether held on by spirit gum or toupee tape, they will occasionally fall off. The only thing the clown can say when this happens is "That's the first time my nose ever ran that far." To be fair to the putty nose, however, it is useful in the "Balancing Feather" bit, which has been employed successfully by Emmett Kelly:

Holding three juggling balls and a feather so that the audience can see them plainly, the clown with the putty proboscis indicates that he intends to juggle while balancing the feather on the tip of his nose. To balance the feather he needs two hands and so places the balls on the ground. Both hands are necessary to stick the end of the feather into the putty of the nose. The only way the clown can bring off this stunt is by cheating a wee bit. Once the feather is in place, the clown carefully kneels to get the balls. His attention is fixed on the feather "balanced" above him. Picking up one ball, he holds it high. He picks up the second and does likewise. But, on the third, he fumbles, and the last ball rolls away. The clown, still carefully balancing the feather, searches the ground frantically with his free hand, but he cannot locate the third ball. Annoyed, he forgets what he is doing for a moment and looks down. The feather, still stuck firmly into his putty nose, does not fall off. He retrieves the ball and suddenly realizes that the jig is up. Sheepishly, he retires in embarrassment.

Cheeks Applied with a brush, swab, or finger, the shapes above will serve to raise or lower the cheek bones artificially and aid in highlighting the eyes. The designs above are normally separated by the nose. Once applied, they should be powdered.

Tears The shapes that clowns sport under and sometimes on top of their eyelids are called tears, for they follow the lines of the face down which tears fall. They can be used to highlight the cheeks as well as bring out the eyes. This last is especially important to the white-face clown, whose foundation erases the features almost completely. His eyes would appear little less than pinpoints without something to adorn them. Tears may be applied with a brush or swab. The finger is too large to be a feasible applicator for this feature.

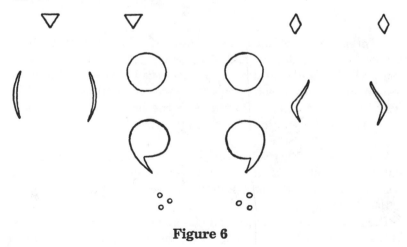

Figure 6

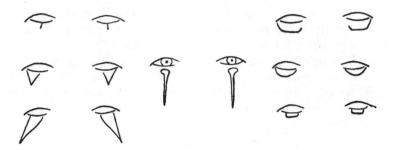

Figure 7

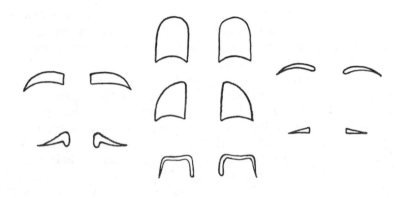

Figure 8

Forehead This area makes use of a variety of eyebrow shapes and other designs and aids in bringing out the eyes. As in the case of the Auguste clown, the shapes can also be used to blend the makeup into a variety of outrageous skull caps or false foreheads. They can be applied with the brush, cotton swab, or finger and, as always, should be set after they have been painted in place.

When the full face has been set and dusted, the clown then outlines each shape with a dark or black line and applies crow's-feet or other character lines if desired. Once these have been set, so is the clown.

The novice clown can pick and choose among the various shapes in the above illustrations in deciding the face he will use. He will find that the original face he chooses will begin to change slightly with repeated applications. Eventually, it will evolve into a set series of patterns as the character develops. This is part of the clown's growth. In any case, by using the shapes above, he will be well on his way. There can be only one possible answer to the question frequently asked by beginning merrymakers:

"How does a clown look?"

With his eyes.

5

Costume

Figure 9

What should the well-dressed clown wear when he gets up before his audience?

The consensus seems to be that clowns wear ill-fitting clothes. This is only partially true. The costumes of most professional clowns fit perfectly. They only appear ill fitting because certain features are exaggerated. The coat looks baggy because it has oversize pockets or the shirt overlarge because the clown makes use of huge cuffs. Such features are determined by the character and should not be randomly tacked on simply because they look outrageous. The clown who does not aspire to social status, for example, would have no reason to sport an overblown dickie that is really a part of formal attire. Likewise, the tramp, whose costume is for the most part a realistic reflection of the real-life hobo, would have little use for multicolored baggy pants usually found on the Auguste. The clown must choose his costume with as much care as he uses in deciding on his makeup.

Another misconception is that the clown costume is a one-piece suit trimmed with ruffles and overlarge buttons. Although some clowns use this type of suit, the majority opt for a multi-piece outfit. The reason for this is that the clown who must make several costume changes during his performance simply does not have the time to remove one costume completely and don another.

A clown with a one-piece costume is also faced with another problem. The costume is a reflection of the clown's character. When he changes to a different costume, he can therefore look like a completely different clown. The illustration at the beginning of this chapter (Fig. 9) demonstrates this. The clown can avoid this when he assumes different roles by incorporating part of his existing costume into the costumes he assumes to play his part. This is difficult to do with the one-piece outfit.

The simplest costume can be sewn together by using a pajama pattern. A small or large pattern may be employed, depending on the character of the clown, and additions may be built into the suit if desired. This is the advantage of designing a costume as opposed to buying one ready-made. Velcro may be used in the seams of a costume to hold it together for a specialty bit such as the one used in "The Clown Band."

During a lull in the program, a group of clowns enter with musical instruments.
ANNOUNCER: Hold it right there! What do you think you're doing
BAND LEADER: We are going to give a concert.
ANNOUNCER: You can't do that. The program is already planned. We have other acts waiting to go on.
BAND LEADER: Yeah, I've seen them. For our first selection . . .
ANNOUNCER: You can't do this!

BAND LEADER: Why not?

ANNOUNCER: I don't even know how well you play together.

BAND LEADER: Oh, we don't play together. We're all soloists.

ANNOUNCER: I see. Well let's hear a sample.

(The band leader motions, and a clarinetist stands. The leader raises his arms, and on the first downbeat, a stream of water shoots from the instrument and hits the band leader. This can be accomplished with the hot water bottle described in Chapter 8.)

ANNOUNCER: This act is all wet.

BAND LEADER: The second one is better.

ANNOUNCER: It better be.

(At a wave, a very small clown trundles an immense bass drum forward. He winds up to beat the drum, and the force of his swing combined with the weight of the drum spin him in a series of concentric rolls. He ends up with the drum atop his prostrate form.)

ANNOUNCER: That does it. . . .

BAND LEADER: No, wait! I've saved the best for last.

ANNOUNCER: You have? All right, I'll give you one last chance.

(This time a clown stands up with a sousaphone. As the leader prepares to direct, the clown in the Velcro costume enters. A piece of heavy elastic, secured backstage, is attached to the back of his costume. He walks forward as far as the elastic permits and leans slightly against its pull. He is almost directly in front of the musician. On the downbeat, the musician gives a blast on the horn, the clown in front of him rips open the Velcro holding his costume together, and the elastic tears the costume from the clown's body. The clown is left standing in a pair of outrageous red long johns. He flees in embarrassment, followed by the other clowns.)

Such specialty costumes are used mainly by professional clowns. The cost of creating them can be prohibitive for the amateur. A tear-away costume like the one described above is the easiest and least expensive to produce. Other costumes in the specialty line inflate, smoulder, spout leaks, and fall apart. The amateur clown will not really need costumes like these for the shows he will do, but many clowns, at one time or another, will have call to use the following accessories:

Collars and Cuffs   A parody of the tuxedo and suit accessories of the past, oversized versions of these can be made from cardboard or highly starched material. They are not connected to the costume and make the use of a shirt optional.

Dickies These are extensions of the collar to include a fake shirt front. When constructed from thin rolled plastic, the shirt front, if not held down, will spring upward. A dickie may also be made from a roller blind, the roller of which is concealed in the collar. When released, it shoots upward audibly.

Gloves These are used to hide the flesh color of the hands. However, the clown may have occasion to remove his gloves. In such a case, he can use one glove with an impossibly long wrist that runs up his sleeve and another with detachable finger tips. This will provide him with an excellent bit before he plays a musical instrument or sits down to dinner.

Hats A simple chapeau can be made by the clown using an empty oatmeal box. By covering it with felt and adding a brim, he will be supplied with a very usable undersize top hat. Rolled into a cone and adorned with pom-poms, felt may also be used by itself. A store derby, which is a mute used by trumpet players, can be painted to provide the clown with another covering for his head. Even old hats can be used by the clown. The choice of hats is simply one of money and suiting the character.

Patches Squares of material can be used to heighten the color scheme of the clown's costume. The only rule to follow in using them is not to overdo it.

Pockets These are optional in the clown costume but are useful to hold walk-around properties. They are also a good place for the clown to put his hands.

Shirts Multicolored pullover shirts can always be used by the clown. The best is an old-fashioned, long-sleeved tank top.

Shorts The clown should never buy his shorts in a clothing store. There he will only find pairs intended for use as undergarments. In a pants drop or similar situation, this will be a touch of reality that could turn his audience off. A pair of baggy, brightly colored shorts made of thick material is preferred.

Skull Caps These head coverings can be constructed from a baby's T-shirt. The shirt is tied beneath the sleeves and the top part cut away. When turned inside out, it will provide the white face clown with a bold appearance. By sewing rug yarn or fake hair to the skull cap, the clown can sport an outrageous hair style. More professional versions can be made by cutting two pieces of cloth in the shapes pictured in Figure 10 and sewing them together.

Socks The style and color of socks are determined by the character of the clown. Usually, any brightly colored pair will do.

Suspenders If the clown does not use a belt, very wide, colorful suspenders are the uniform of the day. They can be especially helpful in keeping the clown's baggy pants looking baggy.

Tights The acrobatic clown will want to wear a full set of these beneath his costume. If his pants split during the show, the last thing he will want to do is embarrass the audience.

The most important rule, no matter what the clown ends up wearing, is that the costume be kept clean. This applies to the tramp clown as well. Audiences never like a seedy clown.

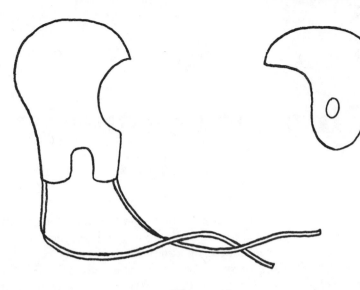

Figure 10

Physical Comedy

For the most part, the clown's movement is dictated by his character. Whether his gestures are broad or subdued, they convey to the clown's audience something about his personality or intent. A clown who intends to sneak up on a fellow clown could use either broad, slow movements or fast, erratic movements, depending on his character. But no matter what movements the clown uses, he must be in complete control of them. Exercises in tumbling, fencing, dancing, or the martial arts can help the clown maintain control over every movement made while performing.

The clown needs surety of movement because his environment is in constant chaos, and the clown himself is the only element that can supply order. In performance, the clown's every movement should be ingrained. If he has to think before he makes a move, his constant pausing will break the flow of his bits, sketches, and routines and quite possibly put his audience to sleep.

SLAPSTICK

Taking its name from the noisy device used by early clowns to safely whack away at each other, slapstick can be used to create low or high comedy. At its lowest, it is simply the acts of falling down, hitting one's fellows, and stubbing one's toes as frequently as possible. It requires little thought.

At its highest, it is a carefully planned series of movements that can make the clown's environment appear to be out to get him. Laurel and Hardy used slapstick in this way constantly throughout their careers. In *The Music Box,* they attempt to move a piano and are constantly foiled by the force of gravity. The subtleties they used become evident when this film is compared to one in which the Three Stooges are given a similar assignment. Laurel and Hardy make use of a logical sequence of mishaps, while the Three Stooges are simply brutal. Timing is the element that makes this difference.

Timing is a flowing progression from one action to the next so that a cause and effect relationship is established. Every action must be tailored to lead logically to the next so that the movement of a bit or sketch runs inevitably toward a predetermined conclusion. For example, in the tippling scene of *The Bohemian Girl*, Stan Laurel is given the job of siphoning wine into a multitude of bottles from an immense vat. He discovers too late that once the siphoning process has begun, it does not stop. To save as much wine as possible when changing bottles, he sticks the hose in his mouth. Unfortunately, the bottles fill faster than he expects, and he ends up with the hose in his mouth more than the bottles. Before long, with only a fraction of the bottles filled, the wine is gone, and Stan is under the table. The comedy of the scene lies in the audience's realizing the inevitability of Stanley's situation. This realization is established by the performer's actions.

While difficult enough for one performer, timing is devilish for two or more. The flow of action must then follow a single path through the movements of all the parties involved. An excellent exercise in timing is *The Broken Mirror*. This sketch was made popular by the Marx Brothers in *Duck Soup* but predates the zany brothers by many years. In it, a mirror is broken by one performer who then takes the place of the reflection. Unaware of the breakage, a second performer enters and attempts to use the mirror, with the first performer mirroring his every move. It is a pleasant, inoffensive routine.

The one danger in using slapstick is that the younger members of the audience might be tempted to ape the performer. Such was the case with Carl Bagessen, a Danish clown whose plate-breaking routine achieved great popularity in 1893. Picking up a stack of plates, he would begin to carry them to a table. With fiendish precision, one plate after another would squeeze out of the stack until they all lay shattered about his feet. While picking up a second stack, one of his hands would become stuck on a piece of fly-paper. After laboriously extricating himself without dropping a plate, the second stack would follow the firse to the floor, and so on. Inspired by the hilarity of Bagessen's performance, many children of the time imitated it at home, only to find that their parents were unamused.

THE TAKE

The take, a silent aside to the audience, can be a look of comprehension or confusion. It is used to point up an important bit of business and punctuate a joke. Oliver Hardy used this to great effect when, in exasperation, he resigned himself to the troubles caused him by his partner. On contemporary television, it is used by Johnny Carson to signal incredulity at a bit of unintentional whimsy made by a guest.

For the clown, the take is a way to accentuate the high points of a piece. An intentional pause in the action of a sketch, its effect is similar to that achieved by the panels of a comic strip. It frames each action and emphasizes through sudden lack of movement. At times, it can even produce a laugh itself.

The double take is an extension of the take. The performer begins to look at the audience but suddenly has second thoughts and directs his attention back to the scene in which he is playing.

TUMBLING

The elementary moves described here should be practiced on a padded surface. None of them are very difficult, but all are essential to clown work. The clown who is interested in developing the more advanced skills of tumbling should enroll in a course, which often can be found at a nearby Y.M.C.A. No book can ever be as valuable as personal instruction.

Forward Roll Squatting with the hands spread shoulder width apart on the floor, the performer tucks his head so that his chin is on his chest and rolls forward to again assume a squatting position. If his head is not bent forward all the way, the performer will land flat on his back, which is painful. It is not advised.

Backward Roll Squatting as for the forward roll, the performer rolls backward, across his shoulders, and reassumes a squatting position.

Standing Forward Roll From a standing position, the performer squats and executes a forward roll.

Standing Backward Roll From a standing position, the performer squats and executes a backward roll.

Leaping Forward Roll The performer leaps forward, landing on his hands, and uses the momentum of the leap to carry him over in a forward roll.

Cartwheel From a standing position, the performer leans to the side, places his hands one at a time on the floor as he kicks his feet, legs straight, over his head, and lands back on his feet.

Tinsica The performer bends forward from a standing position and places his hands, one in front of the other, on the floor. He kicks his feet over his head and returns to a standing position. Basically, this is a cartwheel done toward the front instead of the side.

Backward Tinsica The same as the tinsica but executed over the shoulder.

The tumbling maneuvers described above are arranged in order of simplicity of execution. Anyone in normal physical condition should have no great trouble performing them. For safety's sake, another person should be present during the practice of any tumbling maneuver. This person can come in handy when learning the cartwheel or tinsica by supporting the performers legs the first few times. This will allow the performer to get the feel of the move.

FALLS

Tumbling will help loosen the clown for pratfalls and improve his sense of balance. The pratfall can be performed by itself or included as an extension of a regular tumbling maneuver. There basically are two types of pratfalls: forward and backward.

Forward Fall From a standing position, the clown falls forward, catching himself on his hands. He is then in the basic push-up position. His hands are shoulder width apart, supporting his body, with his feet together on the floor and his legs straight. He lowers himself to the floor, turning his head to one side. Executed quickly, this will look like the clown has fallen. If it is presented by itself, it should be preceded by a trip.

Trip The easiest way to trip is to trip. When walking forward, the clown catches one foot behind the other and intentionally trips over his own two feet. By snapping his head back and thrusting his chest forward, he can make the trip seem very real.

Backward Fall This fall requires a little nerve. The clown bends his knees slightly. Then, splaying his arms backward and to the side, he throws one foot in the air and falls backward, braking the fall with his hands. He should land across his shoulders with his head tucked forward. If he lands in a sitting position or on the small of his back, he can hurt himself. Therefore, he would be wise to have someone help him when learning the fall. After he has been lowered to the ground a few times, he will develop a feel for the move and be able to execute it on his own.

7

A Covey of Clowns

Like birds of a feather, clowns flock together, and when they do, havoc ensues. Or so it seems to the audience.

Actually, a group of clowns are much more organized than they first appear to be. If they were not, the audience would be completely perplexed. They would not know what the heck was going on.

For example, whenever a clown executes a take, the take is taken from the actions of another clown. That means that when only two clowns are in front of an audience, they cannot take together. If they did, the take they took might be mistaken by the audience, which would not be able to tell who was taking who. The exception to this rule of thumb that clowns can take each other only one at a time is anytime three or more clowns are taken together. If one clown blunders, the other two or more take at each other.

Confusing?

The factor that determines how the takes should be taken or any other movement made in a group sketch is the through line of action. This is the path that the action follows to get to the punch line. When several clowns are involved, this line of action can run from one clown to another. The clown who carries the action at any given point is, therefore, given prominence in the routine. As soon as this clown passes the action on to another clown, he sits back to let the other clown carry on.

The simplest example of this is "The Balloon Chase." In this sketch, the action is carried by the clown who carries the balloons. The other clowns simply wait in the background for their turns to come.

Clown One enters with a bunch of balloons. Clown Two decides to snatch them. He calls the other clowns together, and they confer in a huddle. The huddle breaks, and the clowns scatter throughout the arena. Clown Two saunters up to the first clown, grabs the balloons, and takes off with Clown One in pursuit. The chase is on. Clown Three idles across the path of the chase. As Two goes by, Three takes the balloons and runs in the other direction. One sees this and changes course. Four, who has been waiting quietly far from the action, takes the balloons from Three and runs past One. One does a double take and wheels in the opposite direction. Four passes off to Five, who executes an end run, faking to Seven and handing off to Six. Six performs a Statue of Liberty play, and Eight tears off toward the exit with the balloons. Before he gets there, he trips, falls on the balloons, and breaks them.

One looks at the broken balloons and becomes incensed as the other clowns gather to find out what happened. Eight hides behind them. After all, he didn't start the whole thing. Hopping up and down, One stares arrows at the other clowns standing in a line, Two through Eight, in front of him. Winding up, he swings, hitting Clown Two, who wheels and hits Three, who hits Four, who hits Five, who hits Six, who hits Seven, who spins around, missing Eight, and hits Six. The punch continues all the way down the line back to One, who is knocked over. Furious, Clown One climbs to his feet and, flaying the other clowns with the busted balloons, chases them off and out.

For the sketch above to work, there can be no extraneous movement. Only one clown at a time carries the action while the others get ready to join the fun. If Clown Three made merry while Four through Eight were running with the balloons, the distracted audience would miss a good portion of the action.

In a more complex sketch like "The Clown Fire Department," the action and preparations for the action are more involved. Hence, the sketch must be carefully blocked out. The line of action must run smoothly from the snake leaping out of the alarm box to the fire engine. The audience follows the engine to a group of clowns toasting marshmallows who are dispersed by the chief. This gives two clowns a chance to clear the net out of the engine. Meanwhile, the audience follows the chief to the truck, where he grabs a hose. While he runs the hose to its length and executes a fall, another clown grabs the axe. When the chief gets up, he directs the clown with the axe to the building. The clown winds up to swing, and two other clowns grab a ladder. They begin to run to the building, followed by the clowns with the net as the chief gets hit with the ax, stumbles backward, falls over the ladder carried by the running clowns, and lands in the net.

On paper, this looks impossibly complex, but it is not. The audience will always follow the fastest-moving object. Therefore, the clowns who are setting up simply move slower than the clowns carrying the action. In this case, the line of action is indicated, in part, by speed of motion.

The logic of the movement also traces the line of action. One act inevitably leads to another. Once begun, a logical series of actions will drag an audience's attention with it to its pre-established end.

So, in setting up a sketch for a group of clowns, a line of action must be established that moves at a certain rate of speed and contains a logically connected series of actions. Once this is done, the clowns only have to decide who will carry the action. The final result should be a progression of movement toward an absurd end. What the audience should see is a living Rube Goldberg cartoon.

Figure 11

A Clown and His
Equipment

A sense of humor, a character, sensible makeup, and a costume—
these are all anyone needs to become a clown.

Not by a far sight. These elements are merely background
material from which the clown draws to present his own particular
brand of comedy. An automobile mechanic who knows everything
about the operation of the car will not be able to change a tire if he
has no idea what tools are available.

Clowning encompasses only one aspect of the comic while it
incorporates the techniques and comic formats of the other
practitioners of the joyful art. If the only differentiation between
the clown and the stand-up comic is the clown's outrageous
makeup and colorful costume, then the clown is only a stand-up
comic in makeup and a costume.

The clown is a storyteller, a humorist, an acrobat, a puppeteer, a
ventriloquist, a juggler, and a magician. He makes each of these
skills conform to his art by the way in which he uses the
equipment and techniques of the individual skills. Also, the clown
insinuates pieces of equipment that distinctly belong to his art into
the performance of these skills.

How does this make the clown different from the performers
whose skills he borrows?

The storyteller relates an exaggerated tale with an economy of
movement, but the clown over exaggerates in the telling of the tale
as he physically acts it out with incidental props. The humorist
tells an amusing anecdote; the clown *is* the anecdote. An acrobat
tumbles smoothly through a routine; the clown uses the knowledge of tumbling when he fumbles and falls for his audience. A

juggler works hard at each trick he performs; the clown feels no guilt at cheating with specially designed pieces of pseudojuggling equipment to make the skillful balancing of objects no skill at all. Everything that a clown endeavors to do is tempered by his singularly illogical view of the world, and each piece of his equipment is designed to bring a sense of reality to his improbable existence.

Every tool that the clown utilizes must be carefully chosen with his audience in mind. His audience arrives at the theater or tent anticipating an evening of light entertainment. As has been explained earlier in this book (Chapter 2), this anticipation allows the clown to make a meaningful statement because his audience is in a subliminal attitude of relaxed awareness. When a clown plays a practical joke on his audience, he loses their confidence, making them wary of rather than aware of him.

A variety of ordinary objects can be used by the clown, but for some sketches the clown must use objects that are gimmicked or oversized. Many of these gimmicked objects can be constructed by the clown; others, because of the intricacy of their construction, should be made by professional craftsmen. A good number of props can be purchased through novelty or magic shops. When buying equipment at such places, the only thing the clown must worry about is whether or not the item he is purchasing will offend his audience. The purpose of the clown is to create laughter, not play practical jokes on an unsuspecting public.

The equipment covered in this section can be divided into three categories. The first category encompasses ordinary objects and the special uses the clown might find for them. These objects are not gimmicked in any way; they can be found in most homes or may be purchased at any local department store. Their functions as clown props tend mostly toward the slapstick form of humor, and when they are not the focus of the comedic intent, they may be used as a part of the set for a clown sketch or bit.

The second category contains objects that must be specifically adapted by the clown before they can be used in front of an audience. For the most part, these devices are constructed with specific sketches and bits in mind. A few of these devices do have functions that can be generalized so that they may be used as props in a variety of routines. The materials necessary to adapt the devices in this category can usually be found in any hardware store, and their construction is simple. Objects used by the clowns seldom have to appear realistic; after all, the clown himself is a trifle unreal.

The third category consists of props that must be purchased ready-made because their construction is beyond the ability of most clowns. They must either be fashioned by special tools, or their appearance must be fairly realistic. If, by reading the descriptions of these devices, the clown feels capable of putting them together, there is no reason why he should not try. But since these objects are for the most part mass-produced, inexpensive novelty items, the clown does not have to go to the trouble of building them. In short, he should "pay the five dollars."

The only piece of equipment that the clown carries with him at all times is his own body. Gymnastics and circus skills help the clown to use this basic tool better by suggesting new ways to relate to the common objects around him. As with the discussion on physical comedy in Chapter 6, none of the maneuvers suggested are difficult, and all can be performed by anyone in good physical condition.

The remaining pieces of equipment covered in this book are allied to a number of specialized skills. Juggling, puppetry, ventriloquism, balloon sculpture, trained animals, and magic all require a minimum of rehearsal. Some of the equipment used to practice these skills is specialized, but the preparation necessary to make use of them will be time well spent.

The tools and skills described in the following chapters can be used effectively in a great number of bits, sketches, and routines. A "bit" is a short, humorous piece of business that is capable of standing on its own: a visual pun, a demonstrated joke, or a slice of wit in motion. A sketch is a brief play and may consist of a few bits held together by a common theme. By linking several sketches together with a central theme or consistent progressions of thought and action, the clown ends up with a routine.

Unfortunately for the novice clown, not many bits, sketches, or routines are available in writing for his study. The best he can hope to find in this regard are general plot summaries and prose descriptions of other clown's routines. These are adequate for the established clown but are of little use to the beginner. Plot summaries establish a line of physical action for the novice. However, they do not record the comic elements that highlight the action. Unless the clown knows what to look for, he will find these elements only by chance.

Prose descriptions of other's works present a danger to the nouveau funny person. The keynote of the clown's comedy is immediacy: His actions should always appear to be impromptu. By imitating another's work, the clown loses this immediacy, and his performance becomes lifeless. The scripts that serve as examples in Chapters 9–17, as well as those in the preceding chapters, avoid the failings of the simple summary and didactic description. They provide the clown with ways to use specific pieces of equipment while establishing through lines of action and illustrating the comic elements of the plots. Most importantly, the scripts can be easily adapted to fit each clown's needs and character.

The skills required to utilize pieces of specialized equipment ultimately add depth to the clown's performance. They increase the number of options and alternatives open to him in the performance of his sketches and routines. As a joke file allows the clown to ad-lib verbally by readily supplying him with something to say, a variety of skills and equipment allow him to ad-lib physically by giving him something to do. The very nature of the clown requires him to be able to act on a moment's notice, and each new skill that a clown acquires enables him to adapt readily to unexpected situations that always seem to arise during the course of each performance.

The clown will also find uses for these skills outside the performance of his art. Juggling and tumbling are excellent ways to exercise. Puppetry, ventriloquism, balloon sculpture, and magic can be entertaining diversions all by themselves for parties and family get-togethers.

The keynote in working with any of these objects and devices should always be the smoothness of handling. The professional clown must always be familiar with his props so that he doesn't have to pause to remember how to operate the device with which he is working. If the clown laughs at this piece of advice, he should try to remember what it was like as a very young child learning to eat with a fork. The pointed tines always seemed to get hung up on the tongue and gums, but after years of use, the operation of a fork has become imbedded in the subconscious. When a clown performs, this kind of unconscious manipulation is a necessity. If the clown does not have this expertise with a prop, he may forewarn his audience that something is going to happen and lose the element (and laughter) of surprise.

Fortunately, the clown is not expected to be a grand master at every skill he utilizes, but he must have a working knowledge of the skills involved to be able to use his equipment. If he can not use his equipment, he is a very sad clown indeed because his equipment supplies him with the reason to act. The clown's character establishes an inner world on which action can be based. His equipment embodies the external world that creates conflicts to necessitate action.

The equipment listed here is by no means the final word on the variety of tools available to the clown. As a performer, the clown may use any object, device, or skill and should not be confined by a listing in a book. The objects and devices referred to here may eventually lead the clown to related pieces of equipment and more advanced skills. For the clown, the world is his toy, and his play should not be restricted.

Properties
Ordinaire

THE BOARD

To establish two intersecting bisociative fields, the clown has only to pick up a lengthy piece of wood: ply, pine, or two by four. The single requisite for this piece of lumber is that it be longer than the clown is tall.

How does a board (most lengthy pieces of wood are called boards) establish two bisociative fields?

Quite well, actually. The first field encompasses the many uses to which an uncut, unfinished piece of wood might be put. A board may be employed as a brace or fitted to become part of an existing frame. Boards can be used on the outside of a building as a decorative, protective covering. Inside, they may be used to panel walls or build furniture. The list of uses for wood is immense and varied.

A second field is established by the fact that the board is much too long to be carried or moved easily. The point at which these two fields meet is called "the clown."

Gifted with innocent ineptitude, no one can reasonably expect the clown to deal successfully with as complicated an item as a board. After all, a board possesses absolutely no moving parts. It does not have an "off" or "on" switch. It cannot be plugged into a wall socket. All attempts to fuel or put batteries into it will fail. It does not come with directions. Unless moved, it will lie in one place until it rots or fossilizes. IT IS A PIECE OF WOOD. And it cries out to every passer-by, "Use me. Make something out of me. Give me a purpose for being." The clown hears this cry and is more than willing to heed the plea. Unfortunately, the clown has never had so much as one elementary high school shop course and is totally unprepared to deal with the logic of lumber.

He approaches the board as he approaches any newly discovered object: with a sense of wonder. That such an amazing item as this piece of uncut wood can exist is a marvel to him. He has been looking for a board with the dimensions of this one for some time. To reassure himself that the board is just the size he needs, he must measure it. Fortunately, he has an impossibly long tape measure rolled up in his coat. He removes it by pulling one end and letting it unroll from his pocket. It coils around his feet in a tangled mess. Finally, he arrives at the end of his measure and measures the width. Perfect!

Next he must make sure of the length. He places the tape even with his end of the board. Taking the other end of the tape, he starts to walk the length of the board. Unfortunately, he has forgotten that he neglected to straighten out the tangle at his feet, so he falls flat on his face. Undeterred, he walks to the other end of the board, dragging the tangled tape behind him. He places the tape flush with the other end of the board. A perfect fit, he thinks. He is totally unaware that he does not have a true measurement; the other end of the tape lies a few feet behind him.

Cramming the measure in his pocket, the clown prepares to carry the board home. He stands it on end and heaves it to his shoulder. Overbalanced, the board hits the ground, toppling the clown backward. Picking himself up, the clown approaches the board warily. From this moment on, a state of war exists between the clown and the board. Ropes, pulleys, levers, wagons, ice tongs— one item after another suggests itself as a possible solution until the stage is filled and the clown is surrounded by a technological gamut of devices that refuse to meet his needs.

Finally, in a climactic revelation, the clown thinks of the answer to his problem. Extracting a saw from the mechanical rubble around him, he cuts the board into smaller pieces and walks home with the wood under his arm. That the board is now useless for its intended purpose goes unnoticed as the clown revels in his ingenuity at winning the battle.

That story line is not intended to be used as a sketch but as an exercise. The clown must be able to choose alternative movements and properties at a moment's notice, and as with the telling of jokes, practice makes perfect. Ordinary objects such as boards lend themselves readily to improvisation because of their generalized functions.

This is not to say that the above story can be used only as an exercise. With polish, the addition of comedic asides, and the correct pacing, this story could be worked into a sketch containing a steady stream of laughable bits.

Usually, the board as a comedic prop is utilized in sketches involving two or more clowns. These sketches generally use the piece of wood as an oversize slapstick. The use of the board is reduced to one function and becomes merely a bit within a larger sketch. This is true of all board-related sketches but one: "The Carpenter's Helper."

As with most clown sketches, "The Carpenter's Helper" varies in content from one clown alley to another. The script that follows focuses only on the use of the board, but many construction tools may be used successfully within the framework of the sketch, and the script should not be considered as a static scenario followed consistently by clowns around the world. The object of this script, as well as the others in this book, is to provide the clown with old and new material that might spark his imagination and lead him to more original comedy.

As many as six clowns may be involved in "The Carpenter's Helper." They take the roles of the foreman, bricklayers, assistants, architect, employer, and, of course, the hapless helper. For simplicity's sake, the script here has been reduced to the two basic character types used in the sketch to set up the conflict. The first is the person who thinks he knows everything and is represented by the Carpenter. The other character is the individual who knows very little about what he is doing but is so intimidated by the other character that he cannot freely admit his inexperience. This character is the Helper.

The setting is a shop or construction site. The construction setting allows the greater number of clowns to be utilized. Depending on the setting used, the backdrop may be a workbench or the frame of a building under construction. Pieces of lumber are scattered around. Saw horses and other pieces of equipment of the building trade are set up across the stage. Ropes slung from pulleys hang in front of the background. Paint cans, cement troughs, bricks, and other objects may or may not be used. In most cases, the clown will discover that such a set is impractical. Few clown performances are given in the same theater, and the clown is expected to set up and tear down the sets he uses in an impossibly short time. Therefore, the clowns involved in this sketch will usually carry their tools and the offending board on stage with them and carry them off when they are finished.

Two clowns enter. One, the Carpenter, is showing the other, the Helper, around. (If this sketch is presented as a silent bit set to music, do not use the following dialogue.)

CARPENTER: All right! Let's see what you can do. *(He points to the board.)* I need a piece of lumber five feet seven and a half inches long. You can cut wood?

HELPER: Oh, yes. I've cut a lot of wood.

CARPENTER: Here's the saw and measure, and there is the wood. Go to it.

(The Carpenter stands back to watch. At this point, the Helper should work at top speed and appear efficient. He places the board on two saw horses, measures it with the tape measure, and picks up a pencil. But from the moment the pencil enters the Helper's hand, all work stops. He licks the tip of the pencil [to make it write easier], stretches his writing arm [to loosen the muscles], assumes a solid stance [to steady the pencil], and begins to place the pencil to the board. But before he reaches the board, his weight shifts, so he must go through the above again to prepare himself for drawing the line. This bit of business can be elaborated until finally the Carpenter is goaded to speak.)

CARPENTER: Draw the line!

(The Helper lowers the pencil to the board. He quickly adjusts himself, but the pencil will not move. The effort required to move it drives him to his knees. The pencil is shifted from the normal position used in writing to the position used by a young child when drawing with a crayon.)

CARPENTER *(Knocking the Helper aside):* Give me that! *(He draws a line on the board.)* Now, cut it!

(The Helper picks up the saw, obviously flustered, and hurries to the board. In his rush, he neglects to notice one detail. He is leaning on the end of the board that extends far beyond the saw horses. The Carpenter approaches the other end of the board in disbelief and is about to tell the Helper to stop when the Helper makes the first downward sweep with the saw. The board swings up, apparently catching the

Carpenter on the chin, and the saw sticks in the groove. While the Helper, oblivious to what has happened, struggles to free the saw, the Carpenter leans in mock pain on the saw horse. The saw suddenly springs free, and the board slams back in place, apparently on the Carpenter's hand. If other clowns are used, they should be rolling in laughter at the Carpenter's predicament.

CARPENTER: *(After screaming in pain)* Give me that board. *(He tears the board out of the Helper's reach. The Helper, in an effort to explain, starts toward the Carpenter.)* Don't get near me with that saw. *(The Helper stops and sadly puts down the saw.)* Look, maybe you aren't really suited for cutting wood. Why don't you just clean up this area a little. The owner is coming over later, and I don't want him to see this mess. You can start with this board. *(The Carpenter hands the board to his Helper.)* Just put it over there. *(He points in a general off-stage direction.)* Can you do *that?*

HELPER: Sure! *(He tucks the board beneath his arm.)* Right away.

CARPENTER: Good. Then, do it. *(The Carpenter turns to walk away. He sees the saw on the ground and bends to pick it up. The Helper turns upstage as the Carpenter bends downstage, and the end of the board sends the Carpenter sprawling.)*

HELPER: *(Stops after a few steps. He can't decide where to put the board.)* Where do you—? *(He sees the Carpenter on the floor.)* Oh, my gosh! What happened? Are you hurt? *(He drops the board and tries to help the Carpenter up.)*

CARPENTER *(Pushing the Helper away)*: I'm fine! I'm fine! Just take that board away.

HELPER *(Picking up the board)*: Where?

CARPENTER: Over there!

HELPER *(Turns downstage, and the back of the board catches the Carpenter in the stomach)*: Where?

CARPENTER: Oomph!

HELPER: What? *(Turns upstage, and the front of the board knocks the Carpenter flat.)*

CARPENTER *(Climbs slowly to his feet)*: Don't ever do that again. *(He hits the front of the board and the Helper pivots 180 degrees. The back of the board hits the Carpenter in the stomach.)*

HELPER: *(Turning)* Why did you do that? *(The front of the board knocks the Carpenter down. The Helper looks at the sprawled figure for a moment.)* Aren't you feeling well? You keep falling down.

CARPENTER *(Getting to his feet):* I feel perfectly fine! Just get that board away from me!

HELPER: I want to, but . . . *(He begins to turn.)* . . . I don't know where to put it . . . *(Carpenter ducks the board and stands up, self-satisfied.)* If you'd just tell me where . . . *(Helper turns back, and the board clobbers the Carpenter.)* . . . I'll do it. Oh, no! Not again?

CARPENTER: Yes, again! When I get my hands on you . . . *(This last is left unfinished as the Carpenter chases his Helper off the stage.)*

Alternative endings may be used if additional clowns are added to the sketch. The owner of the property may enter to see the Carpenter sprawled on the floor and fire the Carpenter for drinking. Once the Carpenter leaves, the owner discovers his mistake because the Helper innocently begins to knock some stuffing out of the owner's shirt (with the board, of course). If many clowns are used as laborers at the construction site, a Rube Goldberg ending can be set. Through the first part of the sketch, the additional clowns are an on-stage audience. They react, when not working, to the problems of the Carpenter (foreman). By the end, each of them is in a position to be knocked over, tripped up, run down, or otherwise afflicted when the Carpenter (foreman) chases his Helper from the stage. In the act of turning to flee, the Helper hits one clown, which starts a chain reaction that topples the other merrymakers. These clowns join the chase, bringing the ending to a flamboyant harlequinade.

The addition of other clowns to this sketch increases the possibilities of comedy available. Each clown brings with him a number of different fields of thought or action that can be bisociated with the original premise (the board as a useful item and an awkward object). Each field brings with it a variety of approaches to the piece of wood as well as a gamut of tools and props that can relate to the board in manners different from their usual relationships.

Depth is also added to the sketch by sundry bits of business that have nothing to do with the board. These bits are suggested by the bisociation of fields between the board and the other properties.

For example, the difficulty the Helper encounters in drawing a straight line is achieved by the need for precision and the need not to fail. In this script, the bisociation of these needs results in immobility. The Helper cannot get the pencil to move. The board has nothing to do with this bit of business other than to be the passive object on which the line is to be drawn.

Before leaving the board as a comedy item, a mention should be made of the other ways in which it can be used. So far, the obvious has been considered: an uncut piece of wood as building material. A piece of wood can also be used to start a fire, to post a sign, or to make a ramp, as in the following walk-around bit:

A Clown enters, carrying a board and a block of wood. The block of wood should be six inches wide and thick enough to support the board. The length of the block should equal the board's width. The Clown finds a level spot and puts down the block (being careful not to be too harsh since blocks of wood are notorious for their pride). He then places one end of the board on the block and meticulously aligns the other end with some point in the distance. This done, the Clown mounts the high end of the board and strolls down its length. When he reaches the ground, he moves the block to the other end of the board, moves the board ahead so that the board again forms a ramp, and repeats his stroll down the length of the board.

While the Clown is preoccupied with aligning the board properly and walking its length, a Second Clown enters. The Second Clown is obviously intelligent because he seems just as perplexed as the audience about what the First Clown is attempting to do. He watches the First Clown repeat the walk down the board once before he becomes curious enough to speak.

SECOND CLOWN: What do you think you're doing?

FIRST CLOWN *(Pauses just long enough to answer the question and continues as before):* Walking home.

SECOND CLOWN *(Appears satisfied for a moment and then realizes that the answer does not explain the board and the block):* What do you mean, you're walking home?

FIRST CLOWN *(Continuing):* Just what I said. I'm walking home.

SECOND CLOWN *(Ponders this for a moment and then grabs the First Clown):* Hold it! *(He looks at the ramp again to make sure it is there.)* You're walking home?

FIRST CLOWN: That's right.

SECOND CLOWN: And you're in a hurry?

FIRST CLOWN: Correct.

SECOND CLOWN *(Loses control):* Then what are you doing with that board?

FIRST CLOWN *(Not understanding why someone is questioning his actions):* Hurrying.

SECOND CLOWN *(Exasperated at not being able to communicate with the First Clown):* How is that board helping you hurry home?

FIRST CLOWN *(Finally comprehends the confusion of the Second Clown and is amazed that anyone could fail to see the logic behind his actions):* Oh, that's simple to explain. I took a course in physics at (name of local college or high school). *(Starts to go back to the board)*

SECOND CLOWN *(Totally confused, drags the First Clown back):* What does that have to do with that board?

FIRST CLOWN: *(Obviously, he is dealing with a child and only 48 cards.)* If I have to explain, I will.

SECOND CLOWN: Explain! Explain!

FIRST CLOWN: Well, I found out that an object will move faster with less energy if it is going downhill because gravity pulls it along.

SECOND CLOWN: So?

FIRST CLOWN: So if I walk down a hill going home, I'll get there faster than if I were walking on level ground.

SECOND CLOWN: I can understand that, but why the board?

FIRST CLOWN: That's my hill. I build a ramp and walk home on it. *(As comprehension comes to the Second Clown, he begins to move toward the First Clown. Vengeance for being lured into this ridiculous discussion is the only thing on his mind.)* You see, there aren't any hills near my place, so I have to improvise. *(Sees the Second Clown coming and tries to appeal to the Second Clown's better judgment while getting ready to run.)* You'd do the same thing in my shoes, wouldn't you? I mean, why should I wear myself out going home when this is much easier. You can see that. *(He continues in this manner until both clowns break and run simultaneously.)*

From this point in the bit, the clowns may rush to the next point of the performing area and repeat the action. As with most walk-around stunts, this bit can also be used as transitional material or at the beginning or end of a routine. If it is used as a transition or opening piece, the clown should rewrite the material so that it flows easily into the next bit of action. As an ending, it offers the dash and color of the harlequinade since it leads quite naturally to the clown chase.

The one failing of the bit is that to bring the illogical reasoning of the First Clown home to the audience, the name of a local school must be used. This is a cheap shot but an effective one because it adds the element of immediacy to the comic lunacy. Such tricks are many times necessary in the performance of comedy but should be used sparingly. The clown must be able to sustain a prolonged pace of great speed. To do this and at the same. time think on his feet, the clown is forced occasionally to utilize a trite trick. That does not give the clown sanction consistently to choose the easy way out. Inspired originality is what raises the clown's performance to the level of art. Tricks of audience manipulation simply raise the clown's performance to the level of mediocrity.

One final warning to the clown who likes slapstick humor. The board, like the rest of the properties discussed in this chapter, is a tool. By itself, a piece of wood is far from funny. Only when the clown interacts with it does it become a device of comedy. If it is overused, the clown will find himself performing to a silent multitude that has been, literally, *board* to death.

THE CHAIR

Unlike the board, the chair has a very specific function. Or does it?

Everyone knows that a chair is made to sit on, but in a pinch it acquires a great number of alternative functions. As a stepladder, it is more than adequate. The relatively flat surface of its seat can be used as a drawing board. For those who like to eat Oriental in solitary, it can become the table for one. The back of a chair is better able to hold a coat than are most hangers. A single chair jammed beneath a doorknob will secure a door much more efficiently than any other piece of furniture. And it can be used for fending off lions.

"I sing the chair electric," to blatantly alter a piece of superb poetry by Whitman. The chair is as capable of being used in a wide variety of ways as is a piece of uncut lumber. That it is generally assigned a single function is irrelevant because its other uses are just as valid as its intended use.

That its intended purpose is to be sat on only simplifies the job of the clown. Since it already exists in a pre-established field, the clown need only assign one other field to create a bisociative condition.

In this lies the beauty of ungimmicked, ordinary objects. The audience recognizes the object and its function, and when the clown applies to the object an absurd function, laughter will come easily. The reason is the seeming spontaneity of the bisociative fields. Everyone in the audience has at one time violated the assigned function of an object to reach a desired goal. By the same token, they have been hampered by the use of an object just outside the framework of its intended purpose.

For example, consider the clown in the following dumb show entitled "The Snack":

The setting is a living room. The time is just before "the big game" or "favorite program." In the center of the stage sits the chair facing the audience, which has the point of view of the television set. A clown enters. He is overburdened by various snacks: potato chips, pretzels, cookies, a piece of pie, soda. He is in a rush because he does not want to miss a minute of his previously scheduled program. Deftly, he swoops into the chair, maintaining the balance of the snacks he is carrying. Since there is no table, he must hold the food he has brought with him while getting comfortable in the chair.

Settled, he becomes aware that the television is not turned on. Fortunately, his set operates with an automatic control that is on the floor beside the chair. Under normal circumstances, the clown would simply have to reach down and pick up the control unit to turn on the television. This the clown attempts to do without spilling any of the food he has balanced about his person. His movements are slow and careful, while his attention flickers between the control unit and the food. To maintain the balance of the dishes he is holding, his body contorts and twists as his one free arm moves closer and closer to the box. Some of the items begin to *over*balance, and he freezes. Seemingly by sheer will power, he keeps the plates, glasses, etc., from falling and finally retrieves the automatic television control. From this point on, several different endings are available:

1. As soon as the clown hits the "on" button of the control box a spring snake leaps out, startling him and spilling his snack. (For the particulars of the snake box, see "Spring Snakes" in the chapter on store-bought stunts.) The clown exits in disgust.

2. The clown settles in the chair, clicks the television on, and begins to arrange himself for an evening's enjoyment. As he becomes absorbed in the game or show, he absently begins to fumble with the soda can (or bottle). He is thirsty. Unfortunately, the can (or bottle) refuses to open. If the clown were not confined in the chair by the munchables he is balancing, he would find this problem less troublesome. After several futile attempts, the clown throws his whole body into one supreme effort. The container opens, spraying the clown and dumping the food in his lap. The clown exits, dripping in defeat.

3. As the clown settles himself, he discovers he has company in the chair: a fly. Maintaining the balance of his plates, bags, cups, etc., he begins to stalk the fly with a paper or *TV Guide*. Prisoned in the chair by the containers tottering on his lap and one arm, he takes a few experimental swats at the insect. Finally, the fly lands on the food in his lap. The clown slams the paper on the fly, destroying his carefully arranged snack in the process. At first, he is happy over his conquest of the fly. Then he realizes what he has done and claps his hand against his head in exasperation. Unfortunately, the hand he uses has been holding a plate of pie. He leaves to clean up.

By sitting in the chair to eat his snack, the clown places himself in a position that has been occupied by practically every member of his audience: the difficulty of eating in a chair without the benefit of a table. The humor is expanded by the clown's exaggerated movements. Each specific movement will vary slightly from clown to clown and is dictated by the clown's character and agility, but no matter how the movement comes out, the audience will laugh because they know what the clown is going through. They have been there themselves.

Asides may be added by having the clown talk to himself. His remarks on the trials he has been put to should reflect the thoughts of his audience in a similar situation, for the identification with his audience is the only thing that will make "The Snack" effective as a sketch. As with all slapstick bits, lack of audience identification will reduce the material to a nonsensical horror show of cruelty.

For example, without audience identification, the following bit becomes a bit of silliness at which only a sadist would laugh:

The clown comes on stage prepared to lecture. As he makes his opening remarks, he moves to the chair to sit down. Before he sits, he notices something on the seat. He tries to flick it away, but it does not move. Continuing his talk, he removes a handkerchief and tries to wipe the seat of the chair. His rubbing becomes more and more vigorous until the seat is clean. This done, he replaces his handkerchief, sits down, and slides off the chair. He has polished it too hard.

In this bit, whether the clown takes the role of a didact who could put a brick to sleep or a concerned citizen speaking about a picayune problem makes no matter. Unless the audience is able to recognize the character being lampooned and identify with the situation, their laughter will be cruel. After all, they are laughing at someone who has done violence to himself. The clown must circumvent this type of laughter by giving the audience a reason to laugh at his downfall. This is accomplished by the act of polishing the seat. It justifies the slapstick and allows the audience to relate to the subsequent slip of the seat.

The slip itself is performed quite simply by levering forward on one leg while making the torso as limp as possible. If the surface of the chair is smooth, the pratfall is facilitated, but a smooth surface is not essential. The seat of the chair and the seat of the clown do not need to meet.

As a prop, the chair is found in many clown sketches and routines. It is stood on, lain across, and upheld. Occasionally, when it crops up, it is tripped over. And, the clown may sit in it while waiting for his next show.

THE HAMMOCK

According to *The American Heritage Dictionary of the English Language,* a hammock is "a hanging, easily swung cot or bed, suspended by cords between two supports." It is tailor-made for the clown.

No other ordinary object offers the comedic potential inherent in the common hammock. It combines simplicity of construction with a conflict that naturally establishes two intersecting bisociative fields: The hammock is comfortable, but to get in it and stay there requires practice. Even someone well-versed in its usage will occasionally take a spill.

For the clown with acrobatic ability, such a piece of apparatus is perfection. The hammock supplies him simultaneously with a generalized slack wire and a small trampoline. An added attraction is that it packs flat and can easily be transported between shows. All the clown need do to supply his audience with a five-minute acrobatic routine is reach into his suitcase, string the hammock between two supports and try to climb into it.

Unlike any other ungimmicked prop, the hammock itself will join the action. As it sways, zigging to the clown's every zag, it will appear to fight back. The clown will discover that the war he is waging is not with an inanimate object but with an active thing that seems to have a mind of its own.

The routine described below takes into account the hammock's obvious resemblance to a slack wire and adds some bits usually included in the clown tramp (trampoline) act. All of the bits are safe and simple, but the clown should take into account that the ground he will eventually fall on is hard, and mats should be placed beneath the hammock to soften the falls during rehearsals. Also, as was stated in the chapter on physical comedy, before performing any acrobatic stunt, the clown must walk through every move and fall to ensure against being taken unaware by a real spill. The clown must remember that beneath his colorfully absurd exterior lies a flesh-and-blood posterior. He will gain nothing but bruises by tempting the fates. Absorbing each movement a bit at a time, the clown establishes the pattern of action that will offer him the utmost protection against unwanted bruises and backaches.

With all of the preparation behind him, the clown is now ready for a peaceful, relaxing "Lazy Day in the Country":

The clown enters carrying a book or magazine. He has nothing more important to do than to lounge around, and what better way to lounge than in a nice comfortable hammock. There isn't a cloud in the sky—better double-check that. There are only two clouds in the sky. But they are small. Nothing will spoil the day. A good book, a good day, a good hammock, everything anyone could ask for.

The clown sits on the hammock and leans back to enjoy his rest. Oops! he falls backward out of the hammock. How silly of him. He ought to be more careful. He climbs into the hammock with greater wariness. Ah! He has made it and is peacefully reclining in a pastoral setting. Now for the book. He opens it and falls out of the hammock.

This is going to be more difficult than he thought. Maybe if he creeps up on it. First he must allay its suspicions that he is going to get back in it. Just saunter nonchalantly by, then leap. The clown misses the hammock entirely, does a side roll, and springs up beneath it. The hammock slingshots the clown back to the ground, and he slide rolls out to his feet.

This contraption may not be too intelligent, but it is quick. Another play is called for: force. The clown sidles up to the hammock and grabs it. Planting one foot firmly in the material, he spreads it open with both hands and mounts it. He waits until the swaying of the hammock has slowed. His body jackknifed above it, he must now lower himself into it. Unfortunately, whenever he shifts his weight, the hammock begins to swing violently. (If the supports are strong enough, the clown can actually turn in a full circle.) Finally, it steadies, and the clown plummets to the ground.

This is the last straw. No piece of cloth is going to defeat him. In a fury he leaps at the refugee from a dressmaker and twines his arms and legs in its cloth. He intends to ride it out. The hammock bucks and bounces and the clown flails within its grasp. No longer is he on the attack. His only concern now is survival. In the end, he is left hanging on to the hammock, which peacefully sways above him. Its spirit has been broken.

Slowly, the clown rights himself and settles into the hammock. As he does, the sides cover him, and the bucking and swaying resume: The beast was only playing possum. He is jounced and shaken until the hammock opens to deposit him on terra as firma as possible.

The clown stays grounded for a moment in abject defeat. He has lost. Or has he? Inspiration strikes, and the clown climbs to his feet. He unhooks the hammock from the supports and spreads it on the ground. He jumps on it several times, both to make sure that it is now safe and to render it senseless if it isn't. Then he cautiously stretches out on it with his book or magazine. The day is restored to balance, and the clown gets his much-deserved rest.

An alternative ending to this routine can be achieved by bringing in a second clown. After the last desperate struggle with the hammock, which leaves the first clown heaped on the ground, overpowered by a piece of cloth, the second clown goes immediately to the hammock and stretches out in it. He apparently has no trouble making the contraption function as it should. This angers the first clown enough to redouble his efforts to conquer the swinging demon. He dumps the second clown from the hammock and begins the attack again. This time, when the flurry of movement subsides, he is left in the hammock, not on the ground. He relaxes to enjoy his victory when all of a sudden the air is filled with the sound of thunder. The first clown looks at the sky and sees the gathering storm (lightning may be added if feasible). In resignation, the clown climbs out of the hammock and walks off toward home.

The introduction of the second clown also offers another alternative ending. Once dumped from the hammock, the second clown may assert his claim to use the device. If he does, this routine makes a suitable build-up to "Clown Boxing," which is described later in this chapter. After a tussle over the hammock, one clown introduces two pairs of boxing gloves (of the pig-bladder variety), and the clowns square off for a duel of honor.

No matter what the ending or how the clown uses the hammock, the primary rule of slapstick should always be remembered. Never needlessly repeat an action or bit of business. Every movement must be justified within the logic of the routine, or the clown will only bore his audience and make a fool of himself.

HATS

The accomplished clown should be able to use any object to enhance the humor of his illogical universe. Therefore, his costume must be considered as a potential prop. If the clown will allow this precept to roll around his head for a while, he need only consider the hat. This is readily usable because it can be removed easily and manipulated naturally. Although an integral part of the clown's makeup, the hat can exist independently and can be worn or used by anyone. Such properties make it a perfect tool to be used as in the following walk-around bit.

Lifted almost directly from the work of Laurel and Hardy, this bit was suggested by the incidental business with bowlers that was used throughout their incredible careers. Accidentally knocking Oliver's hat to the ground, Stan would bend over to pick it up. When he did, his hat would fall from his head. He would then pick up his own hat and, since one bowler greatly resembles another, would quite naturally mix them up. This would leave Mr. Hardy wearing a hat several sizes too small for his head and looking incredibly silly.

Below is an enlargement of the bit from these two masters of mirth. Dialogue may be used between the clowns involved, but it should be incidental to the business. Just as movement can on occasion act to the detriment of a joke, joking unnecessarily can obscure a piece of physical comedy. For this bit, the progressive series of movements is the important factor. Many clowns forget that humor is an assault on the senses and that the audience can only devote full concentration to one comedic convention at a time. Verbal comedy must be alternated with the physical, only rarely can they function together. So forewarned, the clown is ready to tackle "The Seven and Three Quarters Solution":

Enter two clowns, both wearing hats. From the way they walk, the audience can easily differentiate between the characters of the two clowns. The first clown is apparently sure of himself. He is nattily dressed and carries a cane. He will be referred to as Clown. The other is the familiar stock character of clown comedy, the Dummy. Together, they approach a section of the audience that has very apparently been enjoying the show up to this point. This will ensure that the crowd to which the clowns will be playing is receptive. (To single out the receptive portions of an audience consistently takes experience, but there are certain techniques that are discussed in Appendix I that will aid the clown in reading his audience.) As the clowns stop in front of the chosen section of the audience, the Dummy bumps into the Clown, who drops his cane.

CLOWN: Clumsy! Can't you watch where you are going? *(He points to the cane.)* Now pick that up.

DUMMY *(Apologizes quietly throughout. He stoops to pick up the cane, and his hat falls to the ground. Just as he is about to hand cane to Clown, he notices his hat at his feet. Putting down the cane, he picks up his hat and, after dusting it meticulously, places it on his head. He has forgotten about the cane and stands observing the audience, occasionally waving or reacting to individuals in the stands.)*

CLOWN: My cane?

DUMMY: Pardon?

CLOWN: My cane! My cane!

DUMMY: Very good! *(Points at the cane on the ground.)* Your cane.

CLOWN: Pick it up!

DUMMY: Sorry. *(Runs through his previous actions. His hat falls, he puts down the cane, picks up his hat, dusts it, etc.)*

CLOWN: Must I do everything myself. *(Clown bends and grabs the cane, dropping his hat in the process.)* I only asked you to perform a simple service for—*(He sees his hat on the ground. So does Dummy.)*

DUMMY: You dropped your hat. Let me help you.

CLOWN: Finally, some satisfaction.

(Dummy bends, picking up Clown's hat and dropping his own. Unable to find a place to put Clown's hat while he retrieves his own, Dummy places it on his head. Then he bends to pick up the hat on the ground. Clown's hat falls from Dummy's head. Faster and faster, Dummy puts one hat on, bends to pick up the other, and lets the first one drop. The effect on the audience will be the same as if they were listening to a record that was stuck, for Dummy is bouncing back a groove every time he bends to pick up a hat. He continues, gaining momentum, until Clown stops him.)

CLOWN: Will you cut that out!

DUMMY: *(Thoroughly frustrated, his own hat on his head, he stops for a moment as he is hit by a revelation. Planting one hand firmly on his hat to hold it in place, he stoops with his back erect and grabs Clown's hat from the floor. That his hat cannot possibly fall off when he stoops in this manner fails to prevent him from holding his hat in place. Better safe than sorry. He begins to dust off the hat he has just picked up.)*

CLOWN *(Walks to Dummy with his hands out, ready for his hat)*: Thank you.

DUMMY *(Seeing the outstretched hand, he drops the hat and grasps the hand firmly. As he begins shaking it vigorously, he tramps on Clown's hat)*: I was more than glad to be of service. Anything to make you happy.

CLOWN *(Watching in disbelief, he groans.)*

DUMMY: What's the matter? *(He sees the hat smashed on the floor.)* Oh, I'm sorry. Let me get it for you.

CLOWN: No, I'll get it myself!

(As they bend simultaneously, they both get "it." Their heads meet somewhere over the hat, and they both reel back. Dummy realizes that he is in a lot of trouble. Clown is almost frothing at the mouth. Dummy flees, chased by an angry clown waving the cane over his head. They run to another section of the audience where they repeat the action just described.)

Note should be taken of several important points in considering this bit for use as a walk-around number. Most importantly, Clown should be careful not to strike or shove Dummy in front of the audience. Such a display of physical violence in a bit of this type is unnecessary. The walk around is an intimate performance for a small group of people sitting in a large arena surrounded by an immense crowd. Small groups tend to identify closely with the characters and what they do to each other. This is especially true of the children in the stands, and there lies the danger. To a child, a clown is a real creature. A child who sees one clown hitting another (even in fun) will assume that the blow and not the frustration behind it is funny. Obviously, the clown is not really hurt. The youngster can plainly see the overexaggerated grimaces, and everybody around him is laughing, so hitting a clown must be funny. Countless clowns have their shows disrupted by children who misguidedly hold this false belief. At the high point of the performance, a child will break from the crowd, run at the clown, and with a great big smile belt him in the chops, stomach, or nether regions.

This is not funny.

The clown will be sore pressed (if not just plain sore) to recover from this fancy little bit of upstaging. The clown who does not believe this should try smiling or telling a joke while a freshly beaten muscle is tensing and trembling with pain. Therefore, beware of displaying any sort of harsh slapstick while in close proximity to an audience. Save it for the alienating confines of the stage or ring.

Second, Clown in the above bit is forced to raise his voice several times in irritation. When a clown raises his voice, he must do so only out of frustration. He is exasperated, not angry. His movements must be so broad and outlandish that his audience, even the children, will realize that he is not acting in anger. This is especially important when the contrasting character in the sketch or bit is Dummy. Audiences like to root for the underdog, and Dummy is as under as a clown can get. Besides, an angry clown never sits well with the public. He only makes them feel ill at ease.

Third, because of the repetitive movement in this bit, pace and timing are essential to its success. If the action progresses too slowly, the bit will be monotonous. If it progresses too fast, the audience will not have time to absorb the slightly bent logic of the action, and the bit will become incomprehensible. Pace does not refer to speed but the steady progression of plot from one action to another. The clown will seldom need to rush. If the logic of the situation is strong, the clown will simply need to keep the action going. The speed of presentation will automatically be dictated by the objects with which he works and the timing required to relate effectively to his fellow performers.

Last, several different fields bisect at varying points in the plot of this bit. Since they are easily identifiable, there is no need to list them here. These bisecting points frame the action and are most likely the places that an audience will laugh or snicker. The clown must be prepared to occupy himself in a manner that relates to his situation whenever the audience laughs. If he does not, the action of the bit will be broken, and the clown will have to pick up the momentum of the bit from scratch.

These four points are important to the successful performance of a clown and so will be restressed in a number of the sketches and bits included in this book. The clown must be constantly aware of his audience's sensibilities, which, after all, is paying to be entertained. What the paying public will tolerate and what it likes defines his art. The clown must remain circumspect, treading softly until he is sure of his audience and himself. Then he will be able to leap at those moments when the audience will closely identify with his absurdity.

THE ENDS OF HIS ROPE

Unlike its ungimmicked fellow objects, the rope has been the inspiration for a set clown sketch (a sketch that remains basically the same no matter where it is presented). In this sketch, which is titled "The Strongest Clown in the World," the rope is made to appear something that it is not while remaining a rope to all the characters concerned as well as the audience. In the end, the very fact that it is a rope, as the clowns have been maintaining all along, produces the laughter.

The bisociative fields that intersect are the fields of appearance and reality. Filled with the need to display his uniqueness, the clown chooses a bad way to prove it. Wishing to be recognized for his strength, the clown forgets that he is a congenital weakling and *must* stoop to deception.

His desire for strength, however, is a reasonable one. It is a dream that almost every member of the audience secretly harbors. If they did not, Charles Atlas would not be able to afford the cost of advertising in comic books. The human being's fixation with personal power will help the audience identify with the clown's dream and allow them to laugh at themselves as they snicker over the clown's misplaced pride. They do not know that the clown is prepared to cheat.

Prepared? But doesn't this section deal with ungimmicked objects?

Quite right. The rope is not gimmicked. It *is* the gimmick. The only requirement for the preparation of this sketch is that the clown wear a baggy coat several sizes too large for him. This done, everything becomes self-working.

Since the cheat with the rope is clearly revealed at the end of the sketch, the subtleties of performance and preparation will be discussed after their description. And now the time has come to bring on "The Strongest Clown":

ANNOUNCER: Ladies and gentlemen, boys and girls. (name of the show or organization) is proud to present for your enjoyment "The Strongest Man in the World."

(Three Clowns enter. Two of them lead the way, gesticulating and posturing to prepare the audience for the Strong Man. These Clowns are assistants who will eventually handle the crowd, making certain that they are taken in by this simple-minded ploy. They are followed by the Strong Man, a scrawny specimen wearing a coat several sizes too large and carrying coils of rope in both his hands.)

ANNOUNCER: All right! Stop! Hold it right there! (name of the clown), what do you think you're doing?

STRONG MAN: I am the strongest clown in the world.

ANNOUNCER: Now you can't possibly expect any of us to believe that.

STRONG MAN: Yes, I do. I can prove it.

ANNOUNCER: You can prove it?

STRONG MAN: Yep. Right here, right now.

ANNOUNCER: This I have to see. How do you propose to prove that you are the strongest clown in the world?

STRONG MAN: By challenging anybody to pull these ropes out of my hands.

ANNOUNCER: O.K. You asked for it. Ladies and gentlemen, I'm sorry about this interruption, but (name of the clown) insists on carrying this through to the end. So may I have some volunteers from the audience. *(A lot of truly vicious souls raise their hands. Some of them will really want to tear the Strong Man apart, and these people must be weeded out by the assistant clowns.)* Good! Just come down to the assistants and we'll get this over with.

(The assistants split the volunteers into two groups of not more than 10 each, making sure that each group is evenly matched physically. THIS IS IMPORTANT! Meanwhile, the Strong Man tosses both coils so that they unwind to either side of him. He apparently maintains his hold on the end of each rope. The volunteers pick up the ropes that stretch away to either side of the Strong Man. The assistants position themselves on the ropes right next to the clown.)

ANNOUNCER: That's great. Everybody is in position. Now here is what we are going to do. When I count to three, I want all the volunteers to pull as hard as they can until one of these ropes comes out of (name of the clown)'s hands. Ready? One. *(Drum roll)* Two. *(The Strong Man begins to look worried. He is having second thoughts.)* Three! *(The drum roll continues, rising and falling, as the Strong Man is yanked back and forth by the volunteers. At times, his feet leave the floor, and he appears to be about ready to be pulled apart. Just then, a Fourth Clown enters, dressed as a concessionaire and hawking lemonade.)*

FOURTH CLOWN: Lemonade. Get yer lemonade. Ice cold lemonade, here. Good for a thirsty man. Get yer lemonade. *(Continues.)*

(The Strong Man sees the lemonade salesman, and so does the announcer.)

ANNOUNCER: Well, (name of the clown), you seem to be working up quite a sweat. A nice cool lemonade would probably really hit the spot about now. Wouldn't it?

(The Strong Man nods vigorously and then slips out of the coat to get a lemonade. The coat remains hanging on the one

rope that has been threaded through its sleeves and held taut by the two groups of volunteers, who are straining in opposite directions. The volunteers have actually been having a tug of war with each other.)

ANNOUNCER: Wait a minute! What's this? *(He pauses to allow the situation to come to full realization in the audience's mind: about half a beat.)* Get out of here, you silly clowns.

(The Strong Man and lemonade vendor head for the hills while the two clown assistants collect the rope, thank the volunteers, and send them to their seats.)

So simple, so effective, so easy to muff by adding extraneous movement. This is why the clown assistants are vitally important to the success of this sketch. The risk of extraneous movement comes from the volunteers, not the performers. The assistants must select the appropriate audience members and arrange them with a minimum of confusion. They must make certain that the volunteers understand what is to be done. And by positioning themselves on either side of the Strong Man, they ensure that the rope will be stretched taut enough to allow him to slip effortlessly out of his coat.

The Announcer adds to the smooth operation of the sketch by providing the voice of authority. His amplified repetition of everything that occurs or is said in the arena carries the progress of the action to every member of the audience. He even punctuates the end of the sketch by ordering the clowns to leave and reestablishing order once the merrymakers have gone.

The setup for "The Strongest Clown" is simple. A rope is run through the sleeves of a coat and centered so that the ends protruding from the sleeves are of equal length. When the coat is worn and the ends are held coiled in both hands, the one rope appears to be two separate ropes. The sleeves hanging over the clown's hands conceal the fact that the ropes run up the arms. Thus prepared, the clown is ready to test his mettle against any 20 people in the world without the necessity of extensive physical training or high-protein diets.

THE TABLE

Table stunts are often easier and safer to perform than the common pratfall. Why? Because the surface of the table is closer to the performer than the floor. This does not mean that the clown can allow himself to be careless when using the table as a stumbling block. Anyone who rushes into any acrobatic comedy routine without painstakingly walking through it to check his moves deserves whatever sprains, contusions, or breaks he gets. The clown should always have a healthy respect for the tools that he uses. Even the smallest object listed in this section, the hat, can be harmful—if swallowed whole.

The clown will find that any fall on a table will be enhanced by sound effects. Drum rolls and rim shots punctuate the fall and reassure the audience that the fall has been planned. This reassurance is especially necessary with table falls because the table top, being only a thin piece of wood, makes a louder sound when hit than does the floor. His audience will not enjoy themselves if they believe that the clown is doing real violence to himself.

To do a forward table fall, the clown must stand a few feet in front of the table. If he is too close he will appear to be only lying down quickly on the table's surface. As with the pratfall, the legs should be kicked in the air, which will give the illusion that the clown is not in control of his movement. The distance of a few feet necessitates that the clown make a spring at the table. Later, this spring should be incorporated into the movement involved in tripping or stumbling.

The spring accomplishes three things: It allows the clown to reach the surface on which he will fall. The forward thrust adds to the motion of the fall and will later help the clown direct his movement across the table top, as is needed to perform table rolls, and it will help him clear the table's edge. Clearing the edge will avoid a great deal of pain and undesirable language. After the spring, the clown slaps his hands on the table's surface to break his fall and lands so that his waist is at the table's edge. His legs, which have been kicked in the air, drop to the floor, and the clown slides from the table with a stunned expression on his face.

A variation of this that can be used on the table or the trampoline is the running forward fall. The clown runs to the table with the apparent intention of jumping up on to it. He places one foot lightly on the edge and performs a slip step. (See "Physical Comedy.") Simultaneous with the slip step, he jackknifes forward and hits the table with his forearms. His feet drop to the floor and he crumples to the ground.

The back fall is much easier to perform on a table than it is on the floor. The clown uses the edge of the table as his pivot point. He rocks backward, levering his feet into the air and breaks his momentum by slapping his palms and forearms against the table top.

A more advanced form of this fall is done by vaulting onto the table. The clown faces the falling surface. Placing his right hand and foot on the edge, he springs upward, using the hand and foot on the table as pivot points. His body turns as it rises above the arm and leg, and as he descends, he slams his left foot and forearm against the table to break the fall.

The easiest table roll is not really a roll at all. It is more of a turned-around tabled tinsica. The clown stands with his back to the table. He leans backward as if to perform a table fall but lands on the top at an angle. His legs are kicked up and over his body as he spins his trunk to angle off the table's other edge. As his legs come down, they extend over the table's edge, and their momentum pulls the clown to a standing position on the opposite side of the table from which he began. He ends as he began, with his back to the table.

The side roll is the next easiest. From a spring, the clown rolls across the table on his back from left to right or right to left. There is one minor drawback to this roll. When the clown reaches the other side of the table, he will fall off. To break this fall, he must time the roll so that when he leaves the table he leaves it face down. He may then treat the fall as he would a forward pratfall.

The shoulder roll and the forward roll present a problem when performed on a table. At the end of each, the clown is coming down blind. He cannot see where he will be landing. If he does not locate the correct spot on the table to begin his roll, he could land against the opposite edge of the table or miss the table completely and land on the floor. This can be remedied by placing adhesive tape on the table top at the point where the roll should commence.

The backward roll poses a problem opposite to the one presented by the shoulder or forward rolls. During its performance, the clown cannot see where he is going until it is too late to stop his movement. The backward table roll is identical to the backward somersault. The clown stands facing away from the table. He leans back as if he were going to do a back fall on the table; instead, he executes a backward somersault that carries him to the other side of the table. Taking care to clear the table's edge, his feet drop to the floor, and he rises to a standing position. If the table is too high to allow him to execute this maneuver, the clown may perform a backward leg extension, thrusting his legs up in the air and pushing himself off the table, rounding off on the table's opposite edge.

In all of these rolls, the movement must be followed through so that the clown goes to the ground. The clown must remember that he is falling over the table and not trying to impress his audience with his gymnastic prowess.

The clown is now prepared to tackle a table routine. The routine described below is almost identical to the clown trampoline routine that will be explained later, the bits of business and falls are all the same. However, performing with a table requires that the clown justify any acrobatics he might use. The trampoline is a justifiable piece of apparatus to use in a display of physical ability. Great would be an audience's surprise if a trampoline were not used to dive from or bounce on. The table, on the other hand, *is a table*. Its function is to hold food, although it can be very serviceable as a writing surface, card table, or workbench. If the clown does not seem to have a reasonable excuse for falling all over the furniture, he will receive no laughter for his efforts. He will have seemingly beat out his brains for nothing.

And now, on to "The Recital":

A table sits in the center of the stage. Carrying a large book, the Clown approaches the table and turns to the audience.

CLOWN: I'm going to interrupt the show because I think that all of you have the wrong impression about me. I mean, whenever I come out here, you laugh. Well, I want you to know that I am not just another clown. I've been studying to be a great actor, and I'd like to prove to you that I'm not merely somebody to be laughed at. To do that, I'm going to perform Hamlet's soliloquy. *(He points to the table.)* This is my battlement. I didn't have time to build a real one. Just one moment—I'll hop up on the table and begin.

(He places the book on the corner of the table. Then he tries to step up after it but finds the table too high. He will have to hop up, after all. Placing one foot on the edge, he tries to swing the other on to the table top. The foot on the table's edge slips, and the Clown spins in midair to plummet face down to the ground. Picking himself up, he smiles self-consciously at the audience. Then he turns to study the table. Walking back a few paces, he

runs to the table at full speed, puts one foot on the edge, does a slip step, and falls forward. He bounces from the table top to the ground.

Obviously, he will have to jump higher. Leaping up, he runs at the table again. This time, he does a side roll across the table and falls off the other side. Maybe he ran at the table too fast. He tries again and misses the table completely, rolling under it. Once directly under the table, he springs up, hits the table with a thud, and drops like a rock back to the ground.

He crawls warily from beneath the troublesome piece of furniture and gathers himself for one more assault. He walks to the table and laboriously scales it like a mountain climber. When he attains the top, he looks around, not quite able to believe that he really made it. He stands straight and walks to the book. As he bends to pick up the book, he accidentally kicks it to the floor.)

CLOWN: Oh! *(To the audience)* I'm sorry, I knocked the book off the table. *(He looks at the book on the floor and suddenly realizes where he is standing.)* And it fell all the way down there. *(He is afraid of heights.)* Ah!

(The Clown, shaking, tries to get lower on the table top to keep from falling off. Carefully, he stretches one leg over the edge and uses it to search for the floor. He does not release his hold on the table top until both feet are firmly on the ground. Then he picks up his book and leaves, shaken but wiser.)

If an Announcer is used in the program, the following script is recommended for this routine:

The Clown enters, reading a book.

ANNOUNCER: Well, if it isn't (name of the clown). What are you reading?

CLOWN: *Hamlet.*

ANNOUNCER: *Hamlet?* Why are you reading *Hamlet?*

CLOWN: I am studying to be a great actor.

ANNOUNCER *(Dripping with sarcasm): You* are studying to be a great actor?

CLOWN: That's right.

ANNOUNCER: Are you any good?

CLOWN: I'm the best.

ANNOUNCER: I see. Well, why don't you show all of us how good you really are?

CLOWN: Right now?

ANNOUNCER: Sure! Why don't you read something from your book?

CLOWN: I can't.

ANNOUNCER: Why not?

CLOWN: It's *Hamlet.*

ANNOUNCER: So, what if it is?

CLOWN: To read *Hamlet,* you have to be standing on a battlement. It says so right here. *(He points to a page in the book.)*

ANNOUNCER: Oh, you have to be standing on a battlement. You could use the table.

CLOWN *(He thinks about it for a moment)*: All right. Just hold on a second until I get up.

The action proceeds as in the first script until the Clown knocks the book from the table.

CLOWN: I dropped the book.

ANNOUNCER: Yes, you did. And it fell all the way down there.

CLOWN *(He suddenly realizes where he is standing)*: Ah! *(He climbs down.)*

No matter which script is used, the Clown's reason for using the table must be established before he begins his climb to the top.

WHISKED AWAY

Hasn't one ordinary object been overlooked? What about the broom?

Emmett Kelley's brilliant use of a broom to sweep up a spot of light has been often misused by unimaginative clowns who lack the skill to perform it effectively. No one has ever equaled Mr. Kelley's performance with the broom. His emulators always make the mistake of adding movements and cloudy bits of business that muck up the surreal quality of sweeping the spotlight.

However, there is a bit of walk-around business that makes use of a broom that even the novice clown will be able to perform immediately. The ordinary object used in this business is a whiskbroom:

The Clown approaches a member of the audience.

CLOWN: I hate to bother you, but we have a problem. You see, every day before the show, a man is supposed to come through and clean up the seats. Every seat in the house has to be dusted. Well, today he was in a hurry. He was taking his family to see a circus, and he missed one seat. *(He smiles sheepishly.)* I was given the job of coming in here and straightening out his oversight. Would you mind if I dusted your seat?

(When the spectator stands to help out the Clown, the merry-maker uses the whiskbroom to dust the seat, not the seat the audience member was sitting on but the seat that is firmly part of the human anatomy. The Clown then moves on to another section of the audience to pull the same prank.)

In this bit, the broom has nothing to do with the intersecting bisociative fields. The fields only encompass the variant definitions of the word "seat." The audience establishes the first field by assigning to the word the meaning usually applied to it. When the clown reveals his intended meaning, the fields unite in an explosion of laughter.

The clown will get some idea from the six ordinary objects described in this section of the range of comedy available in ungimmicked items. Ordinary objects force originality on the clown's performance because of the variety of their possible uses. Because the audience can readily identify the objects, they will laugh easily when the clown surprises them with his novel use or misuse of the ordinary. They will not have to strain to grasp the logic of the comedy. One of the great comic minds of the twentieth century, Jonathan Winters, constantly reduces the public to helpless guffaws by picking up a common item and forcing his own peculiar perception of the universe on it. In a similar manner, a clown should be able to create comedy by using the objects found in any room of a house. Any room, that is, but one: The clown should never stoop to bathroom humor.

Objects with a Twist

When a clown alters any object, that object is gimmicked. In intellectual terms, the gimmicked object has two bisecting bisociative fields intentionally built into it. This simplifies the clown's job. All he must do is reveal the gimmick to make the audience chortle with comprehension. He does not, as with ordinary objects, have to establish the two fields of thought through a carefully worked out plan of logic before exposing the cross-referenced divergent comic elements to the audience. The fields lay hidden within the gimmicked object he will use. Therefore, he may devote more of his time to the material in the bit or sketch. By releasing him from the confining logic required to set his audience up, the gimmicked object provides the clown with an opportunity to concentrate on his comedy.

The danger of using gimmicked objects, however, arises from this very fact. His job simplified, the clown may ignore the chance offered to him by the gimmick. Most gimmicks can ride on their own. The audience will laugh when they discover the twist hidden in the object no matter what else the clown has prepared for them. This is what makes a gimmicked property perfect for walk-around bits. The clown only has to bring the object forth, reveal part or all of the gimmick, and his audience will begin to giggle. Such a situation can be tempting for the clown. Being lazy, he may present the gimmick and go no further. He will have received his laughter and think his job is through. Many clowns fall into this complacent trap. They build their routines and shows by stacking one gimmicked object onto another without giving a thought to the comic theme that is necessary to string these objects into a unified whole. The effect is a hodgepodge of unrelated properties: physical comedy Henny Youngman style.

But "Laugh-In" used this style very successfully, didn't it?

No. "Laugh-In" used a fast pace in connection with one liners and blackouts, but the material between each commercial reflected a progression from one thought to another. The show was divided into a series of thematic blocks, with Rowan and Martin establishing the links from one thought to another. The two hosts provided direction for the satirical jibes of the supporting comedians.

A study of his work will reveal that even Henny Youngman, a comedian infamous for his seemingly disconnected rapid-fire comedy, recognizes the importance of maintaining thematic consistency in presenting comedy. His material is arranged in blocks according to subject matter. He only switches to a new subject if his audience does not seem to be warming to the topic he is covering. The illusion of his random style is created by the fact that the individual jokes in each block are not arranged in any order at all.

If the clown is unconcerned with the quality of laughter he receives, then he is welcome to grab a handful of the 24 items listed here and string them randomly together for his act. The serious clown will not have to fear his competition, for although the lazy clown will get laughter, it will not be the kind of laughter that rewards a fine performance

BABY RATTLER

Ingredients   A suitcase, paint, rubber cement, and a baby's rattle.

Construction   The clown glues the baby rattle in the bottom of the suitcase. The following words and phrases are painted on the outside:

"DANGER! BEWARE! BABY RATTLER! OPEN AT YOUR OWN RISK! CAUTION!" The paint should be a bright color that contrasts with the color of the case. The words should be conspicuous, with "BABY RATTLER!" having the largest letters.

Performance   "The Baby Rattler" is a walk-around bit but can be incorporated into a larger sketch. As a walk around, it relies completely on the comedy inherent in the gimmick:

The clown walks around the arena, stopping in front of different sections of the audience. Each time he stops, he holds the case up for the audience to see. He may even point out the words "Baby Rattler!" by underscoring them with his finger. Cautiously, he lowers the case and begins to open it. Fear is written all over him. He hesitantly opens the lid a crack to peek in. As he does, the case begins to vibrate and shake furiously. The clown slams the lid and holds the suitcase tighter until its motion subsides. Then, holding it far away from his body toward the audience, he drops the lid, and the audience realizes that the clown was referring to a "Baby rattler" not a "baby Rattler."

Simple. Yet some clowns feel that the gimmick relieves the clown from performing completely. The lazy clown uses the following version:

The clown stands in front of a section of the audience, holds the case aloft so they can see the writing on it, opens the lid, closes the lid, and walks on.

Admittedly, the lazy clown gets a few titters and an occasional guffaw, but he removes all the joy from the bit. He does not allow his audience to relate to him or the situation. However, when the bit is done well, the audience achieves a certain empathy with the clown. The exaggerated fear he displays is the fear they feel when in the presence of slimy snakes or crawling insects. Therefore, they willingly accept the clown's deception, and their laugh is louder.

As a bit in a larger sketch, "The Baby Rattler" is best suited as a blow off because it establishes a reason for a harlequinade and adds a punch at the end. For example, in "The Animal Doctor," which will be described fully later in this chapter, "The Baby Rattler" can be used in the following manner:

The Veterinarian has finished his examination of the last animal and is about to move on to another when a Clown runs in with a suitcase. The other clowns, sitting patiently with their pets, look on.

CLOWN: Doctor! Doctor! Help me. I have an emergency.

VETERINARIAN: An emergency? What happened?

CLOWN: My poor pet Sammy got hit chasing a car. You've got to help him, doc. Please.

VETERINARIAN: All right. Where is he?

CLOWN: *(Handing over the suitcase):* In there.

VETERINARIAN: In here? *(He looks at the suitcase and begins to read the writing on the outside. DANGER! CAUTION! OPEN AT YOUR OWN RISK! BABY RATTLER! He pauses for a moment and then screams BABY RATTLER! GAH! (He tosses the suitcase to another clown, who in turn passes it to another. All of the clowns are trying to flee and rescue their pets from a clear and present danger. Finally, the clowns in the waiting room have gone, leaving the one with the suitcase laughing uproariously at the havoc just created.)*

ANNOUNCER: Well, you certainly got rid of everybody in a hurry. *(The Clown nods vigorously, weak with laughter.)* Tell me, do you really have a baby rattler in that suitcase?

CLOWN: Oh, yes! Would you like to see it?

ANNOUNCER: Yes, I would, but don't get too close. *(The Clown holds up the case and drops the lid.)* Oh, get out of here, you silly clown!

As can be readily seen, the sketch is more satisfying than the walk around. "The Baby Rattler" provides the reason for the dash and color of the clown chase and provides a reason to clear the stage. Nothing hurts a sketch more than taking too long to clear the set and to go into the next bit. This is always a problem when animals are used. They never seem to be able to follow the script closely. But more about that later.

BEST SEAT IN THE HOUSE

Ingredients Suitcase, paint, and one toilet seat.

Construction Paint the phrase "The Best Seat in the House" on the lid of the suitcase. Put the seat in the suitcase. Close the lid.

Performance This is one of the cruder pranks that a clown can pull on his audience, but they will forgive him for the strained logic of the bit if he works hard enough to set up the situation. The most effective method to present this piece of low comedy is to make the clown a ticket scalper. Most audience members will be familiar with this low-life character and be sympathetic to any comic statement the clown might make about him. Their identification of the character aids in raising the humor of the bit, but if this were the only element at work in the piece, it would not be raised far. It is given an extra life because the clown in effect is saying that the show is not that good, and since he is part of the show, that his performance leaves something to be desired. Otherwise, the item he is offering would not be "The Best Seat in the House."

The Clown sidles up to a member of the audience. Clutched under his arm is the suitcase. Although he must appear furtive, he must speak loud enough for everyone in the immediate area to hear him.

CLOWN: Psst! Hey! Have I got a deal for you! *(He looks around as if to make sure that no one can hear the conversation. Actually, he checks the audience to make sure that they can hear and see what is going on.)* I noticed that you are sitting at one of the worst spots in the audience. If you stay here, you are going to miss the best parts of the show. You don't want that to happen, do you? *He waits for the audience member to respond.)* Well, since I like the look of your face, I'll tell you what I'll do. I was here before anybody showed up to buy tickets, and I got ahold of the best seat in the house. I just found out I won't be able to use it, so I'll be willing to let you have it. Don't thank me. I know how generous I am being. You'll be able to see everything in the show from here. *(This last part is said even if the audience member does not appear ready to thank the clown.)* I don't expect you to take a pig in a poke. I mean, why should you move unless you're sure the seat I'm giving you is good? So . . . *(He looks around again.)* I'm going to let you take a look at it. Would you like to see it?

(When the audience member says "yes," the Clown opens the suitcase to reveal the "best seat" to the audience. He then moves on to another section of the audience and repeats his performance.)

This bit can also be used as incidental or transitional material. As incidental business, the "Best Seat" breaks up action in a larger sketch. To "break up the action" does not mean to interrupt the flow of action, which will only be annoying to the audience, which has been trying to follow the logic of the bit. Instead, it means varying the action for a moment. The flow of action must be kept going, so the business is presented as an aside. This is important in sketches that require a build-up to reach the punch line or blow off. The incidental business allows one or two clowns to hold the audience's attention while the rest of the clown alley set the stage for the madness to come. Incidental business can prevent an audience from putting two and two together and finding out what the clown has in mind, thereby ensuring their surprise and laughter at a quick bit of business. One word of warning, though: The clown must beware of using too many incidental bits, or the comedy of the sketch will be obscured.

As transitional material, incidental bits allow the clown to clear the stage for the next sketch or routine. Nothing is deadlier than asking an audience to wait while the stage is struck. The following script is an example of the way incidental business may be used to hold the audience while the next set is being set up:

The clowns have fled, and the stage is littered with equipment. After the audience has quieted, they become aware of a Clown who has entered from the back of the auditorium or somewhere in the arena other than the performer's entrance. He is carrying a suitcase and hawking "The Best Seat in the House."

CLOWN: Right here, you can get the best bargain in town. First come, first served. Only one left. It's what you've been waiting for.

ANNOUNCER: Hold it, (name of clown), stop right there. What do you think you're doing?

CLOWN: I'm making these people an offer they can't refuse.

ANNOUNCER: What's that?

CLOWN: I'm giving them a chance to buy the best seat in the house.

ANNOUNCER: The best seat in the house?

CLOWN: That's right

ANNOUNCER: But all the seats here are good seats. There is no best seat in this place.

CLOWN: Oh, yes, there is.

ANNOUNCER: Oh, no, there isn't.

CLOWN: Oh, yes, there is.

ANNOUNCER: No, there isn't.

CLOWN: Is.

ANNOUNCER: Isn't.

CLOWN: Is.

ANNOUNCER: Isn't.

CLOWN: Is.

ANNOUNCER: Isn't.

CLOWN: Isn't.

ANNOUNCER: Is.

CLOWN: See, you agree with me. Last chance to get the best seat in the house.

ANNOUNCER: Just a minute. Now every seat here offers a perfect view. Every member of the audience can see what's going on. How can there be a *best seat!*

CLOWN: Take my word for it. I have the best seat here.

ANNOUNCER: O.K. If you have the best seat here, show me where it is.

CLOWN (Holds up the suitcase): Right in here.

ANNOUNCER: In there? I find that hard to believe.

CLOWN: It's true.

ANNOUNCER: Prove it. Show it to me.

(The Clown lifts the suitcase high and drops the lid. If playing in the round, the Clown should use a suitcase that allows both sides to drop so that the entire audience can see the "seat" at the same time.)

ANNOUNCER: I should have known.

(The stage is now ready for the next act, and the show goes on.)

The part of the announcer may, as always, be taken by another clown. An announcer is invaluable in variety shows because he keeps the audience informed as to what they will be seeing next. Without him, the audience would soon be confused and numbed by seemingly random arrangement of the varied acts. The announcer adds continuity.

However, in the clown show, the announcer's function is different. He is there to clarify the action taking place. To do this, he may use two different styles. Like the sportscaster, he may keep up a running commentary: reporting the action blow by blow as a detached observer. Or he may become part of the action, actively conversing with or commenting on the clowns in the performance. This last style has been used very successfully on "The Pink Panther Show." The always silent panther wanders in and out of trouble while the announcer feeds the audience the information necessary to understand the intent of the action. By using this style, the mime or silent clown is freed from the stylized movements required when presenting a dumb show. The announcer will be talking for him.

BOARD, AGAIN

Ingredients   A board, a leash, a piece of paper, a large box with collapsible sides, and a tack or two.

Construction   The box should be large enough to hold three or four clowns, dressed as pirates. For easy packing and shipping, it may be made of four flats. The clowns inside can hold the flats together in a box shape until the appropriate moment when they release the flats, allowing them to fall to the ground. The outside of the box should be painted with the words "X marks the spot. This is it. Secret treasure trove. Gold doubloons. Last treasure trove for 5,000 miles. Pull tab to open." An added touch is to plaster the box with travel stickers from tourist attractions that no self-respecting pirate would dare miss.

The leash is then put on one end of the board. To keep it in place, hammer the tacks through the leash into the board.

The paper should have a large map on one side and on the other, the words "Treasure Map," printed in large letters.

Performance   Since every area in which the clown performs is different, the directions on the treasure map should be worked out prior to each show. If presented on a stage, the directions should keep the clown facing away from the box until the last moment because the stage will frame the clown and box together. If he looks at the box, his audience will wonder why he does not see it. On a gymnasium floor, the clown will be able to wander around freely because the amount of space available to him will separate him from the box in the mind of the audience. An alternative solution to this problem is to have the clown keep his eyes on the map at all times while following the directions.

The clown enters with the map unfolded in front of him. He looks around for a starting point referring to the map briefly before he finds it.

ANNOUNCER: Well, well, if it isn't (name of clown). What do you have there?

(The clown holds up the map so that the announcer, and the audience, can plainly see the words "Treasure Map" boldly written on the back.)

ANNOUNCER: A treasure map! How lucky! Is it genuine?

(The Clown nods his head.)

ANNOUNCER: My, my. Then pretty soon you're going to be very rich.

(The Clown nods again, rubbing his hands together greedily.)

ANNOUNCER: Then let's get started. You're sure you're standing at the right place? Good. Now, the first instruction: "Walk forward six paces."

(The Clown ticks each step off on his fingers.)

ANNOUNCER: "Turn at a forty-five-degree angle and walk three paces." Done? Good. "Take two giant steps east. Turn south and take six scissors steps. Hop five times to the west on the left leg. Face south and back seven steps."

(The Clown backs into the box and falls over.)

ANNOUNCER: It looks like you've found it, or it's found you. Open it up and let us see what's inside.

(The Clown tries to open the box with his bare hands, unsuccessfully. He pries, kicks, and pounds, but it does not open. Picking up some rocks and bricks that are scattered on the ground, he throws them at the box, but they bounce off without doing damage. Finally, the Clown leans against the box in defeat.)

ANNOUNCER: Don't give up now. You've worked so hard. If you could only get a good grip on the box, I'm sure it will come open.

(The Clown straightens. He has suddenly gotten an idea. Walking away from the box, he stoops and mimes, rubbing his hands with dirt.)

ANNOUNCER: Good idea. Now, you will be able to get a grip on the box.

(As the Clown dusts his hands on his pants, the sides of the box fall to reveal a group of clowns dressed as pirates. They see the clown and begin to sneak up on him with evil grins on their faces. The Clown remains unaware of them until they grab him despite the fact that they continually hush each other and chuckle in anticipation.)

ANNOUNCER: Uh-oh! Don't look now, but I think you have company. Too late. Well, what do you think they'll do with you? Hang you from the highest yardarm?

(The pirates like this idea and produce a rope. The Clown blanches.)

ANNOUNCER: Oh, too bad. The pirates don't seem to be able to find a yardarm. Well, you're safe from that. Maybe they'll roast you over an open fire.

(The Clown shoots the Announcer a withering look, and the pirates begin collecting wood, which they heap around the clown's feet. Then they begin to dig into their pockets.)

ANNOUNCER: You lucked out again. They seem to be out of matches. I know, they're going to make you walk the plank.

(The pirates are really enthused by this idea. They bring out the plank. As they look for a place to set it down, the Clown begins to tremble. Finally, they place it over the edge of the stage or simply drag the Clown over to the board. One of the pirates hands the end of the leash to him and at sword point forces the Clown to walk the plank around the block.)

ANNOUNCER: Walking the plank just isn't what it used to be.

Depending on the number of props that the clown wishes to use in the sketch, the walk at the beginning when the clown is following the map may be enlarged by adding incidental bits to the sketch. Not looking where he is going, he can trip over a chair, get tangled in a rope, or discover a fence or tree two paces in front of him when he must walk three paces in a straight line. As the directions become increasingly bizarre, he may even forget to say, "Mother, may I," and be sent back to the beginning. If this is done, the clown should not repeat the directions as before but rush through them as if he were a character in a silent movie.

The pirates should keep up an undercurrent of noise after they appear. Chuckling evilly and filling the silence with pirate language will add to the unreality of the scene. Pirate language consists of words like "aye," "belay," "lubber," and "ahr."

The longer the clowns can hold the attention of the audience with incidental bits of business, the bigger the laugh will be at the blow off. If the audience sees the trick too soon (without the benefit of the build-up), they will groan at the brutality of the visual pun. They must be led to expect something completely different to happen, so the leash on the plank should remain concealed until the very last minute.

BOXING GLOVES

Ingredients (for one glove)   Two pieces of thin, pliable leather with a glossy finish on one side and one piece of quarter-inch-thick stiff leather cut to the shape depicted in the illustration. The thick piece of leather should be cut slightly smaller than the thin pieces. *(Note:* Four gloves are necessary to perform the sketch below.)

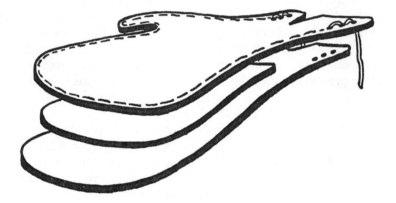

Figure 12

Construction   Sew the two pieces of pliable leather together with the glossy sides facing each other. Turn the glove formed inside out and place the piece of stiff leather inside the glove. The stiff piece of leather should not bend when inside the glove. If it does, the glove will not lie flat and will not produce the loud slapping noise required in the boxing sketches. Trim the piece of leather so that it fits into the glove easily. Make a slit on the side of the glove that covers the back of the hand. The slit will extend from the wrist down the center of this side for approximately four inches. This will allow the hand to slide into the glove without difficulty. With an awl, punch holes that parallel each other on either side of the slit. Thread the holes with a leather thong or a shoelace.

If this is beyond the technical ability of the clown, he should consult a shoemaker or write to:

A. J. Fast
9738 E. M-78
Haslett, Mich. 48840

Although primarily concerned with the manufacture of clown shoes, A. J. Fast may be able to help.

Performance The boxing gloves are a natural outgrowth of the bladder, which is a leather slapstick. Unlike the bladder or the slapstick, however, the gloves are never used to hit anyone; they are slapped together to produce a loud bang. When one clown swings at another, he always pulls up short or misses the other clown entirely. This is made obvious to the audience so that they do not get the impression that either clown can be injured. The sound effect for the hit is made by the clown who receives the pulled punch. He slaps his gloves together as he reels backward. Done smoothly, even though the hits are obvious misses, one clown apparently strikes the other.

As with all slapstick bits and sketches, the humor does not come from the apparent violence done to one clown by another. As stated earlier, in Chapter 6, this is a mistake made by many clowns, comedians, and actors. If the clown makes this mistake when performing "Clown Boxing," he dooms the sketch to failure.

But doesn't the sketch rely on the violence of prizefighting? Yes. However, the clown must remember that the boxing sketch is a parody. It lampoons the brutality of the fight, the arbitary authority sometimes imposed by the referee, and the callousness of the managers who make their living from the pain and blood of the boxer. At the end of the sketch, they get theirs, and justice triumphs.

The Referee enters blowing a whistle. He carries with him a bell that will be used to signal the beginning and end of each round.
REFEREE: Ladies and gentlemen, welcome to the first, semiannual, noninvitational clown boxing tournament. For our first fight, in this corner, weighing in at two hundred fifty pounds, the world champeen of clown boxing, Muhammad (name of clown).
(The Champion enters with his manager, his hands clasped in

victory over his head, and swaggers to his corner to do deep knee bends and other warm-up exercises. His manager, an obvious toady, tries to keep up with him, massage his neck, and caters to his immense ego.)

REFEREE: And, in this corner, weighing in at ninety pounds, the challenger, "Killer" (name of clown).

(The Challenger enters reluctantly, being dragged by his manager. He is a thin clown who has no hope of winning the fight.)

REFEREE: And now, if both fighters will come to the center of the ring, we'll go over the rules.

(The Champion and Challenger come to the center and stand on either side of the referee.)

REFEREE: During this match, I don't want to see any of this— *(He kicks the Challenger in the shins.)*—this—*(He hits the Challenger below the belt.)*—or this—*(He holds the Challenger's head and knees him in the face.)* Have you got that?

(The Champion nods as the Challenger staggers around.)

REFEREE: All right. Shake.

(The Challenger begins to shake violently.)

REFEREE: No, shake hands.

(The Challenger shakes his hands in front of him.)

REFEREE: No, no. Shake hands with each other.

(The boxers clasp hands, and the Challenger is forced to his knees by the Champion's grip.)

REFEREE: Go to your corners and come out fighting.

(As soon as the boxers reach their corners, the bell rings. The Champion barrels out of his corner, takes one swat at the Challenger, and knocks him flat. He turns with his hands clasped above his head in victory and walks away. The Challenger picks himself up. He runs at the Champion swinging, but before he can deliver a punch, the bell rings.)

REFEREE: Round's over.

(The Challenger stares at the Referee in disbelief. The Champion sits down and takes a drink of water while his manager massages his shoulders. The Challenger returns to his corner, but before he can sit down, the bell rings.)

REFEREE: Round two.

(The boxers walk toward each other. When they are in striking range, the Champion points at the Challenger's foot.)

CHAMPION: Your shoe is untied.

CHALLENGER *(Looking down):* It is?

(The Champion swings, and the Challenger falls over. The Challenger climbs to his feet and advances, swinging, on the Champion. The bell rings.)

REFEREE: End of round two.

(Again, just as the Challenger reaches his corner, the bell rings.)

REFEREE: Round three.

(The boxers come out of their corners cautiously and, when they meet in the center, begin dancing together. After a few turns and possibly a dip, the Champion yells.)

CHAMPION: Ah! You tramped on my foot. *(He flattens the Challenger with a swing.)*

(The Challenger jumps up and runs to the Champion. This time, before he attempts the swing, he looks at the Referee. The Referee stands nonchalantly by. Turning back to the Champion, the Challenger prepares to take his best shot. Before he can land a punch, the bell rings.)

REFEREE: End of round three. *(After a short pause, he rings the bell again.)* Round four.

(This time only the Champion gets back to his corner. The Challenger has been standing in shocked disbelief at the unfairness of the match. The Champion approaches the Challenger with his hands held palms forward. Not understanding what the Champion means to do, the Challenger raises his hands to match the way the Champion holds his. When close enough, the clowns begin to play patty cake. They slap their hands together, clap once, slap their right hands together, clap, slap their left hands together, clap, hit their own knees, clap, and as the Challenger prepares to repeat the sequence of claps, the Champion gives him an undercut. The Challenger rises on his toes, then sinks, allowing his torso to hang limply from the waist. Otherwise, he remains in a standing position.)

CHAMPION: And now, for my famous "bolo punch."

REFEREE: "Bolo punch"? What's a "bolo punch"?

CHAMPION: A "bolo punch." Bo lo the belt.

The Champion places one glove behind the bent-over Challenger and, with a swing, slams the other glove against it. The Challenger falls face down.)

CHAMPION: Now I will finish him off.

(The Champion puts his hand beneath the Challenger's chin and lifts the Challenger to his feet. The Challenger's body is still rubbery from the last punch and must be held up. Taking

careful aim, the Champion counts to three and swings. He misses the Challenger, who ducks at the last moment, then leaps up and hits the Champion who has spun 360° from the momentum of his own swing. The Champion recovers and again holds the Challenger up by the chin. The Champion takes three practice swings and follows through on the last one. The Challenger ducks, the Champion misses, and the Champion is again hit after spinning in a circle.

Now reinvigorated, the Challenger begins to bob and weave as the Referee and managers converge on the fighters to find out what is going on. The fighters square off and swing simultaneously. On the back swing, they take out the managers, and on the forward swing, they miss each other and both hit the Referee. The managers and Referee climb to their feet and chase the fighters out of the ring and off.)

The announcer may be added to the list of characters in this sketch. As a sportscaster, he can provide a running commentary on the action, providing the audience with a way to identify with the violence.

As a parody of prizefighting, the boxing sketch above is not always successful in every section of the country. In large metropolitan areas and university towns, prizefighting is looked down on, so the sketch as it appears here in a blatant form would not be acceptable for presentation. However, by adding a justification for the fight and taking it out of the "prize" category, clown boxing is still usable because it makes a stronger statement about the senselessness of physical combat:

Two clowns are having a disagreement. This can be at the end of another sketch or established as the clowns walk on, engaged in an argument. One clown is the self-assured character and will be referred to as Clown. The other is Dummy.

DUMMY: That does it! We are going to settle this right here and now by the rules.

CLOWN: The rules? What rules?

DUMMY: The rules of boxing.

CLOWN: That's ridiculous. The rules of boxing. You don't know anything about boxing. *(Turning to the audience)* He doesn't even have a pair of boxing gloves.

DUMMY *(Whipping out some boxing gloves):* I have two pairs of boxing gloves.

CLOWN: It's still no good.

DUMMY: Why not?

CLOWN: If we're going to do this by the rules, we need a referee. And even if we had one, we don't have a bell to signal the rounds.

DUMMY: I can be the referee. I have a bell. Look, it's a cute little ding-a-ling.

CLOWN: You're a ding-a-ling. Why should I trust you to be the referee?

DUMMY: I'll be fair. I'm an honest person. *(To audience)* Aren't I an honest person?

CLOWN: Well, O.K. You don't stand a chance, anyway. *(They put on the gloves.)* What do we do first?

DUMMY: We come out and shake.

(They both begin shaking bodily.)

DUMMY: There's something wrong here. I know! We have to shake hands.

(They clasp hands, shake, and begin to go to their corners. Unfortunately, their hands stick together. In a gargantuan effort to separate, they both fly backward to sprawl on the floor. After they pick themselves up and go to their corners, the dummy rings the bell.)

DUMMY: Round one.

(They barrel out; the Dummy swings, and the Clown falls flat. The Dummy returns to his corner humming happily to himself. Angrily, the Clown gets up and runs at the Dummy, swinging. Just as he gets to the Dummy, the Dummy rings the bell.)

DUMMY: Round's over. (He waits until the Clown reaches his corner and is beginning to relax. Then he rings the bell.) Round two. *(They advance toward each other, and as they arrive at the center, the Dummy points at something in the distance.)* Look at that!

CLOWN *(Turning):* Look at what? I don't see anything. *(As he turns back, the Dummy hits him.)*

DUMMY: *(Walks back to his corner and waits for the Clown to run at him. He rings the bell.)* Round's over. (He waits for the Clown to get to the corner and then rings the bell again.) Round three.

CLOWN: *(He has caught on and is going to get even. As he meets the Dummy at the center, he points into the distance.)* Look at that!

DUMMY *(Points to the Clown's feet):* Your shoe is untied.

CLOWN *(Looking down):* It is? *(The Dummy hits him and returns to the bell. This time, the Clown walks calmly to the Dummy's corner, picks up the bell, and walks back to his own corner.)*

DUMMY: Where are you taking my bell?

CLOWN: I'm going to referee for a while. *(He rings the bell.)* Round four.

(The clowns advance slowly and begin to circle each other. Their circling picks up speed until suddenly they are dancing together. The Dummy breaks away.)

DUMMY: Ow! You tramped on my foot. *(He hits the Clown and walks to the Clown's corner to stand beside the bell. The Clown rushes at him, and the Dummy hits the bell.)* Round's over.

CLOWN: I'm the referee.

DUMMY: Be my guest.

CLOWN *(Rings the bell):* Round's over. *(The Dummy happily walks back to his own corner. The Clown is having a fit. He can't seem to win.)*

CLOWN *(Rings the bell):* Round five. *(The clowns advance and do the patty-cake business, at the end of which the Dummy clobbers the Clown. The action that follows is the same as for the "Champion and the Challenger." The Dummy lifts the Clown by the chin, swings, misses, and gets hit by the Clown. After this has been repeated, the Clown chases the Dummy off the stage.)*

The bell used in this version of the "Boxing" sketch should be the kind used at counters or hotel desks. Placed on the floor, it can be rung easily with the foot.

The second version of this sketch will be readily accepted by the audience because it justifies the violence used in the performance. Also, it permits audience identification. In it, the two clowns are trying to solve a problem by the rules. Absurdly, the rules they choose are the rules of boxing. Like many members of the audience, the clowns have no idea what the rules of boxing might be. The only thing about which they are sure is that boxing requires the participants to hit each other.

BUCKET OF WATER

Ingredients   One bucket and a lot of confetti.

Construction   The confetti is poured into the bucket until the bucket is one-quarter full.

Performance   This bit is an old standby, perfect as a blow off for any sketch. It involves one clown chasing another with a bucket that is assumed to be filled with water. At the end of the boxing sketch, the bit could appear as follows:

The second version of clown boxing is used here. The Clown, having knocked the Dummy for a loop the second time in a row, goes to his corner and picks up a bucket.

CLOWN: I'm not going to let you off that easily.

(The Dummy, not wanting to be doused with water, heads for the hills. They zig-zag all over the performing area until the Clown traps the Dummy in front of a section of the audience. As the Clown chucks the contents of the bucket, the Dummy ducks, and the contents fly into the audience.)

If done properly, the audience will laugh with relief at being spared a drenching.

Although the "bucket of water" bit can be used in a variety of sketches, it is the traditional blow off of "The Washerwoman" sketch. In the context of the sketch, the bucket of confetti can be made to look as if it holds water. Two buckets are used, and one contains water. The clowns splash some of the water to mislead the audience as to the confetti-filled bucket sitting innocently in front of them.

Two clowns enter in drags, carrying buckets, washboards, and bundles of laundry. They sit beside each other and prepare to wash their clothes.

ANNOUNCER: It's washday, and it looks like two people want to get an early start.

(The clowns have begun their washing. Clown One has the bucket of water, and Clown Two has the confetti. Clown One vigorously scrubs a towel, sloshing water on the ground. He wrings the towel and tosses it aside. The towel hits Clown Two full in the face.)

ANNOUNCER: Oh, oh. There appears to be trouble brewing.

(Clown Two pulls the towel from his face and turns to the other clown, when he is hit by a second towel. Clown One is oblivious to the direction his towels are taking. Clown Two is furious. He begins to swing a towel at Clown One, who stoops to pick up more laundry. The towel misses Clown One, swings around, and Clown Two hits himself.)

ANNOUNCER: These towels are tricky things. Maybe you should try again.

(Clown Two begins another swing but is hit by another towel. Furious, he walks up to Clown One and beans him.)

ANNOUNCER: That takes care of that, but you better watch out!

(Clown One, who is still unaware of the trouble he has started, is now angry at Clown Two. He tosses a towel at Clown Two intentionally. This begins a battle in earnest. Both clowns begin to swat each other with wet towels. The frenzied fight continues until the announcer intervenes.)

ANNOUNCER: Wait a minute! Stop! What are doing? *(The clowns stop the fight.)* You aren't accomplishing anything. Now both of you have a lot of work to do. Why don't you make up, shake hands, and get your washing finished? *(The clowns hesitantly shake hands.)* That's better. Now, back to work.

(No sooner do the clowns begin to wash again than Clown One tosses another towel accidentally at Clown Two. This is the last straw. Clown Two walks over to Clown One, picks up the bucket, and pours it over Clown One's head. Clown One does a slow burn for a three count. Then he stands, picks up Clown Two's bucket, and advances. Clown Two begins to run, and Clown One chases him until he is cornered, then empties the confetti on the audience.)

This sketch combines the madness of the harlequinade with an end in which the audience is tricked. The trick brings the chase to the audience, allowing them to be involved. However, the trick can go sour. At one performance of "The Washerwoman," when Clown Two dumped the water on Clown One, some water was poured into the bucket of confetti. The clowns did not stop the sketch. The result was that some members of the audience were surprised by a wad of wet paper and two pints of water.

They were not amused.

CAMERA

Ingredients   A square wooden box, black cloth, tripod, smoke bomb, lighter, and hot water bottle.

Construction   The box should have one side open. This is covered by the cloth. A lens hole is bored through the side opposite the open end. After the box is bolted to the tripod, it will look like the cameras used by photographers at the turn of the century. The smoke bomb, lighter, and hot water bottle (see "hot water bottle" later in this chapter) are placed inside the box. The bit is now ready for presentation.

Performance   The camera is used to lampoon the photographer: amateur or professional. The comedy is predicated on the seemingly irrelevant and troublesome attention the photographer gives to the camera and the film. He sometimes seems to forget the subjects of his endeavors. The clown will find a great deal of latitude for improvisation in using the camera. By exaggerating the real quirks of the camera bug, he will increase the audience's identification with the bit because everyone has been subjected to the "Family Portrait."

A group of clowns enter, all dressed in their Sunday best. They are followed by the photographer, who carries the camera. He puts the camera down and ducks under the cloth to make sure the view is unobstructed. Then he sets himself to the task of posing the picture. He takes each member of the family and organizes them into a group before the lens. Checking on the grouping, he then begins to adjust the pose. When he is done, the family is arranged in absurd pretzel-like postures. The photographer returns to the camera and checks the light. He is not satisfied. He moves the group three steps left, forward, backward, and catty-cornered until he is satisfied. The group moves each time as one entity, maintaining their poses as much as possible. Finally, the photographer is satisfied. He ducks behind the camera to make sure everyone is in the shot. While under the cloth, he lights the smoke bomb. He begins to count to three, and the camera begins to smoke. The other clowns begin to cough but hold the pose. The photographer ducks under the cloth, this time to locate the water bottle and arrange the tubing in the lens hole. When he comes out, he keeps his hand on the water bottle. Counting to three with his free hand, he squeezes the bottle, which shoots a stream of water and drenches the clown family. They angrily chase the photographer off.

The problem with using a spray or stream of water is that the audience cannot see what is taking place. Water becomes practically invisible when viewed from a distance. To avoid this, the clown should add a few drops of blue food coloring to the water. In nature, water is never really blue, but the audience associates this color with the liquid. They have heard and remember such clichés as "cool blue waters of a mountain lake" and "blue Danube." Therefore, this cosmetic device will go unnoticed but seen.

CAR WASH

Ingredients A wooden frame capable of supporting shower curtains, bicycle, tricycle, shower cap, bathrobe, bath brush, and two clowns wearing identical makeup and costume, one short, one tall.

Construction Fasten the shower curtain securely around the frame. The short clown, tricycle, and a clown wearing the shower cap and bathrobe are concealed behind the curtain.

Performance Unlike other bits, the car wash employs a fair amount of equipment and a relatively large number of clowns. As a prop, the car wash itself cannot be used in connection with any other sketch. It is a piece of specialized equipment. However, the clown will find that the time it takes to set it up and tear it down will be worth his while.

ANNOUNCER: A new business seems to have popped up here—car wash. How convenient. And here is the first customer. *(A clown enters with a bicycle. This is the Tall Clown, who wears makeup and costume identical to that of the Short Clown behind the curtains. He looks at the car wash and checks his change.)* It only costs a quarter and the bicycle does need a wash. Why not?

(The Tall Clown gives his money to the Attendant. Then, mounting the bicycle, he rides it into the car wash. The sounds of clanking and rattling come from behind the shower curtains, and the Short Clown rides the tricycle out the other side.)

ANNOUNCER: Oh, you forgot about shrinkage. Maybe you should have used cold water. *(The Short Clown looks at himself.)* Well, you get what you pay for.
(The Short Clown chases the Attendant around the car wash a few times. Then, they both run through it. They exit hurriedly, chased by the clown in the shower cap and bathrobe who has obviously been bathing inside. To snappy music they all run off.)

CATSUP AND MUSTARD

Ingredients Catsup and mustard bottles of the squeeze variety and red and yellow yarn.

Construction Thread the red yarn through the catsup lid, the yellow through the mustard lid. Knot both ends of each piece of yarn. Place the lids back on the appropriate bottles.

Performance These bottles may be used in different sketches as an incidental bit of business or as a walk-around stunt. When the bottles are squeezed, the yarn shoots out like a stream of mustard or catsup.

CHICKEN DINNER

Ingredients A tray or suitcase, a plastic corn on the cob, glue, and a sign saying "Chicken Dinner."

Construction Glue the corn cob on top of the tray or in the suitcase. Stick the sign on the bottom of the tray or the side of the suitcase.

Performance This walk around is a sight gag that leaves the clown little to do. He simply walks up to a section of the audience, shows the sign, and then reveals the corn. For the gag to work, the clown must react, or overreact, to the audience's response. He has just played a trick on them, and they were fooled. Therefore, the clown feels he has every right to laugh at their mistaken interpretation of his sign.

COLLAPSIBLE CHAIR I

Ingredients Folding beach stool, wide elastic strip, and tacks.

Construction Remove the cloth that serves as the seat of the stool. The cloth is the only thing that holds the stool erect when it is unfolded. Without it, the stool will not stand. Tack the elastic strip to the stool's frame at the point where the cloth was originally held in place. The elastic will stretch when any weight is placed on the stool, and the stool's frame will fold up flat on the ground. As soon as the weight is removed, the stool will spring back to its original state.

Performance The collapsible chair may be used in a variety of sketches: "clown boxing," the "Family Portrait," etc. It may also be used for a walk around. It is one of the many all-purpose props that lend the world of the clown an unreal, cartoonlike quality.

The chair is best used as a blow off to bring a conceited clown down a few pegs and can be used by a solo clown or a group. The number of clowns who become involved with the chair is unimportant because the nature of the chair will focus the audience's attention on the action taking place around it. It offers a comfortable seat as befits the function of a chair but withdraws the offer at the last moment.

Unfortunately, the collapsible chair is too small a piece of equipment to be effective as an acrobatic prop on a stage. But it *is* effective as a two-clown walk around. The "Muscle Man" provides the clown with an excellent opportunity to make use of the collapsible chair. Full of conceit, the muscle man of the title uses his strength to intimidate those weaker than himself. His costume is padded in exaggeration of the body muscle-bound. As with most men who have too many muscles, he swaggers because he cannot move otherwise. He is ready for a long, hard fall. The other clown is by no means a weakling, but like many members of the audience, he does not know how to cope with a show of strength. If not for the special properties if the chair, he would be unable to compete against the "muscle man" entirely:

The Clown enters carrying sunbathing equipment and the chair. He is wearing an old tank suit with outrageous colors. Dumping the equipment, he begins to look around around for a good spot from which he can enjoy the sun. He places the chair in one spot. The chair is adjusted to make the best use of the sun. From the pile of equipment, he picks up an oversized light meter and checks the intensity of the light. Then he unfolds a reflector and prepares to get a tan. But before he sits, he remembers something. Going back to the equipment, he gets an umbrella and sets it up over the chair. He does not want to get too much sun. As he begins to sit down, the Muscle Man enters.

MUSCLE MAN: Hold it right there!

CLOWN *(Looks around to see if the muscle man is speaking to him)*

MUSCLE MAN: You!

CLOWN *(Points to himself)*

MUSCLE MAN: Yes, you! You're standing on my spot.

CLOWN *(Points to the chair)*

MUSCLE MAN: That's right. Now, get out of here.

CLOWN *(He begins to collect his equipment.)*

MUSCLE MAN: Hold it! What do you think you're doing?

CLOWN *(Points to himself, to the equipment, and at a point in the distance.)*

MUSCLE MAN: Oh, no, you don't. You're not taking my stuff anywhere.

CLOWN *(Shakes his head and again points to the equipment and himself)*

MUSCLE MAN *(Picking the clown up by the tank top):* That stuff is on my spot, so it must be my stuff. Right?

CLOWN *(Nods vigorously)*

MUSCLE MAN *(Puts the clown down and swaggers to the chair. He turns with a smile of superiority on his face and sits. The chair collapses, and the equipment topples over him.)*

This is a one-shot bit that can end in either a chase or a blackout. Because of the number of props required, however, it is not practical for a walk around. For that the clown has to use only the chair. He enters in the same costume as above, finds a good spot, and tries to sit down. The chair will thwart his intentions every time he sits, and when he stands, the elastic will return the chair to its. former shape. At first, the clown is confused by his failure to sit down. After one or two tries, he locks with the chair in mortal combat. Leaping, rolling, and falling, he tries to force the chair to bend to his will. The chair refuses to comply with any of his demands. In the end, he admits defeat and walks away to find a more reasonable piece of furniture and a new audience.

COLLAPSIBLE CHAIR II

Ingredients   One folding chair and two strong springs.

Construction Remove the supports that connect the front and back legs of the chair. In most cases, these supports will not be held on by a nut and bolt. If it is, the retaining bolt can be drilled off or the supports can be cut away with a hacksaw (do not use a saw designed for wood). These supports are replaced by the springs. The springs must be strong enough to hold the chair together when not in use, but weak enough to let the chair collapse when sat upon. This collapsible chair will not always spring back, because the legs when opened fully will spread to form an angle greater than 180°.

Performance The appearance of the folding chair limits the uses to which it may be put. Folding chairs can be found only at bridge games and family reunions:

The stage is set with a small table that holds a number of magazines. Above the table, a sign proclaims "Dentist," for this is a dentist's waiting room. Innocently, beside the table waits the chair. A receptionist leads a clown into the room. His head is bandaged as a preventative for a very bad toothache. He wanders about the room, distracted by the pain. Picking up magazines, flipping through them, and tossing them back, he cannot concentrate. Finally, he collapses into the chair, which collapses under him. As he gets up, he spits teeth (corn) on to the floor. The receptionist returns to give him the bill.

FIREHOUSE, ENGINE, AND ALARM

Ingredients Four flats, four lengths of rope, two ladders, fire hats, raincoats, boots, a net, an axe, a tiny cup of water, a snake box, a length of fire hose (or garden hose), marshmallows, sticks, a dummy, and a shopping cart.

Construction Paint the flats to resemble a house. Cut a window in one of them. During the presentation, they will be put together so that they resemble a large box. So that the box will remain standing during the sketch, the flats must be strung together. To do this, drive nails into the frame of the flat so that the nails on the front and back of the house alternate with the nails on the sides. Tie a rope to the topmost nails on the front and back and lace the rope around the nails and tie them securely at the bottom of the flats. Voilá!

The snake box can be attached to the front of the house. It should be painted red, bear the words "Fire Alarm," and have a hinged top. An open snake can may be placed in the box. (See "Spring Animals.") A clasp to hold the top in place will keep the snake coiled in the can. When the clasp is released, the spring in the snake will force the top back, and the snake will spring out.

Traditionally, the engine is constructed from a hand or animal cart and resembles the engines used in the nineteenth century, albeit in miniature. Unless the clown is wild about carpentry, this type of engine is impractical. "The Clown Fire Department" is a parody of the volunteer fire-fighting teams found in many small towns. These teams seldom can afford the most modern equipment. They must make do. Therefore, instead of using a realistic engine, the clown may choose to hang his ladders, hose, etc., on a shopping cart to let the good times roll.

Performance "The Clown Fire Department" is a sketch that potentially has a part for every member of a clown alley. However, as more clowns become part of the action, economy of motion becomes critical to the success of the presentation. The final effect should resemble a Rube Goldberg invention at work: one action relates to or causes another until all of the movements taking place snowball toward catastrophe.

If each clown adds his own personal irrelevant bit, the action of the sketch will become disjointed. The clowns will be competing with each other for the audience's attention instead of directing that attention toward the intended conclusion. This does not mean that the individual clowns involved in the sketch should scrap originality in their presentation of the piece. Room for individual originality always exists as long as it remains germane to the story line. The clown may use the actions of his fellows as spring boards for takeoffs that eventually lead to the prescribed end. There is no room in a group sketch for a "star."

Because of the number of clowns involved in this sketch, the audience will not be able to indentify closely with individual characters. Instead, the audience must identify with the situation. The spectators should be able to imagine themselves as the ill-equipped, untrained firemen who have been forced out of a comfortable office or bed to fight a roaring blaze. Also, they should identify with the bewildered home owner who forgets the danger of remaining in a burning building in order to save as many personal possessions as possible.

The clown will be tempted to rush through many bits of the business in this sketch. This is unnecessary. The faster the clown performs individual bits of the action, the more the audience will miss. The illusion of speed is attained by relating the bits to each other. The sketch is better served if the clown will take his time:

The house is set off center on stage or to one side in the ring. A police clown enters, joking with the audience as he walks toward the house. When he gets near the house, the clown inside it sets off a smoke bomb. The police clown, seeing the smoke, runs to the alarm. He is knocked to the ground when the spring snake leaps out at him. This is the signal for the fire fighters and engine to enter with the clanging of bells, amidst loud, frenetic music. Honky-tonk piano is perfect for this. The engine is preceded by the chief, who is the fall guy for the blunders of the other clowns.

As soon as the engine/shopping cart stops, the clowns whip out marshmallows and sticks and run to the burning building. The chief breaks up the party and sends them to work. The clowns scatter to prepare for the slapstick to follow. One clown grabs the axe and runs to the building. Two clowns pick up a ladder. One or more clowns begin spreading the net. The remaining clowns stand around the building trying to blow out the fire. The chief stands behind the clown with the axe. On the first back swing, the axe hits the chief, who reels backward. Meanwhile, the clowns with the ladder are running to the house with the ladder sideways between them. The chief falls over the ladder. He picks himself up just in time to get tangled in the net carried by the other clowns.

Obviously, if the chief wants the fire put out, he will have to do it by himself. He grabs the hose out of the cart and runs to the building. Unfortunately, the hose does not reach. He sprawls when it uncoils to its full length just short of the house. The only thing to be done is form an old-fashioned bucket brigade. The chief stands by the house with the other clowns behind him. The clown on the end produces a small cup of water. Trying not to spill the contents, the clowns pass the cup toward the house. When it reaches the chief, he drops two Fizzies in it and drains the cup. The other clowns are outraged. They converge on the chief, but before they can do him any harm, a clown appears in the window. The Clown is dressed as a woman.

CLOWN: Save my baby! Save my baby! *(This is repeated periodically until the baby is "saved.")*
(The clowns stretch the net beneath the window and begin yelling, "Jump! Jump!" The Clown in the window ducks back into the house and begins to throw every conceivable object out the window—everything but the baby. The traditional items are flannel underwear, a chamber pot, and an immense bra. As each item lands in the net, the chief removes it and holds it high, saying, "This isn't the baby!" And the other clowns renew the refrain, "Jump! Jump!" Finally, the Clown in the house appears with the baby: a dummy dressed in a flowing nightgown, wearing a baby's bonnet.)
CLOWN: Here's the baby! Here's the baby!
(While the Clown in the house is winding up to chuck the baby, the fire fighters run back and forth with the net trying to anticipate the proper landing spot of the dummy. They finally settle in one location as the "baby" is tossed. The dummy arcs with the nightgown fluttering behind it as the clowns follow its trajectory. It misses the net completely.)
CLOWN: My baby! My baby!
(In complete failure, the fire fighters leave helter-skelter.)

FLOWERS I

Ingredients   Plastic flowers and plastic straws.
Construction   Trim the leaves from the stems of the plastic flowers, leaving a straight, smooth wire. Put the straws over the stems. They should slide off and on easily.
Performance   This walk-around bit blatantly plays on the egotism latent in every audience member. To carry it off successfully, the clown must convince his audience that he seriously intends to give them something and, when he withdraws the gift, walk away as innocently as if he had given the present. Also, the clown must be sure to choose an audience member who will enjoy the joke. He should choose someone who cannot keep from smiling broadly or laughing out loud. These people are easy to find because their teeth are showing.

The Clown approaches an audience member. He carries a bouquet of flowers.
CLOWN: Hello. I've been appointed to present an award. At every

show, all the performers take a look at the people in the stands and hold a beauty contest. We choose four people out of every audience that we believe to be the most appealing, and today you were one of the winners. So I am proud to present you with this flower. It's a token of our esteem.

(The Clown hands the flower to the audience member, making sure that the member grabs the straw. Then he turns and walks on—WITHOUT LETTING GO OF THE FLOWER. The flower should come away easily, leaving the audience member holding only the straw.)

FLOWERS II

Ingredients One large plastic sunflower and a pin.

Construction Make an obvious hole in the center of the flower with the pin. Place the flower in the lapel.

Performance This bit relies on the audience's belief that the clown is going to pull a prank on them and is very good for parties. The clown approaches some members of the audience and asks them to sniff the flower. As soon as they see the hole in the flower they will think that the clown intends to get them with the old squirting flower trick. The flower, of course, cannot squirt water. The audience is deceived by their own preconceptions. This makes the format used on "Truth or Consequences" perfect for the presentation.

Because of the improvisatorial nature of the bit, a script would do more harm than good. The presentation is a test of the clown's ability to ad-lib and read his audience. The people on whom the inverted prank is to be played should be out of the room for a moment so that the clown can let the rest of the audience in on the joke. Then those unaware of the deception are brought back. The first audience member to trust the clown and sniff the flower receives a small prize for his bravery. The other participants will learn that sometimes it pays to trust a clown.

FLUTE

Ingredients Lunch box, fish line, thin wire, safety pin, linked rubber hot dogs, and a plastic flute.

Construction Form one end of the wire into a hook and twist the other end around the flute. Tie one end of the fishline to the hot dogs and the other to the safety pin.

Performance The clown attaches the safety pin to his shirt and places the hot dogs in the lunch pail. He walks in front of the audience, sits as if to eat lunch and takes out the flute. Positioning the lunch box open before him, he begins to play. If the clown cannot play the flute, a simple trill will do. As the clown plays, he snags the fish line with the hook on the flute. By extending the flute forward slightly and lifting with it, the hot dogs will rise like a snake charmer's cobra right to the clown's hand or hot dog roll. As an incidental bit of business, it can be used with "The Carpenter's Helper," "Clown Boxing," "The Family Portrait," or other sketches. It can also be used as a walk around.

HOT WATER BOTTLE

Ingredients A hot water bottle, rope, funnel, two corks, and surgical tubing. Both corks should fit tightly in the mouth of the hot water bottle.

Construction Tie the rope around the neck of the hot water bottle so that the ends of the rope dangle freely and are of equal length. A hole, large enough to accommodate the funnel's spout is drilled through one of the corks. This cork is pushed tightly on the funnel. In the other cork, drill a hole large enough to insert the rubber tubing.

Performance The hot water bottle enables the clown to dispense water whenever and wherever he wants. As used in connection with the camera, it is filled with water and fitted with the cork and rubber hose. By simply squeezing the bottle, water will be forced out in a stream that can be directed with a fair amount of accuracy. Some clowns become deadly shots with this contraption. Until it is ready to be used, a paper clip or clasp should be used to seal off the tubing.

In the feather routine described in Chapter 13, the hot water bottle with the funnel cork can be used to thwart a prank perpetrated by one clown on another. The rope is tied around the clown's waist and the bottle tucked inside his trousers. The clowns enter arguing:

PRANKSTER: You can't.
CLOWN: I can.

PRANKSTER: Oh, no, you can't.
CLOWN: Oh, yes, I can.
PRANKSTER: Then prove it.
CLOWN: All right. Here's the feather. Watch.
(The Clown places the feather on the tip of his nose. His head is thrown back, and the only thing he can see is "up." As soon as he begins his amazing demonstration, the Prankster brings out a jug of water or a seltzer bottle. He dumps the water in the other Clown's pants. The other Clown does not squirm or wriggle; apparently he does not feel the water at all. The Prankster can't figure out why his prank refuses to work. As if to answer, the Clown ceases his balancing act, unties the rope around his waist, and removes the hot water bottle. Then, returning tit for tat, he gives the water back to the Prankster, sans container. The Prankster drips away.)

Rubber cement may be used to seal both the rubber tubing to one cork and the other cork to the funnel. Doing so will insure that the clown will always stay high and dry.

IRONING BOARD

Ingredients An old-fashioned wooden ironing board and a small block of wood.

Construction The hole that receives the support at the tapered end of the ironing board is covered with the block of wood. The support, when placed behind the block, will hold up the board until the square end of the board is pressed gently. Then the tapered end will rise enough to release the support. The ironing board will immediately collapse.

Performance Of all the gimmicked items, the ironing board is the least difficult to alter. The gimmick is practically built into it from the start. Occasionally, if someone looks at it the wrong way, it will collapse all by itself. The supporting brace can not be firmly secured to the underside of the board. Therefore, when the squared end is struck with sufficient force, the ironing board will fold, dumping any clothes being ironed on to the ground. This idiosyncrasy detracts from its desirability as a household appliance, but rigged so that its collapse can be brought about even easier, it is a boon to the clown.

The ironing board is a purely slapstick clown prop that can be used in a number of sketches. Since it is usually associated with the laundry room, it can be an excellent addition to "The Washerwoman" or, as the case may be, "The Washerman." In today's liberated society, the man of the household can occasionally be found doing the wash. But, as in Laurel and Hardy's time, many men have the disadvantage over women. Because they lack practical experience in dealing with the complexities of soggy clothing, they find that their brows crease easier than a simple pair of pants.

For example, the men of two households have a day off. Their wives do not, and the laundry must be done. The men decide to combine forces and discover that their unfamiliarity with the simple procedures makes the chore an almost insurmountable task.

Two clowns enter. Clown One carries a bag of soggy laundry and a bucket. The bucket contains confetti. A small cup of water is nestled in the confetti. If the bucket is not swung, the water in the cup should not spill. Clown Two carries the ironing board and iron.

CLOWN ONE *(Setting the bucket and laundry on the ground):* This won't take any time at all. You set up the ironing board while I separate the clothes. *(He stoops to dig in the laundry bag. Clown Two spins around to set up and catches Clown One with the ironing board as he is bending, sending him head over heels. For a moment Clown One stares at his companion from the floor. Then he rises and walks to Clown Two. In the meantime, Clown Two is studiously examining the apparatus of the ironing board, trying to figure out how it should be put together. He is unaware that he has clobbered Clown One and that Clown One is walking nonchalantly toward him. Clown One stands patiently until Clown Two notices him and smiles. Clown One begins in a friendly manner.)*

CLOWN ONE: I hope you don't mind my saying this, but ... *(He shouts.)* ... watch what you're doing.

(Clown Two flinches at the sudden increase in volume and releases his hold on the ironing board, which falls on Clown One's foot.)

CLOWN ONE: Put up the ironing board. *(Mutters to himself)* Sometimes I wonder about people. They can't seem to do the simplest things without messing them up. *(While muttering, he gathers a small pile of clothing out of the bag and deposits it at the rounded end of the ironing board. He hands a shirt to Clown Two, who, having assembled the ironing board, is checking the heat of the iron.)*

(Clown Two begins to iron the shirt. After doing one side, he sets the iron down on the squared end of the board to flip the shirt over and begin on the other side. In doing so, he presses down on the squared end to release the support on the other end of the ironing board, which then drops. Clown One sees the iron slide down the sloping board toward the pile of clothes and his waiting foot beyond. He catches it and discovers what he should have known before he made the hasty grab. The iron is hot. He handles it like a baked potato, tossing it from one hand to the other until Clown Two resets the board and takes the iron off his hands—by the handle. Clown One runs to the bucket of water and sighs with relief as his hands are supposedly cooled by the nonexistent liquid therein.)

CLOWN ONE *(Slowly walking back to the ironing board as if he is going to verbally lash Clown Two. He stands stewing for a moment; then, shaking his head, he picks up the clothing at the rounded end of the board and moves all the laundry to the squared end.)* I'm not going to say a thing. Let's just get to work. *(He hands another shirt to Clown Two.)*

(Clown Two flings himself into the job at hand. He runs the iron once or twice across a sleeve, sets it on the squared end, flips the shirt, makes a few swipes, puts down the iron, and so forth. Clown One removes his coat and bends over to sort more clothing. His back is just beyond the end of the board. Absently, Clown Two misses the end of the board when he pauses to flip a shirt and sets the iron on Clown One's back. The only reaction that Clown One exhibits is to shoot a take of astonishment at the audience.

When Clown Two picks up the iron, Clown One looks over his shoulder. The middle of the back of his shirt has a hole shaped like the heating surface of an iron cut from it. The edges of the hole are charred. When Clown One sees this, he begins leaping about while trying to put out his burning shirt by beating it. Clown Two, seeing his companion in trouble, tries to help. He runs to the bucket, grabs the cup of water, and throws it on Clown One. Clown One advances on Clown Two, who, in backing up, trips the ironing board. The ironing board col-

lapses, the iron slides, and Clown One grabs it. This time he drops it before it can burn him, and it lands on his foot. This is the last straw. With vengeance in mind, he grabs the bucket and begins to chase Clown Two. At the end of the chase, the audience gets the confetti.)

This sketch may be performed as a dumb show, using either an announcer to carry a running commentary of the action or music to provide an external rhythm to the tomfoolery. The ironing board can also be presented as a solo piece. The clown pits himself against the machine (ironing board) in order to bend it to his will. As usual, the clown gets bent before the machine.

As an afterthought, the clown may not wish to use confetti for this particular sketch. The tiny squares of tissuelike paper are not the best material in the world to hold the cup of water. Fortunately, there is an inexpensive alternative, in many cases less costly than the precut packaged paper carried by novelty and dime stores. This alternative can be purchased ready-made in plain, buttered, or caramel-covered form. Its generic name is popcorn.

The only drawback to popcorn as a substitute for confetti is that it is edible. Some youngsters in the audience might be tempted to pop it in their mouths. Since this product is seldom individually wrapped, and the major portion in the bucket will wind up on the floor, such behavior should be discouraged.

LEVITATION I

Ingredients   One bench, a sawhorse or other object that will serve as a fulcrum, and a long, sturdy board, preferably two inches by six inches.

Construction   None.

Performance   This version of the comedy levitation is meant to be presented on a stage in front of a curtain. It cannot be presented in the round, which proscribes its use as a circus sketch unless one end of the arena is blocked off from the audience's line of sight. The clown may wish to invest in a professionally made backdrop or screen to solve this difficulty. If he does, a tentlike façade is the best choice.

The bench is placed a few feet in front of the curtain. Enough room should be allowed so that the clown/magician can move easily behind the bench. In back of the curtain, directly opposite the bench, sits the sawhorse. Several clowns or an awfully big prop man manipulate the two by six board. The number of clowns and the size of the prop man necessary to move the board will be determined by the weight of the clown/magician.

To carry off this slightly bent illusion, the clown/magician must play his part to the hilt. He really can, through magic or sheer willpower, cause somebody to rise unsupported into space. His power is unquestioned. The only difficulty the clown/magician may encounter is getting his audience to believe this. Impossible? Not at all. By not speaking or acting facetiously but by the simple device of parody, the clown/magician lulls his audience into accepting his ability. In imitation of a famous illusionist, he struts about the stage. With elaborately useless gestures, he prepares his assistant for the demonstration. By the time he is ready to perform the trick, his audience will be so absorbed in his laughably lavish preparations that its attention will be driven away from the obvious fact that it is being set up.

Background music will aid the clown/magician to create an atmosphere that will divert the audience's attention until the final moment of revelation. A great number of instrumental pieces lend themselves to the floating, lyrical nature of the levitation. "The Young and the Restless," which can be found on the album *Nadia's Time,* the opening from *Tubular Bells,* and "Neptune" from Holst's *The Planets* are all excellent selections for a legitimate levitation. These three pieces are only suggestions; in selecting music for this sketch, as with others, the clown must choose a composition that works with his own particular internal rhythm. Some clowns will find that they achieve better results from music with a faster beat.

ANNOUNCER: And now for one of the most amazing feats of modern magic. (name of the clown/magician) will mystically suspend his assistant in thin air without the use of wires, mirrors, or any visible means of support.
(The music begins and the clown/magician, attired in a flowing cape, enters with his assistant. He acknowledges the audience with a haughty bow. Regally, he twirls the cape from his shoulders and flings it aside. Fixing the assistant with a hypnotic eye, he waves his hands briefly before the face of the prospective floater and the assistant's eyes close. Then, the

clown/magician helps the assistant assume a comfortable reclining position before going behind the bench.

As he takes his place between the bench and the curtain, an end of the board pokes conspicuously into view behind him. Whoever is manipulating the board obviously can not see what they are doing. Presumably the board is intended to lift the assistant and the bench, but the individual manipulating the board can find neither. The end of the board taps the floor like a blind man's cane searching for something to guide it. The clown/magician realizes the problem and, covering the assistant with his cape, he ducks out of sight behind the bench to rectify the lack of vision exhibited by his cohorts behind the curtain. Standing, he dramatically raises his hands over the assistant. In the manner of the great wizard he pretends to be, he strains as if he has become invisibly bound to the body on the bench. Slowly, burdened by the weight of the assistant, his hands begin to move upward, and so does he. The clown/ magician was in such a hurry to arrange the board beneath the bench that he arranged it under himself instead. For a moment, he is daunted, but only for a moment. In an all-out effort to

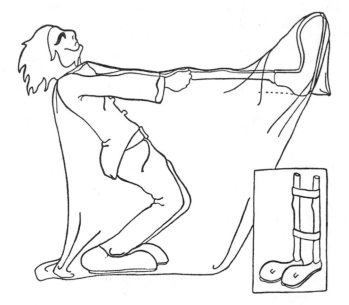

Figure 13

recoup, he grabs a hoop and passes it over his own levitated body. The assistant, realizing that something is amiss, stares incredulously from the bench. As soon as the clown/magician is lowered, he leaves, presumably for more practice. The assistant follows carrying the bench and cape.)
ANNOUNCER: How uplifting.

LEVITATION II

Ingredients Two dowel rods one inch in diameter and three to four feet long, nails, two two-by-fours 18 inches in length, a pair of old shoes, a bench, and a sheet or blanket.

Construction Nail the dowel rods and old shoes to the two-by-fours so that the finished product resembles the assembly in Figure 13. Two broom handles may be substituted for the dowel rods if desired. Also, if desired, two pieces of wood can be nailed to the bottom of the dowel rods to serve as surrogate feet to slip inside the shoes.

Performance The levitation apparatus is concealed beneath the blanket, which is folded in an accordion pleat and placed next to the bench. This method of folding the blanket permits the blanket to unfold curtainlike when the clown/magician picks it up. The apparatus, therefore, remains hidden from the audience. Consequently, this levitation can be performed in the round.

Like Levitation I, Levitation II must be presented in all seriousness to achieve the greatest laugh. For example, when presenting the sketch, one clown, who shall remain nameless, uses a variation on an old joke at the opening of the piece:

ANNOUNCER: What do you think you're going to do?
CLOWN: I'm going to make a clown float.
ANNOUNCER: How are you going to make a clown float?
CLOWN: With two scoops of ice cream, one clown, and some soda.

The use of such a crusty joke at the beginning of the sketch forewarns the audience. From the start, they expect to be deceived. On the other hand, if played realistically, the audience *is* deceived when the assistant levitates from the bench. In some cases, "ooohs" and "ahs" have been elicited. This should always be the reaction for which the clown/magician strives because the way the trick is done is so absurd that the audience cannot help but laugh. That is, laugh at itself for being taken in by such a simple-minded ploy.

The best way to establish realism in this sketch is through the atmosphere established at the beginning. Music is once more the key: music that could be used by a real magician for a levitation. For this sketch, "Heather" from the Carpenters' album *Now and Then* and selections from Vaughn Williams's *Antarctica* are excellent mood pieces that lend themselves to the rise and fall of floating in "An Elevating Experience."

As the music begins, the clown/magician sweeps in with his assistant. Las Vegas style, the performers quickly acknowledge the audience and assume their positions. The assistant stretches out on the bench. Reaching across the assistant, the clown/magician raises the blanket, using it and his body to conceal that his assistant has picked up the false feet to replace his own, which he has dropped to the floor on either side of the bench. The blanket covers the assistant and is tucked around his neck.

The clown/magician passes a hand over the assistant's face, instantly putting him to sleep. The clown/magician gathers the forces within him as he extends his arms over the assistant. His hands are tensed to support the weight of the body on the bench. As his arms rise, so does the assistant. With both feet on the floor, the assistant should be able to raise his shoulders from the bench. The false feet in front of him lift the blanket, giving the covered clown the illusion of floating.

The clown/magician looks to the audience for approval, and as his attention shifts, the assistant begins to sink back to the bench. The magician's hands increase their tension over the body, and the assistant rises higher. Under the blanket, the assistant now stands as in Figure 13. Maintaining his control of the body with one hand, the clown/magician removes the bench from beneath the blanket by sliding it from between the assistant's legs. The assistant is now free to "float" anywhere on the stage by walking around to the clown/magician's command. After causing the body to float freely about for a few moments, the clown/magician steps forward to take his bow. When he does, he steps on the edge of the blanket, dragging on the floor. Unfortunately, no one informs the assistant to cease floating. The assistant continues to walk forward, and the blanket, pinned to the floor by the weight of the bowing clown/magician, is pulled from the apparatus. The deception is revealed, but neither performer notices until the bowing clown/magician turns to point toward the supposed proof of his power. Seeing the assistant exposed and the blanket underfoot, he smiles sheepishly, taps the assistant on the shoulder to let him know that the jig is up, and the two of them sidle off the stage.

Extraneous bits of comedy may be added to the opening of this sketch by bringing on another assistant. The second assistant can help restrain the floater, who does not believe that, once aloft, he can be successfully kept there with any measure of safety. He constantly tries to escape until put into a trance by the clown/magician. His doubts are only confirmed when the first time the clown/magician makes a hypnotic pass, the second assistant is hit with the whammy. However, like the bad joke mentioned at the beginning, such bits are more likely to forewarn the audience and lessen the potential laugh.

If the clown must add to the humor of an already funny situation, his best bet would be to combine Levitation I and Levitation II to form a running gag in three stages. In the first stage, the clowns operating the two by six can not find the bench. Later, for the second try, the assistant is covered, and everything goes smoothly until the clown/magician levitates. Finally, the third stage is presented. Levitation II is offered with the ultimate blow-off and the sheepish retreat of the clowns, who resolve never to try again. Until the next show.

No matter how the clown decides to present the levitation, he will always be assured of laughter. The reason for this is that the audience will be led to fool itself. The punch line of the sketch is established by a third field of thought that intersects unexpectedly with the other two fields. The first field is established by the audience's wariness of the clown. They expect the clown to trick them. The clown answers this expectation by offering them what appears to be a truly magical effect. The assistant really appears to float. The audience is thereby lured into a second field in which it is amazed at the clown/magician's success. Then the third field explodes on the scene. The clown tricks the audience just as it thought he would. The members of the audience can only laugh at their own complicity. They have helped to deceive themselves.

PLATES

Ingredients   A package of paper plates.

Construction   Tear away the plastic or cellophane wrapping. Remove three plates.

Performance   At first, this walk-around bit may appear ungimmicked. The plates are unaltered in any way and remain, throughout the bit, ordinary paper plates. The gimmick is the special way in which the clown handles them to prove that "3 × 3 = 10."

Two clowns approach a section of the audience. They are deep in the middle of an argument.

CLOWN ONE: You're wrong. I don't owe you ten dollars.

CLOWN TWO: Yes, you do.

CLOWN ONE: How do you figure that?

CLOWN TWO: Well, two weeks ago you borrowed three dollars. Right?

CLOWN ONE: That's right.

CLOWN TWO: Last Tuesday, you borrowed another three dollars.

CLOWN ONE: Yes, I did.

CLOWN TWO: And two days ago I loaned you another three.

CLOWN ONE: Right.

CLOWN TWO: That's three times I loaned you three dollars.

CLOWN ONE: So far, so good.

CLOWN TWO: And three times three is ten.

CLOWN ONE: Hold it. That's where you're wrong.

CLOWN TWO: No, I'm not. Three times three is ten, and you owe me ten dollars.

CLOWN ONE: No, I don't. Three times three is nine. You're multiplying incorrectly.

CLOWN TWO: That's absurd. I know what I'm doing.

CLOWN ONE: That's debatable. I want you to prove to me that I owe you ten dollars.

CLOWN TWO: O.K. *(He takes out three paper plates.)* Here are three plates. To find out how much is three times three, all I have to do is count these plates three times in a row.

CLOWN ONE: And if you do, you'll come up with nine. Here. *(He takes the plates and spreads them on the ground.)*

One ... two ... three
four ... five ... six

seven . . . eight . . . nine
See? Nine!
CLOWN TWO: Oh, no. You did that wrong.
CLOWN ONE: How did I do that wrong?
CLOWN TWO: Watch. *(He points to the plates.)*
 One . . . two . . . three
 four . . . five
(He picks up a plate on the fifth count.)
 . . . six
(He picks up another plate.)
 Seven
(He picks up a third plate. He now holds three plates, which he places back on the ground one by one as he finishes counting.)
 . . . eight . . . nine . . . ten. There! You owe me ten dollars.
CLOWN ONE: Impossible! Let me count again.
 One . . . two . . . three
 four . . . five . . . six
(He picks up a plate on the sixth count.)
 Seven
(He picks up another.)
 . . . eight
(He picks up a third. He now holds three plates, which he puts back on the ground one by one as he finishes counting.)
 . . . nine . . . ten . . . eleven
CLOWN TWO: You owe me eleven dollars now. Isn't inflation wonderful.

The clowns move on, still struggling over the complexities of high finance. Most audience members will be so absorbed by the abstract counting of the plates that they will miss the reality that one, or two, plates are counted twice. The clown may wish to perform this bit as a solo, using a member of the audience as a straight man.

One word of warning. The clown should never present this bit for school assemblies. The American educational system has been suffering for the past few years from a disorder whose single symptom is the inability to differentiate between abstraction and practicality. The most virulent strain of this affliction is modern math. It has been known to infect educators as well as students. For example, this bit has been presented as a solo piece in over 45 schools up and down the Eastern seaboard. At each presentation, a teacher was selected to assist the clown in determining the answer to three times three. In every case, the exchange followed these lines:

CLOWN: How much is three times three?
TEACHER: Six.

Unfortunately, there is no known cure for this malady.

RADIO

Ingredients A tape player, a tape that is recorded to alternate between a radio program and static, a small table, and one radio that does not work.

Construction The tape player can be built into the back of the table. However. to ensure that the sketch goes smoothly, the clown may wish to hook the tape player to a public address system and have an assistant operate it from backstage. Magnetic tape has been known to tear or tangle, and if it does so offstage, the assistant will be able to correct the situation.

Performance As a test of pacing and rhythm, the clown will find the radio sketch one of his greatest challenges. Once begun, the sketch can not be stopped until its conclusion. The clown is fixed within a set routine of carefully blocked out moves and responses. For the most part, he will be attempting to fit all of his actions to the sounds that seemingly come from the radio.

A Clown enters with a newspaper. He has spent a hard day at the office and now intends to relax, read the paper, and listen to some good music. He turns on the Radio and finds a station that plays the music he likes. After adjusting the sound and giving the fine tuner one last twist, he heads toward his chair to read the paper.

As he walks away, the Radio fills the room with static. He turns back to adjust it. When he gets near the Radio, the static mysteriously disappears. Probably outside interference, he thinks. Everything seems to be working properly now. He turns back to the waiting chair. The static returns and increases in volume with each step that the Clown takes away from the table. He wheels and runs back to the Radio. It begins to work properly just as he reaches it. This time, the Clown resolves not to be tricked by this conglomeration of transistors and wires. He backs away slowly, keeping his eye fixed on the infernal machine. He reaches his chair this time and settles into it. The Radio apparently is not going to make any more trouble. He opens the paper and leans back. Static immediately fills the room. The Clown, angry now, advances on the Radio. He grabs a hammer or mallet out of the table drawer and raises it to smash the Radio.

RADIO: Ah-ah! Don't touch that dial. We'll be right back. *(Insert the fake commercial of your choice.)* We now return to our regularly scheduled program. *(The Radio continues as before.)*

(The Clown tightens his grip on the hammer. His hands are moist, so he wipes them on his shirt. He takes aim with the hammer.)

RADIO: An important announcement ... *(Sound of a teletype. The Clown pauses to listen.)* ... will be given tomorrow morning at eleven A.M.

(The machine has tricked him again. But no more. The Clown raises the hammer for the last time.)

RADIO: This ends our programming for today.

(The Radio is silent. Slowly, the Clown lowers the hammer and begins to return to his chair. When he gets halfway between the Radio and the chair, "The Star Spangled Banner" begins to issue from the machine. In an automatic act of patriotism, the clown salutes. Unfortunately, he still holds the hammer and knocks himself for a loop. The Radio is the winner and still champion.)

Extraneous business such as attempting to turn off the radio (the radio, of course, keeps playing even if unplugged) may be inserted in the script to make the sketch longer. The clown may also append this sketch to another in order to offer the audience a variety of action. "The Snack" lends itself to this gimmick. So does the hammock or the collapsible chair.

The radio is highly adaptable because it derives its humor from a very real situation. The human body is a natural conductor of radio waves. When in close proximity with a radio or television set, it serves as an antenna. Every member of the audience has seen this principle in action in their homes whenever they have had occasion to adjust the rabbit ears on their television. The picture becomes clear when the antenna is touched but immediately becomes fuzzy when the antenna is released. The audience can identify with the frustration the clown experiences.

RING AROUND THE COLLAR

Ingredients Flour, water, newspaper, poster board, and paint (gold, silver, and red).

Construction Combine the flour with enough water to form a thick paste. This should be done in a bowl. Twist a sheet or two of newspaper into a ring that will slip easily over the head. This will be the frame that will form the band of a very large ring. Tear the rest of the paper into strips. One by one, dip the strips into the flour paste and wrap them around the paper ring until it is completely covered. The strips should be applied in six to eight layers to ensure a sturdy finished product. A "gem" may be added to the ring by taping a crushed paper bag to the edge of the paper circle and coating it with paper strips soaked in flour paste. The ring should be dry enough in 24 hours to retain paint. Gold paint can be used to color the band of the ring and silver to decorate the gem. The red paint is used to make a sign that reads, in easily seen characters, "Ring Around the Collar."

Performance An overblown pun on laundry-detergent commercials, this sight bit is made for the walk around because the only thing the clown need do with it is walk around. The clown places the ring around his neck, holds the sign in front of him, and parades before the audience. The only other use to which this gimmick is applicable is as a throwaway pun.

(The Clown, wearing the ring, approaches Another Clown, who is already on the stage.)
ANOTHER CLOWN: What's that?
RING CLOWN: I have ring around the collar.

Tha-dump *(drum roll and rim shot)*. Vaudeville is not dead. It is only lying in wait.

ROCKET

Ingredients A five-gallon gas can, 100 feet of rope, four large L-shaped brackets, fish line, spring skunk, a safety pin, a firecracker, and one small torpedo or bomb-shaped cyclinder.

Construction A torpedo or bomb casing can be purchased through an Army surplus store. The important feature to look for when shopping around is the presence of fins on the casing. The thing must vaguely resemble a miniature rocket ship. (To cut costs, the clown may want to construct the ship from paper or cardboard, but such materials will produce a product that is easily damaged.) The brackets are bolted to the nose of the rocket. They will eventually support the nose cone (gas can). To give the rocket greater mobility, it can be fastened to a base with wheels by bolting the fins to a board fitted with four rollers. While not a necessity, a base will permit the clown to bring the rocket on and

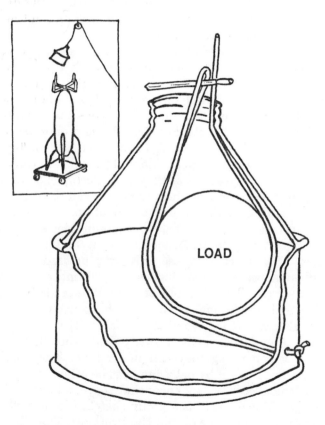

Figure 14

take it off the stage with greater speed. However, the rocket should be able to stand on its own four fins.

To prepare the nose cone, cut away the bottom of the gas can, punch a hole in the side near the bottom, and throw away the cap. If the can is not new, it must be washed out thoroughly because the residual petrol on the walls of the can will damage the load that will eventually be placed inside it. One end of the rope is run through the spout and threaded through the hole in the side of the can. It is then secured by a knot. The other end is strung on a pulley, which should be hung directly over the center of the stage or ring.

Figure 14 depicts the finished product and the manner in which the load (the skunk) is strapped into the craft. The rope loops around the load and back through the spout of the can. It is held in place by a wooden match or thin, easily broken piece of wood.

The manipulation of the spring skunk is described in Chapter 11 in the discussion of spring animals.

Performance The rocket sketch is an absurd reflection of modern technology and the men who ceaselessly try to advance it. In appearance, the rocket is a product of the "paper clip and chewing gum" school of mechanics rather than a piece of sophisticated NASA hardware. In short, it looks like a pile of junk. But the audience knows that it must get off the ground because the rope attached to the nose cone and run through the pulley at the top of the arena is so painfully evident. The audience can relate to this pile of tin with greater ease than to the complex hulks of steel that the government expects them to believe can rise self-propelled above the earth and into the vacuum of space. Although the audience has seen rockets launched numerous times, they cannot really comprehend the tremendous weight and mass of these machines. The object they see thrusting upward through the stratosphere appears only six inches long (12 inches on a 24-inch television screen). That the object actually stands hundreds of feet high and weighs many tons can be conceived of only in intellectual terms. It is beyond their reality. It is mind boggling. Therefore, they will readily identify with the clown's rocket because it is something they can understand. They realize the clown is fooling himself by believing that he is launching a rocket, and they laugh because they know that they could do no better.

Although "The Rocket" is a group sketch, the majority of the action is given to only one clown: the Professor. The other clowns serve as assistants who manipulate the equipment or reactors who point out the absurdities in the sketch to the audience. They grimace and gesticulate to mirror the way the audience would react to this absurd situation if it were real instead of a contrived piece of comedy. The only person who takes the whole thing seriously is the Professor, who has designed "The Rocket."

Preceded by the Professor, who runs about ineffectually coordinating the action, the clowns enter with the rocket. The nose cone is already on the stage or in the ring, rigged, with the rope run through the pulley. The Professor hurries the clowns silently to set the rocket in launch position and complete the final assembly by placing the gas can atop the missile.

ANNOUNCER: Well! What do we have here?

PROFESSOR: A space probe.

ANNOUNCER: A space probe?

PROFESSOR: Yes, we're going to launch a rocket to the moon.

ANNOUNCER: To the moon. That thing doesn't even look like it can get out of bed in the morning.

PROFESSOR: Oh, it can do more than that. It was put together at the (name of a local school or college) laboratories.

ANNOUNCER: I see. And you think that it will really get off the ground.

PROFESSOR: I'm sure of it. All we have to do is count down.

ANNOUNCER: O.K. Ready? Begin. *(As the Announcer counts down, the Professor puts his fingers in his ears. His knees knock and tremble with increasing fear as the numeral One approaches.)* Ten ... Nine ... Eight ... Seven ... Six ... Five ... Four ... Three ... Two ... One ... Blast Off! *(Nothing happens. The Professor realizes that the rocket has not moved. He stops shaking and begins to inspect the machine.)* Just as I suspected. That thing isn't going anywhere.

PROFESSOR: I don't understand what could have gone wrong. *(He turns to the Announcer; so he does not notice one of his assistants placing a firecracker under the rocket and lighting it.)* It should work. It passed all our tests. *(The firecracker explodes, and the Professor is thrown for a loop. Another assistant pulls on the rope and the nose cone begins its ascent.)*

ANNOUNCER: There it goes!

PROFESSOR: It's off. *(Clowns cheer.)*

ANNOUNCER: So are you. *(The nose cone reaches the pulley and bobs up and down.)* Your rocket can't seem to make it out of the arena.

PROFESSOR: What could be wrong now? *(The clown on the rope gives a hard tug, the match stick or piece of wood breaks, and the skunk falls to the ground.)* No wonder. The nose cone was too heavy. There was a stowaway on board. *(He picks up the skunk and begins manipulating it as described in Chapter 11 under the heading of Spring Animals. Another clown attaches it to the Professor's gown.)* A pretty pussy cat climbed aboard when I wasn't looking. Isn't it a pretty pussy cat?

(The Professor begins to milk the audience, getting them to respond actively to the situation. He carries the skunk to a section of the audience that realizes what is being proferred to them. A number of members, most probably children, will try to tell him what he actually has on his hands. The Professor cannot believe what the audience is trying to tell him. He has been around, graduated, seen the world. He knows the difference between a skunk and a pussy cat. To prove this, he checks the animal he is holding by raising its tail to take a look. Not until then does he realize that IT IS A SKUNK. He tosses it away and wanders in the opposite direction, fanning himself in relief. The skunk, attached to his professorial robes, drags behind him. The audience will point out that he is being followed. He tries to run from the creature; the skunk stays with him. Finally, he is chased off the stage, with the other clowns jeering behind him.)

The seemingly unjustified shift from space travel to skunks is a necessary one. Contemporary audiences, bored with the incessant delays and technical errors that plague man's exploration of this solar system, demand a blow off that will strike them out of the blue. The original punch to the line of "The Rocket" was to have the nose cone lowered to the professor, who tears it apart to discover the difficulty. In the nose cone, the professor finds a collection of useless mentionables and unmentionables. Apart from the fact that the sophistication of modern audiences precludes the use of low comedy, this blow off has been overused as a stock out by unimaginative clowns. Everyone in the audience has had ample time in the course of their lives to see undergarments. Therefore, they no longer titter with embarrassment when exposed to such unmentionables. Also, they can easily see what the rocket looks like on the outside. What else but junk could possibly be on the inside. The shift from one set of fields, space exploration and inadequate preparation, to the other, the skunk and the pussy cat, keeps the audience on the edge without any hope of regaining its balance until the clown allows it with laughter.

If the clown insists on putting junk in the nose cone, then he must accept the challenge he has set for himself. Like Jonathan Winters, he must be prepared to present each piece of jetsam economically in an original manner and make certain that the audience can identify with his every action. He must not, as so many clowns have done in the past, expect an object to have humor intrinsically. No object is funny in and of itself. Therefore, the clown can never expect to rest on his laurels, or wherever it is that a clown sits.

SLAPSTICK I

Ingredients   A hinge, some screws, glue, and two pieces of wood 36 inches by 4 inches and ½ inch thick.

Construction   One piece of wood must be shortened by six inches. The six-inch section cut from this piece should be glued to

A   B

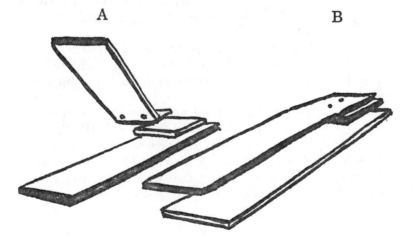

Figure 15

the other piece so that it is flush with one end of that piece. The two cut segments are then rejoined by attaching the hinge as illustrated in Figure 15-A. A shallow gouge may have to be cut in the uncut board at the junction of the hinged pieces. This will permit the longer hinged segment to swing freely. The hinged segment will slam against the uncut piece of wood when the stick is swung. A crack will be produced no matter how hard the board is swung. By rigging the free ends of the stick with a hole and a firing pin, caps or blanks can be used to create a louder sound. (The clown should check the local laws governing such devices before making use of them.)

Performance The slapstick is used by one clown to hit another without hurting him. The slapping noise that the stick produces adds a realistic punctuation to the pulled punch made with the device. The only danger in using it is in overusing it. It can be used to spark business in almost any sketch imaginable.

This particular version fitted for a cap or blank solves the problem of overuse. It is only capable of carrying one charge. Therefore, the clown will be able to use it only once in any particular sketch.

SLAPSTICK II

Ingredients Glue, two boards 36 by 4 inches, and a piece of wood 6 by 4 inches. Both boards and the piece should be one-quarter of an inch in thickness.

Construction The piece of wood is sandwiched between the two boards, and the three are glued together as shown in Figure 15-B. Tape may be wrapped around the glued areas to give them added strength.

Performance This is the original version of the slapstick. Its design predates the Punch and Judy shows of the Middle Ages. When tapped lightly, the ends of the boards clack together to produce the sound effect. The stick does not have to be reset or reloaded. The short piece of wood that divides the two boards ensures that after the fake hit, the boards will separate in preparation for the next swing.

STRETCHER

Ingredients   Two dowel rods roughly as long as a body is tall and a blanket.

Construction   The rods are placed parallel to each other on the ground. The distance between them should be equivalent to the width of the human body. The blanket is spread over them so that the ends of the rods protrude past the blanket's edges. These ends are the handles of the stretcher. Note that the bed of the stretcher (the blanket) is not attached to the rods.

Performance   The stretcher can be used as either a running gag or the blow off to a slapstick sketch. As a running gag, the attendants may begin with a real stretcher and cart everything away but the injured party. Finally, they do pick up the fallen clown and place him on the stretcher. When the attendants stand and run off, they leave the bed of the stretcher and the clown behind them on the ground.

At the end of a sketch, the stretcher can be used to clear the stage of clowns. For example, at the end of the balloon chase, the owner of the balloons ends up slapped down. The attendants enter, place the owner on the stretcher, and leave without their patient. The owner gets up and, with the other clowns, chases frantically after the attendants. Or when the baby misses the net in "The Clown Fire Department," the attendants rush away, with the firemen carrying the twice-dumped baby in hot pursuit.

The introduction of the rigged stretcher adds a twist to the clown's scenes that the audience will rarely expect. The abrupt shift from one subject to another will always take them by surprise and leave them laughing.

TABLECLOTH

Ingredients   One small table, two finishing nails, assorted plastic plates and cups, a tablecloth, and a piece of clear plastic the same size as the table top.

Construction   The finishing nails are driven into two corners on the same side of the table so that they stick up about a half inch from the table top. Two small holes are then drilled into the plastic that corresponds to the nails in the table. The nails should fit easily through the holes and hold the plastic securely to the table's surface. Slits are cut in the tablecloth to allow it to hang naturally over the table's edge, free of the nails. The dishes are glued to the sheet of plastic in a suitable arrangement for a meal. Finally, the cloth is spread on the table top, the plastic is fitted on the nails, and the table is ready to be walked around.

Performance With this gimmick, the clown is able to do that fabled trick: pull a tablecloth from a completely set table without disturbing the dishes. The Dummy and the Braggart are usually set off against each other in this walk around. The two approach the audience, the Dummy, of course, carrying the table.

> BRAGGART: Be prepared to be amazed. I have arrived. Behold! A table. *(He points to his left. The Dummy and table are on his right. He sees his error.)* Behold! Another table. I will now whip the table wrapping right out from under these expensive imported pieces of china.
>
> DUMMY: Made in Taiwan.
>
> BRAGGART *(Pushes the Dummy aside):* Watch closely or you will miss my dexterity. *(He pulls the cloth away, leaving the setting undisturbed.)* Voilá! *(He bows for his applause.)*
> *(As the Braggart bows, the Dummy picks up the table, holding it at an angle so that the audience can see that the setting is cemented to the table top.)*
>
> DUMMY: Are you ready to go now?
>
> BRAGGART: Not yet. I . . . *(Sees that he has been exposed, smiles sheepishly at the audience, and chases the Dummy off)*

For exercise, the clown may wish to experiment with the tablecloth gimmick as part of a larger sketch. Setting the scene in a restaurant or café, the clown, and the alley to which he belongs, should be able to drum up a workable situation that could lead to an elaborate harlequinade.

UMBRELLA

Ingredients Hot water bottle, surgical tubing, tape, and an umbrella.

Construction The tubing is run up the stem of the umbrella and through a small hole in the center of its top. It is taped securely in place. The other end of the tubing is run up the clown's sleeve and attached to the hot water bottle, as described earlier in this chapter. The hot water bottle is naturally filled with water.

Performance The clown walks past the audience with the umbrella opened above him. Occasionally, he stops to see if it has stopped raining. He extends his free hand and, at the same time, squeezes the hot water bottle under his arm. Water shoots out the top of the umbrella. The clown feels the moisture on his extended hand and, since it is apparently still raining, leaves the umbrella open. He continues on his way, convinced that a cloud is hanging over his head.

WASHING MACHINE

Ingredients Four handkerchiefs, four tennis ball containers, one circular piece of wood 20 inches in diameter, six pieces of wood each two feet square, a hinge, a latch, a piece of cardboard, two spring snakes, glue, and sundry nuts, bolts, and finishing nails.

Construction Using the six square pieces of wood, a box is built that resembles the drawing in Figure 16. One square that forms a side of the box must be shortened by three inches to provide an opening through which the clown may turn the wheel made from the circular piece of wood. This piece of wood is bolted to the floor of the box so that it can turn freely like a lazy Susan. To this wheel are glued the four tennis-ball containers. One of these containers is divided into two compartments by inserting the piece of cardboard. A rectangular piece must be cut from the top of the box and reattached with the hinge, as shown in Figure 16. The opening must be large enough to permit a spring snake to spring through unimpaired. The top is then nailed tightly on the box, and a latch is affixed to keep the hinged doorway closed.

Reaching through the opening at the bottom of the box, the wheel is turned until the divided cylinder appears in the doorway in the lid. A neatly folded handkerchief is placed in compartment "A" of the cylinder. The wheel is then turned clockwise until the next cylinder appears in the doorway. A second handkerchief is ripped, shredded, and placed in this second cylinder "B." The wheel is rotated clockwise once again until the third cylinder, "C," is under the doorway. In this container will go a handkerchief that has been torn and burnt. Moving on to the last cylinder, "D," the

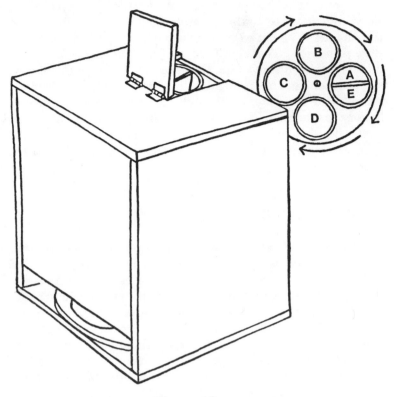

Figure 16

two spring snakes are inserted and held in place while the wheel is turned again so that the divided cylinder is once more in the doorway. The lid of the box will hold the snakes in place. A thick, water-soluble paint is used to make finger marks all over a fourth handkerchief. When the paint is dry, this handkerchief is put in a pocket of the clown's costume, and the washing machine is ready to roll.

Performance Unlike the previous washing sketches, the washing machine uses no water. The comedy comes from what the machine does to the hapless clown. The clown, in this case, represents Everyman in a struggle against the machine.

CLOWN: Let me tell you! You really work up a sweat doing that. *(He takes out his handkerchief to wipe his forehead and sees finger marks all over it.)* Oh, look. I picked up the wrong hanky. Does anyone have a towel or another hanky?

DUMMY: Wait! Hold it!

CLOWN: What is it? Do you have an extra hanky?

DUMMY: Oh, no. I have something better than that.

CLOWN: What might that be?

DUMMY: This! An automatic electric washer and dryer. I just bought it from some guy out on the street. He said it works like a dream.

CLOWN: It looks more like a nightmare. I don't believe it works.

DUMMY *(Insulted):* Give me that. *(He grabs the dirty hand-kerchief.)* You think I goofed again—got taken. Well, I'll show you. *(He stuffs the handkerchief into the machine, using compartment "E.")* There. Now I turn it on and . . . *(Nothing happens.)*

CLOWN: Nothing happens.

DUMMY *(Turns the wheel clockwise):* I don't understand this. It worked for the guy who sold it to me. *(He removes the handkerchief, ripped to shreds.)*

CLOWN: Of course, it did. Ah! What did you do to my hanky?

DUMMY *(Stuffing the ripped handkerchief back into the ma-chine):* Nothing to worry about. It just got caught in the machinery a little bit.

CLOWN: A little bit? It's ripped to shreds!

DUMMY: It still doesn't work.

CLOWN: It'll never work.

DUMMY: Let me take a look in the back. *(He ducks behind the machine with a lighted match or a candle. While back there, he turns the wheel clockwise. Then, leaving the match or candle behind, he comes back out.)* That should do it. *(He pauses suddenly and sniffs the air.)* Do you smell something burning?

CLOWN: My hanky!

DUMMY: Uh-oh! *(He opens the door and takes out the charred remains.)* You can still see the monogram. *(He grins.)*

CLOWN: Why you . . .

DUMMY: Don't get excited. I'll fix it. *(He puts the handkerchief back in the machine and closes the lid. While he kicks and shakes the machine several times, he advances the wheel to the last cylinder.)*

CLOWN: I'm not going to put up with this. *(He pushes the Dummy aside, opens the lid of the machine, and falls over when the snakes fly out.)*

DUMMY *(Looking into the machine):* Your hanky's not there. The snakes must have eaten it.

CLOWN *(Rises menacingly):* That does it!

DUMMY: Hold on! I haven't tried one last thing.

CLOWN: What's that?

DUMMY: The reset button.

CLOWN: The reset button? Do you expect me to believe that a reset button will do any good after all this?

DUMMY: Just let me try. *(He pushes something in back of the machine and turns the wheel to the first cylinder.)* There! *(He opens the lid and brings out the new, folded handkerchief, which is in compartment "A.")*

CLOWN: I don't believe it. You did it. *(To the audience)* Ladies and gentlemen, this is the first thing he has done right this week. *(To the Dummy)* I'm so proud of you.

DUMMY *(Overcome by this unexpected praise, he blows his nose with the handkerchief.)*

CLOWN: No! Don't! Ah! *(He chases the Dummy off.)*

11

Ready-made Properties

No object is funny in and of itself. Some items may be funnier than others, no matter how humorous an item might be, it can never stand by itself. For example, compared to a brick, a flush toilet is a riot. Yet in an episode of "Monty Python's Flying Circus," a single brick received more laughter than 23 flushings of Archie Bunker's off-stage john. The brick became funnier simply because the performers related to it and used it toward a specific, albeit absurd, end. Norman Lear, on the other hand, relied solely on the intrinsic self-conscious laughter provoked by the repeated flushings.

Many clowns become guilty of the same error when they buy a laugh getter at a novelty or magic shop. They feel they need only to sit back and let their new toy do all of the work for them. Consequently, the laughs they receive are weak. Their audiences can tell that they are not doing their job.

But what about Steve Martin? He uses a lot of novelty items, and his audiences never seem to mind.

The important word here is "uses." He uses novelty items to give a bent to what he says or as a transition between spoken bits. When the pace of his act begins to slow, he plays on absurd prepackaged gimmicks to gain momentum and drag his audience into his zany world.

George Carlin may talk about how bizarre it is that a mature man could make a living by dreaming up ceramic doggy doo-doo, but Steve Martin, by example, demonstrates the stupidity of these devices. His well-modulated voice and his radio announcer, Middle American accent belies all of his actions. Because of the way he sounds and his clean-cut appearance, his audience is positive that he is taking nothing that he does seriously. Therefore, his audience laughs with him, not at him.

The clown can not create the same situation with his audience because he is a character. Everything he does derives from the character. If the clown duplicated Steve Martin's act, the audience would laugh at this pitiable creature who is attempting to be funny. The audience sees a character, not a human being. They can identify with the character in an established situation but can not identify with a made-up man in an outrageous costume doing inane things to try to make them laugh. The clown never *tries* to make people laugh: he *makes* people laugh. That is his primary function.

When a clown shops around for a ready-made property, he should always keep in mind that the item he buys must be adaptable to the routine, bit, or sketch for which he is purchasing it. All of the properties listed below can be incorporated into a variety of displays, whether walk around or full-scale sketch. By playing around with the inherent possibilities of each piece, the clown should be able to come up with quite a few new ideas. Each piece lends itself to a specific area of everyday life, so the clown will not have to develop a situation from scratch.

Finally, the clown should practice with each piece of equipment before presenting it to an audience. Smoothness of handling is the only thing that separates the clown from the buffoon.

CAMERA

Unlike the camera described earlier, this camera looks exactly like the modern film devices used today. Only it is about 20 times as big. Many photography stores use gigantic cameras made of plastic for displays. The size of these display cameras make them perfect tools for the clown. The owner of the shop may be willing to sell the model when the display is taken down or refer the clown to the wholesaler who distributes the model. Once the camera is acquired, the clown needs only one more item to equip himself for an excellent walk-around bit: an 8 by 10 photograph of a mule.

If the model camera opens, the clown prepares by placing the photograph inside it. Unfortunately, most of these models do not. In order to perform this bit, the clown will probably have to place the picture face down on the back of the camera. The only problem with using this method is that the picture may slip, exposing itself to the audience. Therefore, in using the second method of preparation, the clown must keep a tight grip on the situation—and the picture.

Excitedly clutching the camera in his sweaty little palms, the Clown runs up to a section of the audience. He is pleased with himself and proud of the camera.

CLOWN: I just bought a new camera. The man who sold it to me said that it is the best one of its kind. You see, this is the kind of camera that develops its own pictures in sixty seconds. He showed me some sample photographs taken with this very camera, and all of the shots were crystal clear. Everything in them was really true to life. *(He grins sheepishly: he is shy about asking the next question.)* You know, I really can't wait to try it out. I wonder if one of you would help me by posing for a picture. How about you? O.K.?

(The Clown leads the volunteer down from the stands and positions him in a well-lighted spot. An oversized light meter or a sextant may be used to determine the best location. The Clown moves carefully back, measuring the distance. He looks into the lens and sees nothing. Realizing his error, he turns the camera around and this time looks through the view finder. He motions the volunteer backward, forward, and side to side until everything is lined up. Finally, he snaps the picture.)

CLOWN: All right! I got it! *(He helps the volunteer back to a seat.)* Only sixty seconds. Can somebody time it? Who has a watch? *(He thinks for a moment.)* Oh! I have one. *(He stares at his watch intently.)* I don't know if I can wait. Twenty seconds to go. Well, let's take a look at it.

(He opens the camera and removes the photograph, or peels it from the back of the camera, without letting anyone see the print. After looking at it for a moment, he smiles at the audience.)

CLOWN: It could have stayed in a little longer, but I think it didn't turn out all that bad. *(He turns over the picture of the mule.)* Do you?

(While the audience laughs, the Clown moves on to another section, resetting his apparatus for a repeat performance.)

Since it plays on the vanity of the audience, this sketch can come very close to insulting the person who volunteers. The clown must be careful to pick a good-natured Joe; someone who has been laughing even before the clown begins the bit is the best bet. Never pick someone with a bored expression. Chances are that such a person feels himself above the childishness of humor and good fun.

The clown can always avoid a possibly unpleasant situation by remembering to stress the time factor at the end of the bit. If the audience is fully aware that the picture is being removed before the time is up, the good-natured insult will be smoothed over by giving the clown's stupidity full credit for the failure of the picture to develop properly. However, there has never been a report of an audience angered or affronted by this piece. Everyone, including the volunteer, always seem to enjoy the jibe poked by the clown. Only a very large ego could ever be insulted by a simple jest.

FIRECRACKER

The bisecting fields of "The Firecracker" sketch are simple. An immense firecracker, which looks as if its bang would rival an SST breaking the sound barrier, is presented to the audience. It is actually a dud. As soon as the audience and the clown who owns the firecracker discover this, another clown sets off a miniscule firecracker that blasts the first clown off his feet. The sketch consists of a fake-out that is blown away by subsequent events.

Several novelty companies carry oversized firecrackers that look very realistic. These plastic dummies come equipped with several feet of fuse that can be cut to the desired length and inserted into the plastic shell. The clown can also construct a passable fake from an ice cream container like those used in soda fountains or ice cream parlors. Painted red, such several gallon containers will resemble a large firecracker. The clown then only need worry about finding a fuse.

Since a real firecracker is eventually used in the sketch, the clown would be wise to check with the local authorities to find out if the use of such explosive devices is permitted in that area. Laws governing the use and possession of fireworks and related small explosives often differ greatly from one community to the next. Knowledge of the law in this case will save the clown no end of embarrassment, not to mention any possible fine or imprisonment.

"The Firecracker" may be presented as a solo piece or as a group sketch. The group sketch is always preferable for any kind of presentation even though, as in this sketch, only one clown is the focus of attention. A group of clowns adds color and dash to a sketch and can transform it into a spectacle. Also, the reactions of the clowns who are just along for the ride aid in focusing the audience's attention on the main performer.

The challenge that this sketch presents to the clown is to make the play comprehensible to the audience. There is practically no plot and absolutely no relevance in the sketch that might allow the audience to relate to the action. The only thing the audience can identify with is the clown's character. If the clown forgets to relate with his audience, he will end up with a big flop instead of a "Big Bang."

A small group of clowns enters bearing the firecracker. They strain under its weight as they maneuver it into position. One of the clowns is apparently in charge. He makes sure that the firecracker is placed "just so" by gesticulating to the other clowns. When the device is in place the clowns step back.

ANNOUNCER: What have we here?

CLOWN: A firecracker.

ANNOUNCER: It's awfully big.

CLOWN *(Considers this):* It's a big firecracker.

ANNOUNCER: Well, you can't bring it in here.

CLOWN: Why not?

ANNOUNCER: It might go off.

CLOWN: That's the idea.

ANNOUNCER: Why would you want to set it off?

CLOWN: I'm going to celebrate the Fourth of July.

ANNOUNCER: Isn't it a little early *(or* late) for that.

CLOWN: I want to get a head start *(or* "I'm making up for lost time.")

ANNOUNCER: I see. But that thing looks dangerous.

CLOWN: It's perfectly safe. I'll show you. *(He lights the fuse, and the other clowns scatter.)* It'll only make a little bang. I only planned for a small celebration. *(He is still standing by the firecracker.)*

ANNOUNCER: Oh. Don't you think you better move a little further away, just the same?

CLOWN: Why?

ANNOUNCER: Because, you're standing alongside a lighted fire-cracker—a big one.

CLOWN: Yes, I know.

ANNOUNCER: And it's lit.

CLOWN: Right. I just lit it. *(He realizes what he has done and where he is standing. With a scream of terror he turns his back to the firecracker and puts his fingers in his ears. His knees begin to knock together. The fuse fizzles out. Realizing that nothing has happened, the Clown takes his fingers out of his ears and turns to the firecracker.)*

ANNOUNCER: You're lucky. It fizzled out.

CLOWN: Rats. And I wanted to hear a bang. *(Another clown sneaks up behind him and lights a small firecracker.)* Nothing ever works right for me. *(The firecracker explodes and sends the Clown reeling.)*

(Two clowns run in with a stretcher—see "Stretcher" in Chapter 10—and exit, chased by the Clown they left behind.)

HANDCUFFS

A set of realistic-looking metal handcuffs can be purchased at just about any good toy store. The only catch is that they have a catch: a small protrusion attached to a spring with which the cuffs may be sprung. With practice, the clown can remove the handcuffs and replace them in less than a second. Without practice, the process takes two seconds. This means that for the price of a toy the clown can become "The World's Greatest Escape Artist."

M.C.: And now, ladies and gentlemen! The World's Greatest Escape Artist, (name of the clown).

(The Clown enters, majestically holding the handcuffs aloft in one hand. He bows to the audience and hand the cuffs to the M.C.)

M.C.: In less than one minute, (name of the clown) will escape from this pair of stainless steel handcuffs. Are you ready?

(The Clown nods, and the M.C. places the cuffs tightly on the Clown's wrists in front of him. The Clown snaps the chain between the cuffs taut in front of him several times to prove that the cuffs are solid and lets the M.C. lead him behind a screen.)

M.C. *(Looking at his watch)*: Begin. *(He counts the seconds aloud in 10-second increments while the screen shakes and shud-ders behind him.)* Fifty ... forty ... thirty ... twenty ... ten ... nine ... eight ... seven ... six ... five ... four ... three ... two ... one ... *(The screen stops shaking.)* And here he is! *(He pushes back the screen to reveal the Clown still in the cuffs.)* Well, maybe (name of the clown) needs a little more time. (He replaces the screen.) And now, presenting (the next act).

(After the act is over, the M.C. checks the progress of the escape artist. This time the Clown's hands are behind his back. The M.C. gives the Clown more time by presenting the next act. After it is over, the Clown is shown with the cuffs attached to a wrist and ankle. After each new act, the Clown is revealed, more tangled in the cuffs than he was before, After the last act, the M.C. goes to the screen.)

M.C.: I don't think we even have to look this time. *(To the clown)* Are you out?

CLOWN: Almost.

M.C.: Well, that's some improvement, but we've run out of time. It's time to go home.

CLOWN: But we can't. I'm nearly out of these things.

M.C. I think you've wasted enough of our time. *(He reaches behind the screen to grab the Clown.)* Ladies and gentlemen, good evening.

(The M.C. leaves with the Clown, the two of them handcuffed together.)

This is only one direction that a parody on escape artists can take. For the clown who eschews the heavy makeup commonly associated with the white face or the painted beard of the tramp, another dimension may be added. Each time the clown is revealed, he has gotten no further with removing the cuffs than he had at the beginning. In fact, he hasn't even changed position. The only difference each time is that he is a little bit older. At the end of the show he is a white-haired old man, and when the screen is whipped back for the last time, the resulting breeze blows him over.

LARGE THUMB

This plastic prosthesis can add to the cartoon-like quality of the clown. If he hits his hand or catches a thumb in a mouse trap, instead of only feigning pain, he has the option of displaying the injured appendage. The grotesquely swollen rubber thumb appears so unreal that it actually serves to reassure the audience that the clown has not really hurt himself. Practically every novelty or magic shop carries this incidental prop.

NETS

A butterfly net can provide the clown with an excellent walk-around bit. The only additional piece of equipment he will requre is an oversized paper butterfly, which can be bought in some of the better card shops or made from several sheets of brightly colored tissue paper.

The premise of the bit is that the clown who is searching for a rare species of butterfly is unaware that the fauna in question is glibly sitting out of sight above the clown. This is a situation parallel to looking for a pair of glasses, not realizing that they are perched all the while above the brow. The play on the reality of the search brings the bit home to the audience. All the clown need worry about with this sketch is that he does not milk the crowd too long. If he does, they will become bored with his antics.

On tiptoe, looking cautiously from side to side, the Clown moves slowly past the audience. He does not wish to frighten away any rare butterfly that might be lurking about before he has a chance to snare it. The real reason he moves slowly is to give the audience time to react to the multicolored insect swaying gently atop his hat. With luck, some sharp-eyed tyke in the crowd will spot the butterfly and attempt to convey to the Clown that it is fluttering over him. Soon the whole audience will be pointing at it. If, however, no one in the audience musters the courage to speak out, the Clown will have to take matters into his own hands.

CLOWN *(After locating a receptive section of the audience, he stops his stalking to make an appeal):* Excuse me, but I'm looking for a very rare insect. *(He proceeds to describe the butterfly on his chapeau in intimate detail.)* Has any one here seen it? *(If no one speaks up here, the Clown should stalk to another section of the audience. Generally, someone will say, "Yes.")* You have? Thank goodness, I thought I'd been looking in the wrong place. Exactly where did you see it? *(The audience member will point and say, "There." Misunderstanding the gesture, the Clown turns and looks in the direction of the pointing finger.)* Where? I don't see anything. *(From this point on, the Clown ad-libs to everything the audience says. The rest of the sketch is a battle of wits between the Clown, who must at all costs avoid finding the butterfly, and the audience, which is desperately trying to communicate the location of the critter. When the audience finally shouts that the insect is on the Clown's hat, the Clown prolongs the bit by avoiding the top of the hat where the butterfly sits. He removes the hat and looks in it, not at the top of it. When told to turn it around, either he turns around himself or else revolves the hat.*

Finally, in frustration, he scratches his head with the handle of the net, snagging the hat on the handle. Only then does he comprehend what the audience is saying. He reaches for his hat to find that it isn't there. It is on the handle on the net. The audience, in frenzied frustration, tries to tell him the location of the hat to no avail. Finally, the Clown drops his arms in defeat. The hat falls to the ground. As the Clown turns to walk away, he sees the hat with the appended insect. In a stealthy leap, he snares it with the net and runs to another part of the audience to repeat his performance.)

Although the blow off to this bit is weak, the bit is a popular one because it relies heavily on the comedy of the moment. It is, as Stephen Leacock might call it, a super comedic bit. If the clown attempts this bit, he is recommended to view a number of the films of W. C. Fields for additional ideas on how to handle the hat with the handle of the net.

PHONE

The phone consists of a plastic telephone receiver on an elastic or plastic card connected to a safety pin. Usually, the pin is fastened to the coat under the arm, and the receiver is tucked into the inside pocket of the jacket. The phone has been used as a comedic device by such performers as Bob Newhart and Shelley Berman. The routines of these comedians give the audience a chance to be passive participants by silently filling in the unspoken portion of a telephone conversation. This device works just as well for the clown as it does for the stand-up comic.

For the clown, the phone can also be an excellent device for crowd control. At parties, or even larger gatherings, the children in the audience may become a little rambunctious, and their excited jabber may drown out the clown. In such a case, the clown is presented with two choices. He may stand still until the audience quiets down, or he can whip out the phone. The majority of the audience will automatically become less noisy whenever a clown picks up another object and begins to work with it because they will want to know what he might be up to next. The rest of the audience will become quiet when the clown begins to speak. The monologue might be something like the following script:

> CLOWN (*Holding the phone receiver to his ear*): Hello? Hello? ... Oh, yes! How are you? (*To the audience*) It's a friend of mine. (*Back to the friend.*) Why, yes, I am. How did you know ... I see. (*To the audience*) He says he heard I was at a party. (*Listens to the phone again*) I'm sorry, he says he heard the party I was at. (*To the phone*) Of course it's noisy. Everyone's having a good time. ... I see. (*To the audience*) He says that the party sounds so great he wants to come over and join us. (*He listens to the phone.*) But he doesn't want to miss anything, so he asks that you hold the noise down until he gets here. (*To the phone.*) How long do you think it will take you to get over? ... O.K. (*To the audience*) He says he'll be over in a few minutes. (*To the phone*) See you then. All right. ... Good-by. (*He hangs up the receiver in his jacket.*) While we're waiting for my friend, I don't want you to get bored, so I have a few things left to do. Would you like to see them? (*And the clown continues the show to a quieter audience until it is time to bring out the "friend"—the ventriloquist's dummy.*)

Some phones come equipped with a battery-powered box that, when turned on, emits a ring like that of a phone. With it, the clown can give a touch of realism to the above call. Also, the ring will help quiet an audience by itself. When someone hears a phone ring, their first reaction is to stop what they are doing and answer it. The ring may also be used in other clown sketches to provide sound effects. For example, the device can be rung during "The

Washing Machine" sketch to signal that something is wrong with the machine. It can also be used as part of the alarm in "The Fire Department" sketch. In short, it is a good all-purpose prop.

RUBBER CHICKEN

Of all clown properties (natural, gimmicked, or ready-made), the rubber chicken has the greatest innate comic potential. An audience really has only to look at it to begin snickering. This does not mean that all the clown need do is run through the audience swinging a rubber chicken over his head. He must do something with it. Even a real chicken has to cross the road to get a laugh.

Because this prop is rubber, it can be folded and stuffed into a variety of different routines and sketches. It can be placed in the nose cone of the rocket, the back of the washing machine, or inside the radio. In "The Fire Department," it can be chucked out the window, and in "The Family Portrait," it can be the birdy that everyone watches. However the clown uses it, he should remember that it should be used only once a show.

SPONGE ITEMS

Like the rubber chicken, sponge-rubber objects can be compressed and placed just about anywhere. For example, the clown may begin to limp sometime during the show. He obviously has a pebble in his shoe. But because of the nature of sponge rubber, instead of removing a pebble, he pulls out a stone the size of a fist. No wonder he was limping!

Other sponge items, like the linked sponge hot dogs, can be used in conjunction with other props. One clown with the "Lion's All-Star Circus" used the hot dogs, sponge fish, rubber chicken, and sponge bread to do a takeoff on a fast-food chain. Stopping before a section of the audience during walk around, he built a sandwich from these items, which were arranged on a tray. When he had finished building his monster meal, he held the sandwich in one hand and flipped the tray over. On the back of the tray was painted, "I'm having it my way."

The budding clown dentist will find the next sponge-rubber device a great boon: an oversized spongy molar. Entering the dentist's office, the clown's next patient stumbles to the chair with a grotesquely swollen cheek. He obviously has a toothache, but the swelling is not caused by an infected tooth. It is the result of having the molar stuffed into his mouth. After a thorough examination, the clown/doctor decides that the tooth must be removed. He enters the mouth with a monkey wrench and firmly grasps the rubber tooth. When he pulls, the patient clamps his teeth on the sponge tooth. The molar will stretch out of the mouth as if it does not want to be removed. Finally the patient releases his hold and the tooth springs out to assume a recognizable shape.

The entire dentist sketch will not be presented here since W. C. Fields in *The Dentist* covers all the classical bits of comedy that can effectively be used in such a situation. The clown who wishes to perform the sketch should see the Fields film and construct his material from the bits he will find there. If he does so, he should remember to switch all material used so that it suits his character and abilities. Not everyone can be the great W. C.

SPRING ANIMALS

Unfortunately for the clown, the spring animal most associated with merrymakers (the snake) cannot be purchased separately. Practically every novelty house in the country carries the spring snake only as an adjunct to the peanut brittle prank. This prank consists of giving someone a can of candy that, when opened, releases a spring snake into the face of the unwary dupe. It is available in two sizes, but the clown will find that the large can is preferable to the small because it contains the superior product. The large can contains a durable cloth-covered snake that will last for years. The small cans hold tissue-covered springs that tear easily.

When used in various routines, the can can be utilized as part of the equipment since it is usually unseen. In "The Fire Department," the snake and can are both placed into the fire alarm box. The can may be substituted for container "D" in the washing machine. It can be used to hold the snakes inside the radio if the clown wishes to incorporate these spring animals in that sketch. Or the entire can may be placed in the rocket as part of the load. The only care the clown must take with the snakes is not to overuse them.

Another spring animal that is adaptable to a wide variety of sketches and bits is the spring skunk. The clown must attach a grommet under the skunk's nose and tie one end of a piece of transparent fish line to it. The other end of the fish line is tied to a safety pin. When pinned to the clown's jacket, the fish line will pull the skunk across the ground so that it appears to chase the clown. By winding the fish line around the snout of the skunk, the clown will ensure that the line will not become tangled. The fish line is unwound when the clown pets the skunk as he manipulates it. With each stroke, more of the fish line is tossed from around the skunk to the ground. This action is covered by the movement of the skunk. The skunk is made to move by placing the index finger on the first spiral of the spring and moving it back and forth.

WHIP

The whip referred to here is not an ordinary whip. When dealing with potentially hazardous tools (i.e., props that may be used as weapons), the clown should always pick up a toy version of the item. This will ensure that no child in the audience will go out, buy a real whip, and begin to flay his friends. A toy whip is shorter than the real thing and therefore less dangerous to use. The end does not attain a speed great enough to do real damage.

When would the clown possibly use such a device?

When he parodies the whip cracker, he spoofs the variety performer whose only call as a performer is a practiced ability in the use of the whip. Armed only with a toy whip, a pile of paper, and a blindfold, the clown is ready to prove his boast that he is the world's greatest "Whip Cracker":

The Whip Cracker, dressed in Western garb, enters flamboy-antly, followed by the Dummy, who is absorbed in reading the newspapers he is carrying.

WHIP CRACKER: Ladies and gentlemen, tonight you are in for a veritable treat. I am going to give you a thrilling demonstration of my consummate ability in the art of cracking the bull whip. *(He waves the ludicrously small toy whip about his head. Meanwhile, the Dummy has sat down in a chair on the stage, engrossed in the paper.)* Helping me is my lowly assistant, (name of dummy.) *(He notices that the dummy is sitting down.)* Get up. *(The Dummy does not hear him. He walks to the Dummy and taps him on the shoulder.)* I said get up on the chair. *(The Dummy points to himself.)* Yes, you. Get up on the chair and stand there. *(He turns.)*

DUMMY: Stand here behind you?

WHIP CRACKER: Yes, stand behind me! *(The Whip Cracker walks away with the Dummy right behind him. When he stops and turns again, the Dummy stays out of his sight behind his back.)*

WHIP CRACKER: I swear, the help you get these days. You ask someone to do some simple thing, and can they do it? No, they *can't. They just cause trouble. (To the audience.)* As I was saying, helping me is my lowly assistant ... *(He notices the assistant is gone. Walking to the empty chair, he looks around and under it. Finding no one, he turns, shrugging to the audience, and sees the Dummy reading the paper. The Dummy waves. Smiling, the Whip Cracker saunters up to his assistant; then, suddenly showing the anger he feels, he grabs the collar of the assistant's jacket and drags him back to the chair.)* Can't you listen. Get up there and stay there.

DUMMY: Stay here?

WHIP CRACKER: Yes!

DUMMY: Right here behind you?

WHIP CRACKER: Right behind me! *(As the Whip Cracker walks away, the Dummy follows, mimicking the other clown's every move. When the Whip Cracker turns, the Dummy stays behind him.)*

WHIP CRACKER: Some people! Now, as I was saying, I am going to ... *(He sees the empty chair. However, this time he is not fooled. He whips around, glares at the Dummy, and points at the chair. The Dummy points to himself. The Whip Cracker nods, and the Dummy picks himself up by his own coat collar and drags himself back to the chair.)* And stay put! Now I will demonstrate my skill by separating the paper held by (name of dummy) into two parts with the whip.

DUMMY: What?

WHIP CRACKER: I'm going to rip the paper in your hands with the whip.

DUMMY: Oh. *(Then he realized what his friend has just said.)* No! *(He is too late. The whip cracks, not even getting near him or the paper, and the Dummy rips the paper in half. If done simultaneously, it will give the audience the illusion that the paper is ripped by the whip. With the paper divided, the Whip Cracker takes his bows. The Dummy stands holding the torn paper in a state of shock.)*

WHIP CRACKER: And now I will perform the same trick over my shoulder with the aid of a hand mirror. *(The Whip Cracker picks up the hand mirror, back toward him, and discovers, after looking for a few moments, that he cannot hope to see anything holding the mirror this way. He reverses it so that the reflecting side faces him. This time, something in the glass captures his attention: his face.)* Hey, good looking! *(He begins brushing his hair into place. Meanwhile, the Dummy has gotten bored waiting for something to happen. He sees the Whip Cracker staring intently at the mirror and steps off the chair to find out what has so taken his partner's attention. Cautiously, he peers over the Whip Cracker's shoulder. The Whip Cracker frowns. Something is marring the perfect reflection in the mirror. He tries to flick it away and, when this fails, turns to see what the cause of the bad reflection might be. He sees the Dummy and starts with a scream.)*

WHIP CRACKER *(Holding his chest to contain his pounding, frightened heart)*: Get back up there and don't startle me again. *(The Dummy shrugs and returns to the chair to hold up the paper. The Whip Cracker sights the newspaper in the mirror, and as if the paper were really before him, he snaps the whip IN FRONT OF HIM. The Dummy tears the paper as if the whip parted it, and the Whip Cracker steps forward to take his bow. If the audience was taken in by the first display, they surely aren't by the second.)*

WHIP CRACKER: And for my final demonstration, I will rend the paper asunder blindfolded. *(He holds up a pair of panty hose.)*

DUMMY: Oh, no, you don't! *(He gets off the chair and walks into the audience.)*

WHIP CRACKER: What do you think you're doing?

DUMMY: I'm going to watch the show from here on in.

WHIP CRACKER *(To the audience)*: One moment, ladies and gentlemen. *(To the Dummy)* Get up here!

DUMMY: Nope.

WHIP CRACKER: Get back on the chair!

DUMMY: Make me.

(The Whip Cracker pauses for a moment, then bolts toward the

Dummy. He chases his assistant through the audience, on to the stage, and back up on the chair.)

WHIP CRACKER: And stay there! *(The Dummy stands holding the paper, nearly blubbering in fright. The Whip Cracker resumes his position with the panty hose.)*

WHIP CRACKER: One last time—blindfolded. *(He pulls the panty hose over his head.)* On the count of three. One ... Two ...

(The Dummy begins to rip the paper. The Whip Cracker tears off the blindfold and stares at the assistant in anger. The Dummy tears the paper into smaller pieces and then tosses them in the air. He holds his hands over his face protectively and waits. Nothing happens. He peeks and sees the Whip Cracker staring at him.)

WHIP CRACKER: Well, you've really done it this time, and you are going to get yours.

(At this point, the "Whip Cracker" sketch can be blended into "Clown Boxing" or ended outright with the bucket of confetti or the chase. If the chase is used at the end, it should be omitted earlier in the script.)

WILTING FLOWER

This device can be purchased at most magic shops and is an easy-to-operate walk-around prop. By pulling a ring on a string, the flower held by the clown can be made to wilt. The merrymaker approaches his audience and offers an audience member a chance to sample the flower's fragrance. When the audience member gets near the gimmicked posy, it suddenly keels over. As always, when performing a trick on an audience member, the clown must be sure to choose someone who will be willing to go along with the joke.

Gymnastics and Circus Skills

Like tumbling, the use of gymnastic and related pieces of equipment promotes balance and coordination. This can only benefit the clown. The practiced maneuvers acquired when working on the balance beam, horizontal bar, stilts, trampoline, or low wire can be related to many of the properties with which the clown will come in contact during his performances. For example, many of the moves that can be performed on the slack wire can be directly related to the hammock described in Chapter 9. Likewise, the trampoline offers a number of bits that can be transposed to a stationary table. And the stilts can provide the clown with material that can be carried over to "The Fire Department" sketch.

Since the basic "how to" of performing on gymnastic apparatus has been amply covered elsewhere, the focus of this section will be on the relation of performing on these pieces of equipment to the art of the clown. Additional, detailed information can be obtained from *Enjoying Gymnastics* by the Diagram Group, *Basic Circus Skills* by Jack Wiley, and *Circus Techniques* by Harvey Burgess. Here, even more than in tumbling, the clown will find personal instruction important. Also, whenever he practices, he will want to use mats and spotters because he will be performing above the ground rather than on it.

BALANCE BOARD

Also known as the rolling cylinder board and rola-bola, this nifty little contraption can be the clown's salvation or downfall (both literally and figuratively). It consists of a hardwood roller approximately six inches in diameter and a length of inch-thick board 30 by 10 inches. The top of the board is usually covered with skid-resistant contact paper, but since this wears quickly, it is better to cover the board with a skid-resistant paint mixture. Nonskid compounds that combine with paint are available at most hardware stores.

To use the balance board, place the board, nonskid side up, on the cylinder so that one end rests on the floor and the other is raised. Put one foot on the lower end. Until the board is to be used, the weight of the body should remain on this foot. The other foot is placed on the raised end of the board. When ready to perform, the clown increases the weight of the foot on the raised end. This will lever the lowered portion into the air with a seesaw effect.

The object from this point on is to keep the board balanced on top of the roller. The basic stance is with the legs spread, one foot on each end of the board, and facing forward toward the long side of the board. Parallel stance is facing one end of the board, both feet pointing toward the end of the board. The squat stance is a variation of these two. The legs are bent so that the performer appears to be surfing on the board. Other skills on the balance board include feet together forward and sideways, the jump, jump with a half twist, jump with a full turn, and if the performer knows how, juggling. To keep both ends of the board in the air during all this, the performer only need remember that the roller always marks his center of gravity; by matching his center of gravity to the roller, balance will always be maintained.

For the clown, the balance board offers itself as a bit of excellent incidental fun. The board, resting on the roller, is set up on the stage. Unaware of its existence, the clown crosses the stage, burdened with a host of objects (packages, full tea service, or whatever). In his hurry, he absently steps on the board and, before he realizes what has happened, is airborne. His object at this point is to get back on solid ground without dropping the objects he is holding. He turns, squats, kneels, and finally manages to return to earth. He sighs with relief, looks scornfully at the board, and, turning to go, trips over his own feet, dropping everything in his arms.

The clown should note that this suggested bit contains only one fall. Any more falls than that would just be playing for a cheap laugh. The balance board limits the number of falls the clown can take. He can only sprawl off it in the manner of someone sent flying by a loose roller skate or a banana peel. His audience will not tolerate more than two such falls a show. Someone who has fallen thus would hardly have a reason to climb on the roller skate again. This would be like a man intentionally standing in front of a moving truck a second time because he couldn't believe what hit him. The audience will cease to laugh after the first fall.

One unfortunate merrymaker from Pennsylvania did not realize this and treated a local television audience to five minutes of getting on the balance board and falling off. Each fall was a repetition of the first. By the end of the first minute, the camera men were yawning, and some members of the studio audience began to rest their eyes. However, to be honest, at the end of his act, he received spontaneous applause. On his last fall, he broke the board.

BALANCE BEAM

As the name implies, this piece of apparatus is a beam on which one balances. Made of wood, it is generally supported above the ground by metal braces and has a nonskid adhesive strip running the length of its top. The gymnast uses the beam to perform basic tumbling stunts. These maneuvers are made more difficult since the beam is narrow and several feet from the floor. It tests a performer's balance. Women competing in the Olympic games are expected to use the entire length of the beam, avoiding too many sitting and lying positions. Fortunately, the clown can profit from familiarity with the balance beam and need not concern himself with the graceful leaping and posturing maneuvers usually associated with this piece of equipment. The clown only need act naturally.

The beam itself is the only piece of gymnastic apparatus that can be incorporated into a clown set without the necessity of disguise. In "The Carpenter's Helper," the frame of the building being constructed can be the beam. As such, it can be used by either an acrobatic clown or the dummy. During the sketch, the clown walks onto the beam and, in the process of doing his job, drops his hat or tool. He tries to reach it and overbalances as he strains. Shooting up into a shoulder stand, he rolls out and, allowing his legs to swing on either side of the beam, rocks forward to fall on his face. Stunned by the fall, he regains his footing and proceeds to stagger away, nearly losing his balance or missing the beam with each step. Swaying woozily back and forth, he never loses his balance entirely.

Another scenario might have the clown, absorbed in reading, accidentally wander on to the beam. Finishing the article, the clown closes the book or folds the paper. Only then does he realize where he is. His problem now is to get off the beam without falling, for he is terrified of heights. He shakes as he inches his way back to the end of the beam and safety. His dilemma may be aggravated by some clown workmen who entered behind him and are sitting on the beam eating their lunch. To return to a solid mooring, the clown must get past (i.e., over) them. Or on his way back, the clown may drop his hat or book, which lands directly on the beam. To retrieve it, the clown must bend over and sacrifice the shaky balance he is fighting to maintain.

Finally, a mock balance beam can be made by placing a four by six between two saw horses. Such a setup would work very well in the circus ring. Also, good for the ring is a narrow scaffolding suspended from the top of the arena. The adventuresome clown could ask for nothing better than this free-swinging beam from which to operate.

BANDS

Usually used in women's gymnastic dance competition, the band is a long piece of cloth or ribbon that trails behind the performer like an after-image. It describes the flow of motion followed by the performer. The band has an analogue in the movement lines used to give cartoon characters the illusion of motion. In effect, it emphasizes each movement and carries it to the audience across great distances.

The clown can make use of a device like this in many group sketches. Substituting balloons or oversized handkerchiefs for the bands, the clowns can underscore the logical flow of motion. Also, when attached to clown props or carried by clowns, the bands help to add a flurry to the excitement of the chase.

However they are used, each clown should remember to choose a band with a distinctive color that is different from the ones used by his fellows to ensure that the audience can tell one band and one movement from the other.

CYCLING

The unicycle is often associated with the clown, which is unfortunate because little can be done with the one-wheeled device that is funny. It can be ridden in a variety of patterns or over hurdles and seesaws to display proficiency in its use. Two or more people can balance off the rider of the cycle, or the rider may decide to present the audience with a demonstration of his control by juggling while riding. However, these are feats of skill that cannot be used readily as comedy.

Still, clowns do ride unicycles in parades or try to milk the machine by repeatedly falling off it and trying to get back on it again. Such uninspired uses do nothing for the clown as a performer. At best, he will be able to hold an audience's attention with the peculiarity of the piece of equipment he is using.

This is not to dissuade the clown from using the unicycle because it does not lend itself to the chase as an encore. After being pursued about the ring, the clown being chased leaps on to a nearby bicycle. He may even take it from another clown, who then joins the chase. The group of enraged merrymakers run after the unfortunate clown, who pedals for his very life. He rides out of sight, followed by his fellows. The audience is then treated to a large crash. If the show is staged in an auditorium with a sound system, the clown might want to use a taped sound effect of an auto collision. At this point, if a band is used, the music takes on an off-key quality, and the bike rider re-enters. Now he is on a unicycle. In front of him is the forward assembly of a bicycle with a badly bent wheel, Pushing this before him, the clown wobbles once around the ring and away. With this disjointed bike, the clown will only add to the happiness of pursuit.

HORIZONTAL BAR

As with all pieces of gymnastic equipment, the clown should be proficient with the stunts he intends to perform. If he cannot execute the necessary maneuvers, he should not be in front of the audience for that particular part of the show. This is especially true of the horizontal bar because the bar cannot be disguised as anything other than a six-to-eight-foot-long steel bar mounted high and anchored to the floor. To use it, the clown must become part of the regular act. Each performer addresses the bar and performs a stunt. The clown then approaches the bar to immitate his betters, only to fall flat on his face.

Paradoxically, in this case the clown *is* one of his betters. Usually, the clown is chosen to perform on this piece of apparatus because of his proficiency on the bar. At the end of the routine, the clown must be able to strip off his motley and outstrip the other performers in a solo demonstration of his prowess. The audience, which always wants to see the underdog make good, will go wild when this happens.

Unfortunately, not every superb athlete makes a superb clown. A performer who is so absorbed by his own excellence will have a very hard time making anyone laugh. He will be unable to humble himself enough to play the fool. The most advanced stunt he must expect to do before his solo spot is a single-knee circle or a propeller spin. The rest of the time he must simply miss the bar or muff the trick and quietly return to the end of the line behind the other performers. Except for those moments when he is on the bar, he must let the other acrobats have the full spotlight.

LADDERS

The standing Roman ladders can be used by the clown in two different ways: as a direct parody of the circus spectacular and as a bit within a sketch. The ladders are simply ladders. Placed side by side, two performers mount them by climbing between them. The performers' bodies become the supports that hold the ladders in an upright position. Other performers then climb the outside of the ladders and style off to the side. A rectangular frame to hold the bottom of the ladders steady will help during practice and can also be used when the ladders are used on a smooth surface like the floor of a gymnasium.

In spoof of the circus spectacular, the clowns enter, preceded by a number of feather-decked, caped show girls. The women remove their capes and acknowledge the audience while the clowns set up the ladders. Then, in a last-minute reversal of roles, the showgirls take their places between the ladders as the supports, and the clowns climb the outside to style the audience. The postures that the clowns assume when they hang from the rungs of the ladders should be exaggerated attitudes of graceful deportment. Since clowns are not the most graceful creatures, their posturing will be closer to that used by Groucho or Harpo Marx instead of that used by the women they replace.

In the carpentry sketch, ladders can be used as part of the chase for the blow off. The carpenter and helper climb either side, trying to catch or evade the other, while the poor clowns who are supporting the ladder sway back and forth, straining against the shifting weight. In actuality, the assistants bear very little weight because they make the ladders sway away from the heaviest side, changing the direction of the sway every time the weight shifts.

In "The Fire Department" sketch, the ladders become another means of frustrating the hapless fire chief. Riding atop the ladders, every time he stretches to save the woman from the burning building, the ladder sways in the opposite direction. Finally, in desperation, he calls for the net.

PARALLEL BARS

The parallel bars cannot be used in a clown sketch because, like the horizontal bar, they defy disguise. Yet they bear a resemblance to a piece of clown equipment already mentioned: the stretcher.

Without the blanket, the poles of the stretcher, held at shoulder level by the attendants, are a good substitute for parallel bars. The attendants run to the fallen clown, carrying two poles. The clown is placed on the pole so that his arms and legs, draped over the side, support him. Then, picking up the "stretcher" and hoisting it on to their shoulders, the attendants race off. The clown, aware of the absurdity of the equipment, levers up on the poles, swings his legs backward between them, and holds himself over the bars on his hands and feet, facing down. He watches the ground pass beneath him and does a take at the audience as the attendants exit with him.

This would make an excellent addition to the use of the stretcher as a running gag. It avoids repetition and allows the clown's frustration to build to greater heights.

STILTS

Although Napoleon might have benefited from a pair of stilts, little is added to the clown's performance by the increase in height. On stilts, the clown may walk forward, walk backward, turn, hop, kick a ball, walk up and down a flight of stairs, or juggle. He certainly cannot run or leap, and he definitely cannot fall, for "the bigger they are, the harder they fall."

Why, then, should a clown learn the skill of walking on stilts?

The stilted clown is a popular parade attraction and, in preshow parades, will always lure people to a show. A clown on stilts is a novelty. For this type of work, strap-on stilts should be used. These, once fastened to the legs, can be concealed beneath a long pair of trousers to make the clown appear gigantic. Strap-on stilts can be ordered through some of the larger sporting goods firms. The preferred type for parade work are metal and are equipped with a system of hinges that permits the leg of the stilt to lean forward from the base the way the human leg bends at the ankle, providing the clown with greater stability.

The skill of stilt walking is also useful to the clown in a number of sketches. By gimmicking a ladder to come apart and reinforcing the rungs so that it becomes a pair of stilts, the clown is able to add a bit of insanity to "The Fire Department" or "Carpenter's Helper." The gimmicked ladder is also an excellent bit of business to use by itself.

The clown, hoping to use the ladder to reach some out-of-the-way object or replace a light bulb, climbs up. Once up, the ladder divides in two, thus creating a pair of crude stilts. The clown off balance, careens across the stage through an obstacle course of objects. Around tables and chairs, up and down stairs, turning and twisting, the stilts assume a life of their own and finally carry the clown off stage, where a confederate creates the sound of a crash.

TRAMPOLINE

As with the horizontal bar, the clown on the trampoline is a skilled performer. However, the trampoline clown is not only concerned with attempting to imitate the skill of his fellows. His problem is compounded: To perform on the trampoline, he must first get up on to it. In doing this, he may use all of the falls and rolls used in performing with the table. The height of the trampoline will require him to alter each of the moves slightly. For example, in rolling across the trampoline and off the other side, the clown must slow his roll before falling, or he will turn in midair and land on his back or side.

Once on the trampoline, his job is almost done. After a number of false starts, the clown traditionally goes into a solo performance, which proves him to be the featured performer of the group. But his performance will receive little notice if he has lost his audience before he takes the spotlight. Here again, repetition is a danger, but so is length. Because of the variety of bits that can be used on the trampoline (see "Table"), the clown's opening performance might run too long. This will tire his audience, and a tired audience is not too appreciative. One performer made this mistake in "The Lion's All-Star Circus" and strung the audience along for 15 minutes (more than half the running time of the entire act). At the end of that time, the audience was so bored that they were ready to applaud ecstatically for another performer whose boast was the ability to do 20-some consecutive back flips. An awesome feat, true, but once you've seen one back flip . . .

WIRE WALKING

Traditionally, the wire-walking clown is a high-society tippler or a tramp. The tippler is coming home from an all-night bash when he stumbles on the wire. He weaves his way across with a number of strategic pauses (to remove a piece of lint from the wire) and perhaps a fall (onto the wire, not off it), from which he must pick himself up (no mean feat on such a slender strand). All of these maneuvers are complicated by the basic position his feet must assume to maintain his place above the ground. The feet are placed so that the wire is centered between the big toe and the one next to it. The performer should never look down but feel his way across. In effect, the performer must play a tippler who can walk a straight line. Finally, the tippler is revealed to be a real wire walker who finishes the presentation with a display of his skill.

The tramp clown is generally a member of a wire-walking troup:

a minor member. He tries to imitate his fellows and finally takes the spotlight himself. He is, like all clowns who use such equipment, very skilled in his art.

The clown unskilled at walking the wire should not be discouraged, however. There is a comedy wire-walking routine that requires no skill at all. When the announcer or ring master introduces a world renowned wire walker, the clown enters. His wire is already strung in the ring or on the stage. He mounts the pedestal and with a flourish does walk the wire. Only in this case, the "wire" is a piece of rubber or elastic. It and the clown sink to the floor where the walk can be made safely without the use or necessity of a net. To carry this off effectively, the clown's equipment should closely resemble the real thing.

Juggling

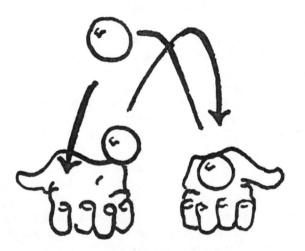

Figure 17

The skill of juggling is not hard to acquire. Patience is the only requirement. The clown must be prepared to start slow and develop each move. In time, the clown will have established the reflexive moves that will allow him to juggle without worrying about dropping the balls. This worry is the biggest block the clown will encounter in learning this skill.

To begin, hold one ball cupped gently in the right hand so that it rests on the ridge of skin at the base of the fingers. Imagine that the ball is a small furry animal and do not squeeze it tightly. The hand should be about waist level. Next, open the hand quickly as far as possible. This will cause the ball to pop into the air. Keep repeating this movement until the ball goes straight up to the eye level and returns with relatively little spin. If the ball moves away from the body or toward the body, it is being held incorrectly. Reposition it as described above and begin again. Switch hands every so often and practice until this first skill is learned.

The second step in learning to juggle is to toss the ball in an arc from one hand to the other. The hands should be held level at the waist as if a tray were resting on them. They should not move more than a few inches. The arc of the ball should be about eye level. When this can be performed smoothly, hold a second ball in the left hand and continue as before. Do not toss the second ball. Simply be content with tossing the one.

The third step is to add the second ball. The second ball should be tossed just as the first ball passes the top of its arc. After the second ball has been tossed, stop, check the position of the hands, and repeat the toss. After the pattern of the two balls has become stable, hold a third ball in the right hand, but do not toss it. Continue for a while with the two balls.

The fourth step is to add the third ball. When the second ball moves past the top of its arc, toss the third ball. Do not hurry since there is plenty of time to get the third ball off. Also, do not be discouraged by dropped balls. After the last ball has been tossed, stop, check the position of the hands, and repeat. This is one complete pass. From here, on in, the juggler adds one ball whenever he becomes comfortable with the tosses being made. Occasionally, the pattern (Figure 17) will break up. To correct this, the number of passes being made or balls being tossed should be reduced until the pattern becomes stable.

Patience is always the watchword. Some people can learn to juggle in two weeks, others in two months. The time to learn juggling is not only determined by the amount of practice but also by the attitude of the person learning. Coordination has nothing to do with it. An uncoordinated person with a good attitude will learn faster than a highly coordinated person with a bad one.

What is a good attitude?

An attitude that is typified by the following statement: "This is fun. It is like a game." Music playing in the background while tossing even one ball, as in the first step, will help keep spirits up during the learning process and will cover the noise of dropping the balls so the neighbors won't complain. For additional information on juggling skills, the clown can look in *The Juggling Book* by Carlo.

Once the clown has learned to juggle, he is ready to move on to comedy juggling equipment. Although many of these properties are self-working and require no skill, the clown will receive better laughs from his audience if they do not know whether he is serious or pulling their legs. If they have actually seen him juggling, they will never know for sure, and the clown will have the element of surprise on his side.

BALANCING BALLS

Ingredients   Three Styrofoam balls, three nails, and one dowel rod.

Presentation   The clown, after giving a short demonstration of his skill, boasts that he can do better. He states emphatically that he can balance three balls on top of each other on the end of a pole. Picking up the pole (the dowel rod), he reaches into his pocket or bag and produces a ball. Unknown to the audience, his hand covers the nail sticking out of the ball's bottom. With great care, he places the ball on the pole, slipping the protruding nail into a hole at the end of the rod. Removing a second ball, he places it on the first, fitting the nail in the second ball to the hole in the

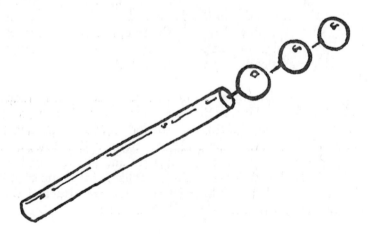

Figure 18

first. Then he removes a third ball and "balances" it on the first two.

All of his movements must be measured as if he were really balancing the balls. Finally, with extreme care, he lifts the pole and points to it while looking at the audience for approval. When the audience applauds, he bows, forgetting about the balanced balls. The pole tilts, and the clown is revealed for a fake. The balls are stuck to the pole and each other and naturally will not fall off. The clown retreats, embarrassed by his mistake.

This bit relies completely on the clown's acting ability. He must convince his audience that he is really balancing the balls. If the audience fails to believe that he is doing so, he will only be fooling himself.

Related bits are the balancing tray and the glass on tray. If one of these three bits is used during a show, the other two should be avoided because of the similarity of the effects.

BALANCING TRAY

Ingredients A tray, a dowel rod, a set of plastic or metal tumblers, a plastic or metal pitcher, several lengths of light chain, confetti, and assorted nuts and bolts.

Construction Bolt one end of each chain low on the side of each tumbler and the pitcher. The other ends of the chains are brought together and held in place by a bolt running through the center of the tray and into the dowel rod. Sprinkle the bottom of the tray with confetti and arrange the tumblers and pitcher on the tray. Since the objects on the tray are held fast by a chain, they will wobble realistically when the clown "balances" the tray on the rod.

Performance During a lull in a regular exhibition of juggling, the clown enters, balancing the tray on one hand. He weaves about the stage, losing more control over the rod and tray with each step. Finally, when he nears the audience, the rod tilts too far. The clown grabs it too late, and the tumblers and pitcher topple from the tray. Only then does the audience realize, as they are sprinkled with confetti, that the objects on the tray are attached with a chain and the clown has been putting them on.

BALL ON STRING

Ingredients   A piece of elastic string, a ball, and safety pin.

Construction   Run the string through the ball and hold it in place by knotting one end. Tie the other end to the safety pin and attach the pin to the coat. The string should be long enough to permit the ball to swing between the clown's legs without touching the ground.

Performance   This bit of whimsy requires that the clown be able to execute a number of juggling passes, stop, and pick up the motion of the balls again. The practice required to execute this effect will be well worth the effort, and the clown should find the challenge fun.

During the show a juggler allows one of the three balls he is tossing to drop, bounce once on the floor, and return to his hand as he continues to juggle. The clown, hoping to duplicate this feat, stands forward. He executes a few complete passes with the balls and then lets one drop, as did the juggler. The only difference between the two maneuvers is that the ball the clown lets fall is the one on a string attached to his jacket. The ball plummets, but instead of hitting the floor, it swings between the clown's legs. Once it reaches the end of the string, it swings back, and the clown begins to juggle as before. The ball never hits the floor.

BOXES

Ingredients   A large stack of boxes wrapped for shipping and a long piece of string.

Construction   Run the string through the boxes so that they are loosely joined like beads in a necklace. A foot of string should be between each box. The string must be knotted at the top and bottom of each box to hold them in place. So constructed, the boxes will wobble realistically when piled in a high stack for the clown to carry.

Performance   The clown enters, balancing the pile of boxes. He staggers along under their weight as he crosses the stage or ring. Another clown, who is absorbed in watching a bit of action elsewhere, barrels toward him; in the ensuing collision, the stack of boxes topple and scatter on the ground. The clown looks at the mess made by his fellow and, pulling the boxes by the string, exits with the boxes trailing behind him.

FEATHER AND TUBE

This excellent balancing effect may be purchased from Larry Weeks, its originator, for relatively little money. It consists of a plume and a hollow tube. The clown places the feather in the tube and blows it straight up into the air. While in the air, the feather turns over and begins to descend slowly. This gives the clown plenty of time to position himself under the feather so that he can catch it on his nose. Once he has the feather balanced there, if he begins to walk forward, he just lowers his head, and the feather will remain on his nose. The feather's design causes the air currents created by walking to hold it in place. It will fall only when the clown stops moving. Very little practice is required to accomplish this amazing feat, and in no time the clown will have a perfect walk-around stunt.

GLASS ON TRAY

Ingredients One glass, a tray, and glue.
Construction Glue the glass to the tray.
Performance This property may be used to good effect by the clown waiter. In crossing the room with the glass on the tray, the waiter encounters a group of arriving clown customers. He wades through, is pushed, prodded, and tripped, but does not lose control of the tray. Only when he is past the other clowns does he turn and glare at them, his hands on his hips and the now obviously glued glass on the tray by his side.

As with the balancing balls and the balancing tray, the clown must handle this prop as if the glass were not attached to the tray. The audience will only laugh if they are fooled, so the clown must act the scene to the hilt.

RUBBER EGGS

Here again, the clown must be able to juggle to carry off the joke. Bragging that his skill at juggling is so great that he can juggle eggs, the clown has a bowl of eggs brought to him. He breaks one of the eggs to prove that his claim is in earnest. Then, taking three eggs from the bowl, he begins to juggle. After a few passes, one of the eggs drops past his hand, hits the floor, and bounces back. Three of the eggs in the bowl are rubber; they can be purchased at most magic stores.

THE THREE-CIGAR-BOX ROUTINE

Ingredients Three cigar boxes and a piece of stiff wire
Construction Attach one end of the wire to one of the cigar boxes and bend the other end as shown in Figure 19. Make sure that the lids of the boxes are sealed tightly with tape.
Performance This is a direct parody of the juggler's art. The manipulation of the cigar boxes has been around for years, and the audience will recognize the intention of the juggler when he brings them forth. A cigar box is held in each hand, and these are used to support a third box between them. The juggler then proceeds to move the boxes on the end by flipping them over and back again. The object is to do this without dropping the box in the center.
The clown eliminates all skill from this feat with the device in

Figure 19

Figure 19. The bent wire is slipped behind the clown's belt, and the box at the other end is "supported" by two cigar boxes held in both hands. The audience should be unaware that the center box can hang there by itself until the clown takes his bow. Therefore, the clown should put together a fairly realistic short-box routine to precede the inevitable discovery by the audience that he has hoodwinked them again.

An alternative method that can be used to support the center box involves a piece of cork fastened to the belt buckle. In this case, the wire is straight rather than bent and the free end is stuck into the cork. This version permits the clown to set up the effect right before his audience's eyes without giving away his secret until the end.

UMBRELLA AND BALL

Ingredients   An umbrella, a piece of string, and a metal washer.
Construction   Run the string through the ball and knot the end

Figure 20

so that the ball will not fall off. Tie the other end around the washer and place the washer over the pointed tip of the umbrella. Two washers may be necessary to keep the ball and string anchored to the umbrella. An alternative method of anchoring the washer in place is to put a rubber tip at the end of the point.

Performance During a juggling routine, the clown enters holding an open umbrella and a ball. He obviously intends to outdo the real jugglers. He tilts the umbrella and, placing the ball at its edge, begins to spin it like a top. The spinning motion apparently keeps the ball balanced at the umbrella's edge. Like a treadmill, the revolving umbrella holds the ball in one position as it keeps rolling from the force of gravity down the tilted top of the bumbershoot. The clown, who, after a few moments, is very pleased with himself, looks back at the other performers to see if his apparent prowess is impressing them. As he does, the umbrella tips lower, and the ball on the string leaves the top to dangle in midair. The clown remains unaware of this development until he looks back to the audience. With laughter all around him, the clown realizes he has balled things up again and sidles off the stage.

Puppetry and Ventriloquism

What do puppets have to do with clowns?

Basically, they are the same type of creature. Both are exaggerations of the human being. Either can function within a logic of unreality in his own magical world. They are living cartoons trapped in a world not of their own making. Neither can be seriously injured. Resilient, they bounce back no matter what befalls them. The only difference between them is that the clown is not confined to the unseen hand that manipulates the puppet. This frees him to manipulate the puppet himself.

Why would the clown want to use the puppet?

In solo performances, the puppet makes the clown's job easier and adds variety to the show. Any audience will become bored if they are treated to the same face and character for a long period of time, but sometimes the clown must go on alone. Whatever the reason, lack of funds to support more than one performer or the unavailability of a partner, the clown will sometimes find himself on stage with no other clown around. When this happens, the puppet provides him with a ready partner. The puppet and the clown are of similar natures. They both dance to the tune of a different drummer. They are a perfect match because they *are* the same performer. When the clown manipulates the puppet, he is his own partner.

The combination of the clown and the puppet brings about a grand reunion. Punch the puppet evolved from Pulcinella the clown. Puppets existed before this, being a natural outgrowth of the doll, but until Punch hit the scene, the puppet was only a flat representation of the human being.

This was especially true of the shadow puppets used in China. Projected on to a screen, the two-dimensional images did little to relate to the audience: They were merely a means to highlight a story. Perhaps the two dimensionality of the Chinese puppet is the reason that puppetry has remained a static art form in that country throughout the centuries. Today, shadow puppets are seldom used except in the Far East, but the clown should not underestimate the value of this ancient art. In a pinch, the knowledge of how to shape a few hand shadows can permit the clown to improvise a puppet show anywhere against a wall.

The first mention of the puppet, as it is known today in Western society, was made by Horace in 300 B.C. He describes the movements of a man in terms of a wooden puppet pulled by wires. Such a puppet is a marionette and is the puppet of choice for many professional puppeteers. It is not, however, the puppet of choice for the clown. The marionette is best suited for puppet theater work, not for the walk around or full stage show. In full view of an audience, the marionette loses the lifelike quality it possesses in the puppet theater. All attention will be focused on the manipulation of the figure, and the marionette will have become a mere toy.

In addition, in a walk-around situation, the puppeteer will find that many children will want to hold or touch the puppet. The possibility of breaking a costly figure prohibits the use of a marionette, not to mention the ever constant danger of some child breaking or tangling the strings. Only one marionette circumvents these problems: the chicken/ostrich/turkey/peacock marionette, hereafter, for simplicity's sake, designated the Bird. The Bird looks like a toy and pretends to be nothing else; therefore, its manipulation is the show. Also, it is inexpensive and can be constructed easily at home. These qualities make the Bird a perfect walk around.

To construct the Bird, the clown needs two wooden rulers, a ball of string, construction paper, a magic marker, one Styrofoam ball 12 inches in diameter, a Styrofoam ball four inches in diameter, two nails, a needle, and 31 Ping-Pong balls. Cutting the odd Ping-Pong ball in half will create a flat surface to serve as the Bird's feet. Ten Ping-Pong balls are threaded on each of the two pieces of the string, with a half ball at one end to form the legs. The string should extend a few inches past the last ball so that it can easily be glued or taped to the large Styrofoam ball that is the body. The remaining 10 Ping-Pong balls are strung on a piece of string so that the string extends a few inches beyond the end balls. By gluing or taping each end of this string to the two Styrofoam balls, the neck of the Bird is formed. The head is the smaller ball. The construction paper is used to create the wings, feet, tail, beak, and, if necessary, comb. The eyes are painted in place by the magic marker. Paint can also be used to color the Bird.

The rulers nailed together to form a cross will serve as the Bird's controls. The body is supported by a string glued or taped to the center of the larger ball and the centers of the crossed rulers. Two strings run from the Bird's feet and, tied to the opposing ends of one ruler, will move the legs. To move the head and neck a string must be run from the small ball to one end of the other ruler. Finally, running a string from the Bird's tail to the remaining free end of the rulers will permit the Bird to bow, bend forward, and peck while maintaining mobility of the head and neck.

With a minimal amount of practice, this absurd creature will be ready to appear before an audience. Strangely enough, this homespun creation usually receives more attention than the carefully constructed marionette, proving once again that the audience is always on the side of the homely underdog, or, in this case, bird.

Despite the Bird, the puppet of choice for the clown is the hand puppet. The reasons for this are that the movement of the hand puppet is realistically smooth, it has a mouth that moves, the audience does not see the actual manipulation that creates the movement, and it is durable enough to be touched by the audience. One of the simplest hand puppets to construct is the sock puppet, which is made from, strangely enough, a sock. The basic sock puppet resembles a snake and can be used by the clown in a variety of ways. Using a basket with a small hole in its side, a snake charmer with his sidekick can tour the audience during a walk around conversing or arguing. By stuffing the sleeve of his coat and attaching it and a false hand to the side of the basket, the clown can slip his arm through the hole in the basket and into a snake puppet that can pop out to talk with the audience. The same idea can be adapted to a hollowed-out stack of books, in which case the snake becomes a bookworm, an excellent gimmick to use when performing for libraries. Ron Hull, an exceptional comedian, has even used this device to create a life-sized emu.

As a partner, however, the simple sock puppet will not do. It looks too much like a sock. What the clown needs is a realistic companion that can converse and react to him. The style of puppet used on "Sesame Street" would be about the best. These wide-mouth hand puppets have the same cartoonlike quality possessed by the clown, and audiences love them. The secret behind their appeal is that each one is indelibly stamped with his own personality. This is what made Punch popular. Their appearance is so important that unless the clown is very skilled at creating puppets, he should not attempt to make one. His audience expects a professional product and, since they are paying, should get one. Information on this type of puppet can be obtained by writing to Puppet Productions, Inc., P.O. Box 82008, San Diego, California 92138.

MOVEMENT

Perhaps the most glaring mishandling of puppets is in regard to movement. The personality and very life of the puppet are derived from its movement. The most common error is to hold the puppet still when it is not speaking. The human body, even at rest, is not stationary. Why, then, should a puppet, a thing that pretends to life, ever be motionless? It should not.

Several methods may be used to give life to a puppet. The easiest, and the one that can be of immediate use to the beginner, is to move the head of the puppet so that its nose shapes a figure eight in the air. This movement requires little thought to keep going, so the beginner can concentrate his attention on other areas while learning to control the puppet.

A more advanced technique for endowing the puppet with life is to give him something to think about. At the start, this may simply be a piece of music that is running through his mind. Later on, the puppet may be preoccupied by solving a problem. With something on his cloth-covered mind, everything that comes within the puppet's sphere of vision will be looked at or reacted to differently than if the figure were just an automaton waiting for his cue.

Eventually, the puppeteer should be able to make his charge react to his immediate surroundings. Staring at unusual objects or people, considering the scenery, grooving with the music, the puppet assumes an aura of reality. The puppet's audience relates to him, and even solemn adults will answer automatically a question posed by a puppet handled naturally.

If the puppet has hands, idiosyncrasies can be added to the movements required by the script. The puppet may gnaw on a thumb or scratch an itch. He may drum his fingers or hold his head. The only rule to remember is that the puppet, when silent, should exhibit the same type of human traits as when he speaks.

The puppet's speech is another area that gives new puppeteers problems. Only the lower jaw of the puppet should move when it talks; many beginners make their charges speak by raising the top portion of the head. This manner of handling the puppet will make it move like a doll being manipulated. The audience will readily believe in the puppet if, like an honest man, he looks them straight in the eye.

The only exception to this is when the puppet must use the letters **B, D, F, K, P, R,** and **T.** To pronounce words beginning with these letters, the puppet juts his head forward in a short emphatic movement and raises the top part of his head slightly. This same forward movement is used also with softer consonants such as **C, G, J, V,** and **Z.** Words ending with the letters f and r receive a variation on this movement. The motion of the head remains the same as above, but the puppeteer does not say the sound until the head of the puppet has begun its journey back to its original position.

All of the above information holds equally true for the ventriloquial figure. This figure, also called a dummy, is a variation on the hand puppet. It is hand-held, but it is operated from a keyboard on a pole connected to the head. The keyboard is out of sight behind or inside the dummy and can have as little as one or as many as 20 or more keys, depending on the number of facial movements desired by the performer. Since the clown usually works in close proximity to his audience, the figure he will want should be inexpensive and sturdy. However, it should not look cheap. Fortunately, two durable, low-cost figures of professional quality are available. One is a fuzzy-headed, freckled little tyke, and the other is a clown. Each has only one key to move the lower jaw, but each carries the attraction of having empty sleeves through which the performer can slip his own arm to give the figure a flesh-and-blood hand. These figures are sold by Show-Biz Services, 1735 East 26th St., Brooklyn, N.Y. The clown can receive, upon request, a catalogue of their complete line of vent figures but should keep in mind that an expensive figure is not always the best one. The clown must always consider the types of shows and the audiences with which he will be dealing.

VENTRILOQUISM

Giving voice to the puppet is a lot simpler than might be expected. By endowing the puppet with lifelike movement, half the job has been done. Although ventriloquism is the art of speaking without moving lips, its greatest practitioner, Edgar Bergen, openly violates the precept. His excellence lies in the believability of his vent figure, Charley McCarthy. Another performer, Weyland Flowers, openly moves his mouth, only bothering to change the quality of his voice. His creations, Madame and her coterie of companions, survive entirely on the absurd realism of their characters. Therefore, the clown should not be discouraged if his lips move slightly during his presentation. If he handles his puppet properly, the audience will still respond to the puppet as a separate entity.

In learning ventriloquism, the clown should begin with the figure or puppet he intends to use in performance. This is the beginning of a relationship. As the clown progresses, the figure will begin to acquire a personality of its own. The use of a cheap practice figure may set the clown back when he changes over to his performance puppet. This is because each figure or puppet has a different feel. The key on one figure may be harder to operate than the key on another, or the weight of the head heavier or lighter on different puppets. These factors can throw a performer off.

To speak without moving the lips, the jaw should be relaxed with the front teeth approximately a quarter inch apart. The lips are slightly separated. With the mouth in this position, the clown is ready to begin. And what better place to start than with the alphabet. Some letters are always more difficult to say with the lips stationary. Surprisingly enough, these vary from person to person. There are a few letters, however, that do give everyone problems: **M, B,** and **P.** The clown should not worry about them, just about keeping his jaw relaxed

For this reason a mirror should be used only occasionally to spot-check the progress being made. Constant practice before a mirror will have the clown straining to avoid all movement of the lips, promoting a style of presentation that resembles lockjaw. One young ventriloquist who had this problem noticeably set his jaw in what he thought was the "proper" position every time his dummy spoke. The effect of this was the same as the operatic soloist who, before each aria, faced the audience, clasped her hands beneath her bosom, positioned her chin back to open her throat, and straightened her back in an overly correct posture. Such an attitude is only displaying the instrument, in this case the voice. The last thing a ventriloquist wants to do is display his voice. When the dummy speaks, the performer must be unobtrusive. To do this, he must relax.

The problem letters can be handled in four different ways. One, they can be avoided. The dummy's part is written so that he never says words that contain **M, B,** or **P.** Two, substitutions may be made for each of these letters: **NG** for **M, V** for **B,** and **K** for **P.** When used in the context of a sentence, the audience will seldom notice. Third, every time one of the difficult letters must be pronounced, the performer de-emphasizes it or uses a glottal stop. (By quietly mispronouncing the letter and stressing the rest of the word, the audience will mentally "hear" the correct pronunciation. The glottal stop, accomplished by cutting off the sound with the back of the tongue, omits the offensive letter altogether. An example of this is the way a cockney would say hospital: 'ospi'al. The ventriloquist simply adds the 'T' and omits the 'P': hos'ital. The audience will supply the missing letter.) Four, the performer relies on the characterization of his figure and, taking a cue from Edgar Bergen, moves his lips. The preferred method of handling these letters is to use whichever way seems appropriate at the time. The clown will eventually find that he uses one method more than the others, but the chosen method varies from performer to performer.

Once comfortable with this manner of speaking, the clown is ready to tackle a routine.

MATERIAL

Writing a ventriloquial routine is made easier by the fact that the relationship between the figure and the ventriloquist is very well established. The only consistently successful relationship is the ventriloquist as the straight man and the figure as the wise guy. Others have been tried, but this seems to be the one that audiences prefer. For the rest, the same rules apply for writing the ventriloquial dialogue as apply to creating comedy and character. The important item to keep in mind is the audience. The vocabulary used for older children and adults will probably not do too much for the kindergarten youngster. If the clown comes up with a good routine, he may want to write two versions to cover both younger and older audiences. At all costs, he should avoid anything that is risqué.

For the clown who cannot come up with any material at all, two superb pamphlets of dialogue and instruction can be purchased through most magic outlets. These are *Ventriloquism and Television Ticklers* and *For Ventriloquists Only,* both by Paul Stadelman. If the clown needs further material, he should have the courtesy to subscribe to a comedy service and not steal from some hard-working, successful comedian.

15

Sculpturing
the Balloon

The only difficulty in making balloon sculptures is blowing up the balloon. The type of balloon used is made of a thin plastic with great elastic properties. It may be purchased under a variety of brand names and is known generically as the "260 A" or animal balloon.

To blow up the balloon, the clown should be aware of a number of facts. It will be easier to inflate if it is first stretched. Body heat, transmitted by the breath, will also facilitate this annoying necessity. By blowing enough air into the balloon to fill it without inflating it, the clown will be able to soften the plastic a bit to enhance its elastic properties. A steady stream of air should then be directed into the balloon until a bubble is formed near the open end. When the bubble appears, the job is almost done. A second steady stream of air should inflate the rest of the balloon. The clown may have to pause several times to catch his breath at first, but after a while, he will find that he will be able to inflate the devilish things in one blow. Finally, at no time should he have to puff out his cheeks when blowing into the balloon. Doing so will only reduce the force of the air flow.

These balloons always inflate naturally in the same direction: from the open end to the tip. If, however, the clown holds the balloon tightly with only the tip free, the bubble will be formed at the closed end. Once this is done, the balloon will inflate toward the open end. For a bit of fun, the clown can blow the bubble at the tip and offer the closed end to a child, asking the youngster to help blow up the balloon. When the child blows on the closed end, the clown blows into the open one. To the audience, the child will appear to be inflating the balloon by blowing into the wrong end.

One word of warning: The clown should not strain too hard to blow up the balloon. The air pressure required to inflate the things could build up in the sinus cavities and cause serious medical problems. For this reason, the clown should never give uninflated balloons to children in the audience without clear instructions on their use. If the clown becomes dizzy while blowing up balloons, he should stop to rest for a while. A bicycle pump will make this job simpler. By attaching the device used to inflate volleyballs, basketballs, or footballs to the pump's hose, the clown will be able to blow up all his balloons in no time.

Once inflated, the balloon must be tied at the open end. Directions for doing this are usually included in the package with the balloons. If the clown cannot find or understand these directions, he will find help never far away. He can either ask someone older than himself or go to the nearest street corner and ask a kid.

The sculptures themselves are made using two different types of twists: the ball twist and the "S" twist. The ball twist, as shown in Figure 21, consists of twisting the balloon so that a ball is formed. By twisting a series of these balls, the clown will be able to form the legs and ears of the various animals he will eventually sculpt. The first and last twists in each series of three are in turn twisted together, and the appendages of the animals appear.

The "S" twist is made by folding the end of the balloon into an S shape, as in Figure 22. The S formed is then twisted along a dotted line right down the middle. It is predominantly used to form ears, but if the "S" used is large enough, it can be used to form a sculpture that will stand on its own.

With these two twists and a bag of balloons, the clown is ready to begin the show. He should be prepared to handle a roomful of children, who will not let him out of their sight until they each have a balloon sculpture all their own.

APPLE

The balloon required to form this shape is not a 260 A but a special balloon named the "Apple Blossom." Each box of these balloons contains specific instructions on how to make the apple.

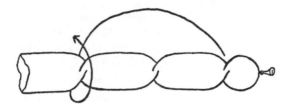

Figure 21

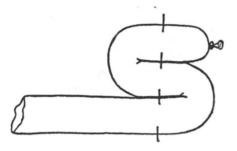

Figure 22

Figure 23

Briefly, the balloon is inflated halfway and knotted. The knotted end is pushed into the center of the balloon with the left index finger. The finger tips of the other hand push the base of the uninflated portion into the balloon to grasp the knotted end. The left finger is removed, and the balloon is rotated several times in one direction. The knotted end and the uninflated portion become twisted together. The right hand releases its grip, and an apple is formed.

The apple makes an unusual walk-around bit. The clown approaches the audience with a lunch pail. He is hungry and so sits down to open the lunch pail. It is empty save for the balloon. He is saddened by this state of affairs until he is struck by a bright idea. He inflates the balloon, makes an apple, and goes merrily on his way.

An interesting sidelight is that when the teeth are drawn over the surface of this balloon, it produces a squeak that sounds like a bite being taken from the real thing. Therefore, the clown can be munching as he walks away.

BALLOON CONTEST

Gathering three volunteers, the clown explains that a contest is going to be held to find out who can blow up a balloon the fastest. Each contestant, including the clown, receives a 260 A. The clown intends to join in the fun because he has been practicing and wants to see how fast he is. At the count of three, all the contestants begin the race. All, that is, except the clown, who calmly takes out a pump and inflates his balloon the easy way. Naturally, he wins, but since he did cheat a little bit, he forgoes the prize and awards a balloon animal to all the other contestants.

DOG/AARDVARK

The dog is made from a single 260 A, using only the ball twist. Beginning at the tied end, the clown makes three twists, one short and two long. The longer balls are of equal length and fold together to make a twist at the areas designated by circles in the illustration. This forms the rear legs and tail. The next part of the balloon will become the body, and its length will determine

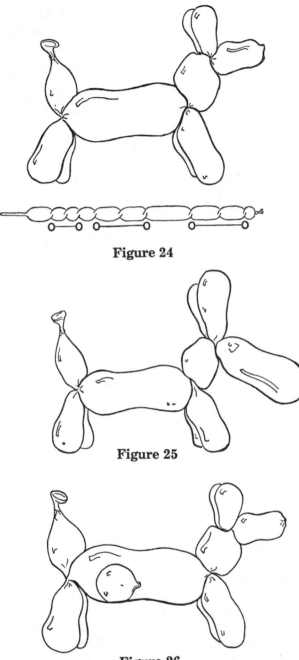

Figure 24

Figure 25

Figure 26

whether the sculpture is a regular dog or a dachshund. Three twists are made farther along. Again, the balls are twisted together at the areas designated in the illustration. These form the front legs. The last three twists form the ears and head. The dog is now ready to give away.

Sometimes the clown may miscalculate in his haste to finish a balloon dog: The body and legs of the animal may be too short. In such cases, the head of the sculpture will be misshapen, frequently having the appearance of a banana. The clown will be unable to correct his error. To save the situation, he need simply announce that he has found an aardvark. Surprisingly enough, many children prefer the aardvark to the dog, perhaps because they are familiar with the aardvark on "The Pink Panther Show." No matter. Any dog that ends up not looking like a dog is an aardvark, saving the clown time and balloons.

DOG AND MEATBALL

This sculpture is made just like the dog above. The difference lies in what happens to it before it is sculpted. The clown twists a ball the size of the tail at the knotted end. He then pushes it into the balloon, grasping a good portion of balloon around the place the ball has been pushed into. The end is then ripped or cut, allowing the ball to fall free inside, and the new end formed is tied. The dog is then constructed so that the free-floating ball is in the body of the animal.

DROODLES

Popularized by Roger Price, droodles are line drawings with important details left out. The 260 A can be used as a three-dimensional version of one of these. The clown blows a bubble in the center of a balloon. He then holds it up between his hands and asks, "What is it?" Chances are that no one in the room will ever guess that it is an earthworm that has swallowed a golf ball.

Figure 27

GIRAFFE

The construction of the giraffe is the same as that for the dog; the difference lies in the length of the balls formed before the animal is twisted together. The legs are longer, as is the neck. The body is shorter. And the ears are as small as possible. The head can be molded easily to the shape in the illustration by squeezing it. A larger giraffe can be made from three 260 As, using the design of the horse described below.

HORSE

The horse is a three-balloon animal, using one 260 A and two ordinary oblong balloons. The oblong balloons are twisted at the center around the areas marked "X" in Figure 28 to form the legs. The ears are made the same way as the dog's, using the ball twist.

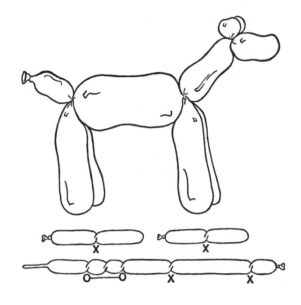

Figure 28

HUMMINGBIRD/BUMBLEBEE

The hummingbird is constructed from one 260 A and a rocket balloon. By tying the ends of the 260 A together and twisting the circle formed at the center of the balloon and the knot, a pair of wings are formed. If twisted onto the rocket near the pointed tip, a hummingbird is formed. Twisting it near the knotted end produces a bumblebee. An interesting note is that both of these constructions are aerodynamically sound and will float on air currents much as their namesakes fly.

LION

Constructed in the same manner as the dog, the difference here lies in the formation of the ears. The lion's ears are made with an "S" twist. The mane is a 260 A partially inflated, with its ends tied together beneath the lion's chin. The "S" twist ears hold the mane back around the lion's neck.

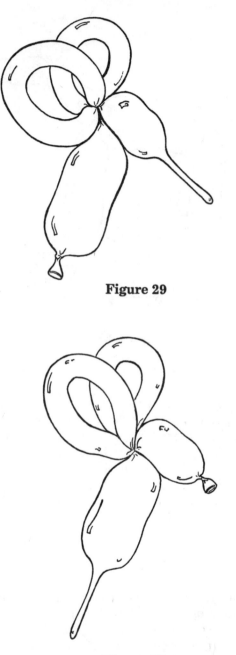

Figure 29

Figure 30

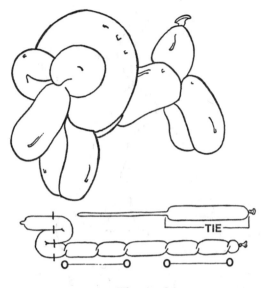

Figure 31

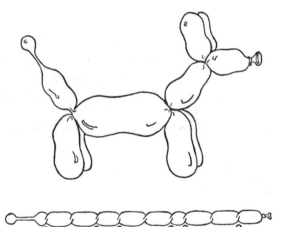

Figure 32

POODLE

The poodle is a backwards dog with a bubble in its tail. In this case, the knotted end becomes the head and the knot the nose.

Figure 33

RABBIT

The rabbit is put together as in the illustration. Beginning at the knotted end, a small head is formed, followed by two large ears, a very short neck, short forepaws, a longer body, very long hind legs, and a small ball tail. The forepaws of the finished product are stuck between the two hind legs, leaving the bunny in a sitting position.

REINDEER

This two-balloon concoction is always popular and simple to make. Begin to form the dog with a 260 A, but do not make the ears. On the ends of the second 260 A, form an "S" twist. Then twist this balloon to the first balloon at the points labeled "X" in the illustration. By putting a bubble in the tip of the first balloon, the clown can end up with Rudolf the Red (or green or blue or yellow or orange) Nose Reindeer. The clown will find the audience willing to persuade him that the only nose possible is red.

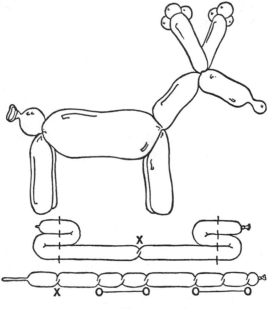

Figure 34

ROCKET

This is the type of balloon used for the body of the hummingbird or bumblebee. The clown should know that it has an interesting property all its own. If the index finger of the hand holding the balloon is inserted halfway into the balloon at the knotted end, the plastic pushed in with the finger will act as a spring. When the balloon is released, it will fire like a rocket. This principal can be great fun at children's parties since, if the fired balloon hits something, the balloon will break before the object it strikes.

SNAPPING THE BALLOON

When the clown is stretching the balloon prior to blowing it up, he loses one end, which snaps back to hit the other hand. This is just as easy (or just as hard) as falling over. The same principle applies to both. The clown must not look as if he is planning to fall down or to snap himself. If he does, his actions will carry no surprise, and he will lose his laughter.

SWALLOWING THE BALLOON

For a bit of whimsy that parodies the sword swallower, the clown only need place the tip of a blown-up untied balloon in his mouth. Just as the balloon inflates in one direction, it deflates in the opposite. When the air is let slowly out of a 260 A, the balloon deflates from the tip toward the open end. By pushing the balloon into the mouth as it deflates, the clown appears to be swallowing it; when he is finished, he licks his fingers and goes off in search of dessert.

SWAN

This sculpture offers a short routine to the clown as he constructs it. He twists two 260 As together at their centers so that they form a cross. Then the four ends of the two balloons are knotted together, as in Figure 35A. On its side, as in the illustration, the balloons twisted this way will resemble a football. Turned 90 degrees and placed over the face, they become a face mask. Worn on the head, they are a hat. By tying a third 260 A to the end of the shape, the clown makes a raccoon-skin cap. Finally, by thrusting the tail of the raccoon-skin cap through the center of the shape, a swan is born.

The swan can be given wings by twisting a fourth 260 A as in the hummingbird/bumblebee sculpture. This balloon is then inserted sideways through the body of the swan.

TEARING THE BALLOON

At one time or another, two children in the audience will begin vying for the next balloon. To quiet them and reach an equitable solution, the clown only need tear a balloon. He ties a knot in the center of an inflated 260 A. Then he rips the balloon in half. One half is knotted; the other is not. The troublesome children are given a choice of the balloons the clown holds. The child who chooses the tied balloon receives the next sculpture. The other child receives the pleasure of seeing his half balloon shoot to the ceiling. It beats drawing straws.

A   B

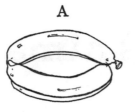

Figure 35

Figure 36

16

Trained Animals

For some reason, animals keep cropping up with clowns. Whether this is a hangover from the days of the fool, when the lighthearted dimwit was thought to possess the singular ability to communicate with the lower forms of life, or due to the advertising of the unknown publicity-minded performer who bills the animals in his act as "natural" clowns, the modern clown is stuck with the image.

Some audiences will actually assume that the clown will appear with a live animal when he is contracted to do a show. There is no way to avoid disappointing people with such expectations, but if they look hard enough, they will find a clown who presents a trained animal act of some sort.

The clown who uses animals is sometimes simply a lazy performer who has decided to employ an automatic crowd pleaser. An untrained animal running about the stage will often please an audience as much if not greater than a well-behaved, trained one. As soon as any animal steps into view, the audience will "ooh" and "ah," and some will even make clucking noises to attract the animal's attention. This makes an animal a difficult partner with which to work. The clown can expect to be upstaged by the beastie's very presence. For this reason, the novice clown should avoid working with animals. He will have enough trouble controlling his own performance without the headache of controlling the animal.

Once the clown is secure in his own character, he is ready to tackle, or be tackled by, an animal. Some performers prefer to train their own charges, but many are not capable of that. Rather than let the quality of his show fall, even for a moment, the clown will be better served by buying a professionally trained partner. By scouring the pages of *Amusement Business,* the national periodical of outdoor amusement businesses, he should be able to find any type of trained animal, from dove to elephant. The animal of choice for most clowns is the dog.

DOG

The temptation, when working with a canine, is to present a standard trained-dog act. Why any clown would want to don makeup and costume to present just another performing mongrel is anybody's guess. But year after year clowns hit the road with their tried-and-true packs of prodigious puppies. They put their charges through the same tired paces and then move quickly on to their next show. The audience applauds, true. Their canines perform all of the prescribed maneuvers on cue, true. Then what is wrong with this act?

It is not enough.

The trained dog must do more than go through its paces when he performs with a clown. The animal must appear to think for himself, to have a mind of his own. Otherwise, the clown is simply another animal handler.

The clown must have something to react to, something to struggle with. The trained dog can supply him with this. In fact, the animal *must* supply him with this. Most of the members of the clown's audience have seen Benji or remember the days of Lassie and Rin-Tin-Tin. They secretly harbor the hope that all dogs can act like these paragons of canine excellence. And they would be greatly disappointed to discover that dogs like these are the exception to the rule if they exist at all.

Therefore, the dog used by the clown should be very well trained, and the cues to which it responds should for the most part be silent, visual cues. As to the choice of breed, the clown should take *his* cue from what his audiences want, and his audiences want a mutt. The popularity of Benji is proof of this. If, however, the clown insists on a pure-bred animal, he should choose one as outrageous as the clown himself. Opinions may vary as to which pure breed this might be, but the clown will be hard pressed to come up with a more outrageous animal than the Pug.

DONKEY

Traditionally, the donkey or, better yet, burro, is used by the clown in one way that requires the animal to know only two cues: stop and go. The act would run as follows:

> ANNOUNCER: And now presenting (name of the clown) and Edgar Rice, the trained burro.
> *(The band strikes up a lively march and the Clown appears with the burro, who obviously does not want to go anywhere, anyway. Throughout the next few minutes, the Clown drags and pushes the animal onto the stage or into the ring. As he arrives at his destination and pauses to wipe the sweat from his forehead, the Announcer speaks.)*
> ANNOUNCER: I'm sorry, but you've run out of time. We have to move on to the next act, so you'll just have to go home. *(And for the first time the burro moves by itself. It walks out, leaving the Clown bewildered and the audience amused.)*

DUCK

Trained ducks have never played a large role as performers. Generally, they have been used in the walk around. The clown enters, followed by the duck, and together they walk around.

That's it.

Presumably, the audience is supposed to laugh because of the way the duck waddles when it walks.

GOAT

The goat is usually used in parades and opening spectacles. Hitched to a goat cart, an outmoded form of transportation, the goat pulls a clown, who waves and gesticulates at the audience while riding past.

PIG

This animal can be the funniest in the clown's repertoire. The little pig is usually trained to follow a bottle of milk. This it will do with a single-mindedness that is possessed by no other animal. With the milk bottle, the clown leads the piglet to a small sliding board where the pig climbs to the top and slides down the other side to reach its reward. The picture of the pig sliding down the board is priceless. A mercenary clown might even take a picture of the event to sell as an oddity to the audience or, better yet, to use as a giveaway to get more shows.

"TRAINED" HORSE

The major problem that the clown will have in working with any animal will be in getting his charge to perform comedically on cue. Felix Adler, one of America's all-time great circus clowns, was continually beset by this difficulty. In his act, he used a mule cued to resist every attempt to push or pull it. During one performance, the mule, tired of being shoved through the same old routine, sat down. Unfortunately, Mr. Adler was attempting to push the animal at the time, and the end result was that the mule sat in his lap. Now, mules are, almost without exception, very heavy, and Mr. Adler immediately desired to extricate himself. His futile attempts soon had his audience weak with laughter, and the mule, in a supercomic bit of brilliance, kept turning his head toward the prostrate clown and hee-hawing as if laughing at his poor master. When the performance was over, the circus owner offered Adler more money to keep the bit in the act, but Adler was never able to make the animal do the deed on cue again.

To circumvent this problem, the clown has one option open to him: He can use the "trained" horse. This animal always responds on cue because it isn't an animal at all. The horse, in this case, consists of two clowns with a blanket tossed over them. In back, the blanket sports a whiskbroom for a tail. In front is a papier-mâché horse's head that juts from the blanket at an absurd angle. Once the "horse" is put together, the clown is ready to unveil "Stanley the Wonder Stallion."

ANNOUNCER: And now, for your delectation, feats of equestrian skill performed with Stanley the Wonder Stallion and his trainer (name of the clown).

(The Clown enters followed by his moth-eaten blanket of a horse, and the "duo" proceed to the ring or center of the stage. The Clown, who plays the role of Stanley's backside, obviously cannot see a thing during this entrance. He weaves back and forth, making Stanley appear to be walking beside himself at times.)

ANNOUNCER: Hold it right there! What do you think you're trying to pull? What is that thing?

CLOWN: Stanley the Wonder Stallion. The best-trained horse in the world!

ANNOUNCER: He may be Stanley, but I doubt if he's a horse. Exactly what is that thing supposed to do?

CLOWN: Well, he can dance.

ANNOUNCER: He can dance?

CLOWN: That's right. Watch. *(To the band or tape deck)* Hit it!

(The music begins with a fast rumba beat, and the Clown begins to prance in front of Stanley like a real handler demonstrating his charge's terpsichorean capabilities. Stanley, however, seems to have a small problem; the two clowns beneath the blanket can not decide who is to lead. The music stops.)

ANNOUNCER: Do you call that dancing? *(Stanley nods.)* What else does he do?

CLOWN: I've taught him to sit.

ANNOUNCER: O.K. Let's see him do that.

(At a command, the intrepid stallion approaches a chair. The clown in the back sits down. Then the clown in the front sits on the lap of his better half. Once seated, both clowns simultaneously cross their legs, and the trainer styles the absurd-looking sitting pair.)

ANNOUNCER: So he can sit, too. Does he do anything else?

CLOWN: He knows how to add, subtract, multiply, and divide.

ANNOUNCER: He does? That I'd like to see. Well, stand him up and let's see how well he does. We'll start off with something simple. How much is two plus two?

(The Clown grabs Stanley by the reins to haul him to the center of the ring. When Stanley stands, only his front half gets up and moves away. As the blanket is pulled off Stanley's back half, a

clown is revealed sitting in the chair, furiously working at a calculator.)
ANNOUNCER: What's this? Oh, get out of here, you silly clowns!
(The clowns flee in embarrassment to a burst of music.)

17

Winsome
Wizardry:
The Magic Clown

What is a magic clown? Isn't he a clown who does magic tricks? He puffs himself up and makes grand gestures to convince his audience that he is about to present the most miraculous illusion seen by man. Then he fumbles everything. He drops the object that he was going to vanish, or if he does make the object disappear, everyone can see it bulging beneath his jacket. No matter what he tries to do, his tricks never work. That is a magic clown.

Not exactly.

Then, what is a magic clown?

A clown who uses magic.

How is that different from a clown who does magic tricks?

Using magic is a very different thing from doing a magic trick. When someone does a magic trick, they present a puzzle intended to bewilder an audience. The puzzle is usually a self-contained unit, a routine. Once the trick is done, the conjurer must move on to the next effect. For example, the trick most commonly used by so-called magic clowns is a throwaway that requires little skill. The clown takes out a handful of brightly colored paper, rips it to shreds, and transforms the pieces into a hat that sports a colorful flower. During the trick, the clown grimaces and gesticulates while spouting jokes and flirting with his audience. Once the hat has been produced, the clown must move on because the trick is done.

Any competent magician could present the same effect more effectively because the audience does not expect him to play a prank. A modern audience expects the clown to perform some prank, so when he does a magic trick, his audiences are seldom amazed. They expected the clown to trick them, and he did.

By using magic, the clown can avoid this pitfall of his profession. To use magic is to adapt a trick to a larger whole; the trick is no longer an end in itself. Incorporating the hat trick into "The Balloon Chase," switching the pieces of colored paper for the balloons, the clown would be *using* a magic effect.

The use of this trick in conjunction with this sketch provides the plot of the "Balloon Chase" with a socially acceptable resolution, which is absent from the original routine. Instead of entering the arena selling balloons, clown number one enters selling cards or whatever else the multicolored paper might be made to represent. Clown number two, the prankster, grabs the paper and leads a merry chase, aided by the other clowns in the troop. At the point where the balloons are usually broken, the paper can be torn in a struggle for possession of the colorful contraband. The basic cruelty of the routine, that is, the destruction of the balloons or papers, is countered by the transformation of the shreds into a useful object: a hat. The effect is no longer a trick but is instead a way to resolve a practical joke gone sour. Clown number one need not leave the performing area in tears. Utilized in this manner, magic can be made to illustrate a point or deepen the plot of a story or sketch. The clown is able to create any number of special effects that allow him to make the improbable possible and the incredible happen.

A clown should "do" magic only when he is satirizing the pretentiousness of his magical fellow performers, but when he does so, he really has no need to perform any magic trick at all. The sketches available to the clown who wants to parody a magician (see "Levitation I" and "Levitation II") are far superior to any fumbled magic effect. In short, comedy magic should be left to comedy magicians and not be allowed in the realm of the clown. However, a clown can always "use" magic to good effect. Through magic, the clown can make his universe come alive. Objects can appear and disappear, wrongs can be righted instantly, and inanimate objects can appear to have lives of their own. As a living cartoon character, the clown is a parody of the human being, and his humor is derived from the human condition. To poke fun successfully at his fellow man, the clown can never allow himself to be tied down the immutable laws of nature that govern the rest of us. Magic can release him from these natural laws and possibly increase the pungency of his wit. Magic can give the clown the freedom to soar.

Like comedy, magic is a bisociative art. The magician leads the audience through one field of thought and at the last moment hits them with an entirely different field. Only the audience never realizes that the second field exists. All they can see is the bright pieces of shredded paper held by the magician. They do not realize that behind the shreds is a very whole piece of paper shaped like a hat.

Hundreds of magical effects can be adapted for use by the clown. This chapter details only 27 such effects and suggests routines in which they may be used. The effects were chosen because of their simplicity of construction or their easy availability. The majority can be made from common materials such as newspaper, cotton washline, zip-lock bags, pipe cleaners, fishing line, thread, cloth, coat hangers, fruit, and rubber cement. Every other item can be obtained at just about any magic shop.

A few of the effects in this chapter do require some practice before they can be presented, but they receive such a positive reaction from the audience that they are well worth the time spent rehearsing them. These effects were not only included in this chapter because they are outstanding stage illusions. They are also fun to work with, and if not for the secrecy that has been placed on their workings by the magician's fraternity, some of them could easily become fad items that would rival the hula hoop popularity.

The routines suggested in this chapter are not meant to be the last word on how these magical deceptions might be used by the clown. No routine can be performed with the same success by everyone. However, these have been tested before many audiences by several performers and have proven effective. It is hoped these suggestions will serve as springboards for other performers and spark a few new ideas.

Magic and the clown were made for each other because both are the stuff of fantasy. A magician must believe in his illusions, but a clown must live them.

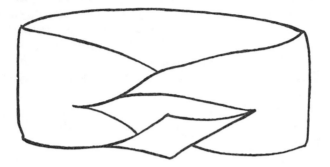

Figure 37

AFGHAN BANDS

Effect A wide loop of paper is cut in half to produce two loops of the same size. These loops in turn are halved. One becomes a large ring of paper twice the size of the original loop. The other becomes two rings inexplicably linked together.

Ingredients A strip of paper, tape, and scissors.

Construction Cut a strip from a sheet of newspaper that is approximately 30 inches long by 6 inches wide. The length of the paper strip will determine the circumference of the loop. If a smaller or larger loop is required, adjust the length of the paper strip accordingly—shorter for a smaller loop, longer for a larger loop. Fold the strip of paper in half so that both ends meet and cut a slit five inches long directly down the center of the paper at the ends. Unfold the paper and place it down so that its length runs from left to. right. Precut two lengths of tape each three inches long. Bring the two ends of the paper below the slit together, giving the end on the right a half turn. Tape the ends together. Next, join the ends above the slit, giving the end on the right one full turn and tape them together. Once the ends of the strip are joined, the effect is ready to be performed.

The trick is self-working. The performer has only to cut the bands along the center beginning at the slit. To avoid a possibly awkward moment during the presentation of the effect, the performer might want to cut starting slits down the center of the joined ends. The loop formed in this manner actually forms two

Moebius strips joined side by side. A Moebius strip can be made from a length of adding machine tape. Simply join the ends of the length together, giving one end a half or whole turn. The loop formed when cut in half will result in one large ring or two rings linked together, depending on the type of twist made in the loop. From this moment on, the only problem is how the effect should be presented.

Presentation   Henry Hay's routine is probably the best one in existence for a solo presentation of the Afghan Bands. He suggests a story about how the bands were used to save the day at a circus sideshow. In using such a story, the performer must make use of specifics. He should name the circus, tell the audience when he saw the show, and describe how he became involved in the action. All of this is part of the art of storytelling, something in which every clown should be well versed, and lends credence to the truthfulness of the story. Unless the audience believes in what the performer is telling them, their attention will wander. They realize that hiding behind the mask of clown makeup is John or Jane Doe; therefore, they must be convinced that the story they are listening to is at least possible. For example, assume that Clyde Beatty Cole Brothers Circus played in Baltimore, Maryland, two months ago on July 26. The shows were at two P.M. and eight P.M. It rained that morning. Now, come back to the present. The Afghan Bands are going to be a part of a show being given in Essex, Maryland, just outside of Baltimore. The story might be told like this:

> Back in July, I went to see the circus at the Civic Center and you wouldn't believe the problems they were having. Some of you might remember that it rained that morning. Well, when the costumes arrived, some clown managed to knock them into a large puddle in the street outside. *(Grin sheepishly and snicker.)* The manager of the circus was pretty mad. You see, he had extra costumes, but he was short a belt for the fat lady and a belt for the Siamese twins. (Clyde Beatty Cole Brothers Circus doesn't have a fat lady or Siamese twins, but most people actually believe that all circuses carry such human oddities.) The only extra belt he had belonged to the sword swallower—*(Hold up the Afghan Bands.)*—and he wasn't very neat. He kept sticking his swords through the back when he was finished with them. *(Turn the bands and show the audience the side where the ends were*

joined.) I took one look at that belt and told him that his problems were solved. He asked me what I meant, and I said, "You need two belts? Well, all you have to do is take a pair of scissors—*(Take a pair of scissors.)*—and cut this belt right down the middle—*(Cut the band down the middle.)*—and you end up with two belts." He said, "I thought about doing that, but if you cut the belt down the middle, you end up with two belts that are both the same size. *(Hold up the two halves of the band so that the audience can see them. Then toss the band with the full turn over one arm.)* That doesn't help me out at all." I said, "Wait a minute. I'm not finished. If you cut this half of the belt in half, half your problems will be solved." *(Begin cutting the band.)* He said, "I don't see how. I just saw you cut the belt in half, and you ended up with two equal halves. One won't fit the fat lady, and the other won't fit the Siamese twins." "Just watch," I said. And sure enough, when I was done, I had a belt that was fit for the fat lady. *(Hold up the large loop.)* He said, "You tricked me." I said, "You're right." "But what about the Siamese twins?" he said. "That's simple," I said. "Just take the other half of the belt—*(Take the other half of the bands.)*—and cut it in half—*(Cut it in half.)*—and the other half of your problems will be solved." He said, "Now, I can believe that you could trick me the first time with that belt, but this time I'm going to watch you closely, and I bet you a free ticket to the show that you can't solve my problems by cutting that half of the belt in half." "It's a bet," I said, and held up two belts linked together and fit for the Siamese twins. *(Hold up the two loops linked together.)*

The Great Merlini suggests another excellent way in which this principle may be used in a solo performance. He recommends a Moebius strip race, using members of the audience. He also notes an additional curiosity of this effect. A Moebius strip with a half turn when cut a third of the way through instead of divided down the center results in a large loop linked to a small loop. No matter how this trick is performed, it is a definite crowd pleaser. The Afghan Bands may also be used in a clown stretch as a test of coordination. It is the type of thing a clown doctor, policeman, or driving instructor might devise to determine the amount of control that another clown has over himself in a given situation. Play around with the idea and, above all, have fun!

THE COAT PENETRATION

Effect   Two ropes are run through the sleeves of a coat worn by the clown so that the ends are of equal length. One of the ropes is tied in front of the performer, and the ends of both ropes are held tightly by two members of the audience. The performer appears to be securely constrained by the ropes. At the count of three, the volunteers from the audience both pull the ropes, and the performer, in full view of the audience, steps free of the ropes that a moment before confined him.

Ingredients   Two ropes approximately 20 feet in length, thin cotton thread and a coat.

Construction   Find the center of both ropes and use cotton thread to tie the ropes together at this point. To ensure that the thread does not break before it is supposed to, use a double thickness. Now bring the ends of one rope together and stretch them away from the other rope. Place the ends of the other rope next to each other and stretch them away from the first rope. The ropes are now folded in half and linked by the thread at their centers. When the link is concealed by a hand, the ropes will appear to run side by side for their full length. Push the ends of the linked ropes through the sleeves of a coat or jacket, and the effect is ready for presentation.

Presentation   The clown enters with the ropes already threaded through his sleeves. The clown does not try to hide that he is up to something.

Today I am going to teach all of you how to do a clown stunt. The stunt I am going to teach you is called "The Strongest Clown in the World" and is very easy to do. All you need to do this trick on your friends are two ropes like these. *(The clown tosses the ends of the ropes to the ground.)* "You can use one rope, but I like to use two in case one breaks. Just run the ropes up one sleeve, across your back, and down your other sleeve. Then coil the ropes around your hands so that it appears as if you are holding separate sets of ropes and you are ready to begin.

Find two friends and tell them that you are the strongest man, or woman, in the world. To prove it, give each of them the ends of the ropes and tell them to try to pull the ropes out of your hands. You see, they don't know that the ropes run up one sleeve, across your back, and down the other sleeve. They actually end up having a tug of war with each other.

Now let me show you exactly how this works. I need two volunteers from the audience. How about you and you? *(The clown picks two members of the audience. When the volunteers are on the stage, the clown introduces them and continues.)* There is one thing I forgot to mention about this trick. If you use two ropes like I do, you have to be very careful not to get the ends tangled. *(He ties two of the ends together, one end from each sleeve.)* When that happens, and your friends pull on the ends of the ropes, the ropes will pull tight against you, and you could get hurt. So don't forget to keep the ropes separated. *(The clown forgets to untie the rope.)* Now, you take this end and you take this end. *(He hands the ends of the ropes to the volunteers.)* At the count of three, I want both of you to pull as hard as you can on the ropes in your hands and don't stop pulling for anything. Ready? One! Two! Three! PULL! *(The clown steps back free of the ropes and starts to root for one volunteer or the other. Urging them to pull harder, the clown may even help one of the volunteers if the volunteer is losing.)*

(The effect happens so fast that many times the clown should pause a second after being released from the ropes to allow the audience a chance to realize what has taken place. Usually, the volunteers do not realize what has happened until after the trick is over. The tug of war absorbs them completely.)

Suggestions on handling By holding both strands of the rope that run from the sleeves for a split second, the rope may be made to appear as if it drew tight around the body and then, in the manner of a cartoon penetration, popped through.

CUT THAT OUT

Effect A newspaper column is folded in half and its middle is removed with a pair of scissors. Instead of being divided by the cut, as one would suppose, when the column is unfolded, it appears to be completely restored. This is repeated several times.

Ingredients   One newspaper column, rubber cement, baby or talcum powder, a brush, and a pair of scissors.

Construction   Clip a column from a newspaper. For this effect, a column from the want ads is preferable since the jumble of small type found there runs together and conceals the fact that the column is never completely restored. Cover the middle section of the column with an even coat of rubber cement, making sure to spread the cement to the edges of the paper strip. Allow the cement to dry. Repeat this process two more times, permitting the rubber cement to dry completely before adding each coat. Sprinkle the powder over the coated section of the column. Always use white powder because it blends with the color of the paper. The powder will remove the shine of the rubber cement and make it invisible to the audience. Using a soft-bristle brush, remove the excess powder from the surface of the column. Turn the column over and repeat the treatment given to the other side. Once this is done, the effect is ready to be presented.

Presentation   At the conclusion of a show, two clowns are left on stage. They seem to be perplexed.

CLOWN ONE: Well, what do we do now?

CLOWN TWO: I don't know. You are in charge of this show.

CLOWN ONE: That's right, but I forgot what is supposed to happen next.

CLOWN TWO: Didn't you write down the order of the show?

CLOWN ONE: I didn't think I had to. The order of the show was printed in the local paper. I just cut it out and put it somewhere. *(Searches through his pockets)*

CLOWN TWO: What does it say?

CLOWN ONE: It doesn't say anything. It just kind of lies there.

CLOWN TWO: Be serious. They're waiting for us to do something. *(Points to the audience)*

CLOWN ONE: All right, it says that (name of Clown Two) is going to leap from a platform suspended thirty feet above the ground and land in a glass of water.

CLOWN TWO: What?

CLOWN ONE: That's what it says.

CLOWN TWO: Give me that. *(He reads the column.)* I can't do that!

CLOWN ONE: Then what are we going to do?

CLOWN TWO: Cut it out. *(He produces a pair of scissors and snips the stunt from the center of the column.)* Now let's see what's next. *(He opens the column that appears not to have been affected by the cut. It is whole.)* This is no good, either. *(He cuts it out.)* And this? No way. *(Repeat the cutting and restoration. Continue in this manner until the column is substantially shortened.)* Well, that does that.

CLOWN ONE: What does it say?

CLOWN TWO: Nothing. I cut out everything we were going to do.

CLOWN ONE: Then we might as well go home. *(Both clowns wave to the audience, bow, and leave.)*

The dialogue of this sketch during the actual performance of the effect was intentionally left vague since each clown must suit his dialogue to the character of the other clowns he performs with as well as to his own. No clown can successfully use the exact wording of another clown's routine.

Suggestions on handling Do not handle the clipped column too harshly, or it will come apart and ruin the effect. The rubber cement does not make a permanent bond between the two halves of the column. If the column should come apart in the middle of a performance, continue the routine as if nothing is amiss, and the audience will never know that something went wrong.

DANCING HANDKERCHIEF

Effect A handkerchief is dropped to the floor in front of the performer and proceeds to leap and dance about as if endowed with a will of its own.

Ingredients A piece of thread, a handkerchief, and a safety pin.

Construction Tie one end of the thread to the handkerchief and the other to the safety pin. Attach the safety pin to the shirt or jacket.

Presentation The arrangement described above should be familiar to the clown. It is the setup for the spring skunk used in "The Rocket" and other sketches.

What does the skunk have to do with the dancing handkerchief?

The dancing handkerchief provides an excellent example of how magic can be "used" to create a special effect. By using the basic move for the handkerchief after the skunk has been thrown away, the clown is able to add life to the fur-covered piece of metal. He

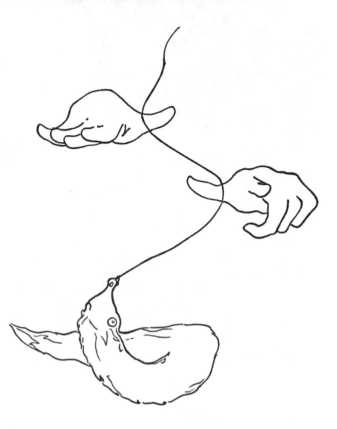

Figure 38

backs away from the skunk, waving his hands back and forth to ward the animal off. Every now and again, his thumbs snag the fish line, as shown in Figure 38, and the skunk appears to leap after him. In effect, the skunk has become a one-string marionette. The skunk will move whenever the clown uses his hands and make the chase a lively one.

THE HINDUSTANI ROPE

Effect   A four-foot length of rope is made to stand rigid. It can regain its flexibility on command.

Ingredients   A four-foot length of magicians' rope, a one-foot 10-inch length of solder wire, and thread.

Construction Magicians' rope may be obtained anywhere that magical supplies are sold. It is the essential item of this effect because it is flexible and can be hollowed out easily. Closely resembling cotton washline, it consists of a woven shell that surrounds a core of cotton fibers. These fibers can be easily pulled from the shell. For this effect, only the shell of the rope is needed. Remove the core from the rope and insert the length of solder wire. Make certain that the solder wire is slightly shorter than half the length of the rope. Tie both ends of the rope with thread to ensure that the solder wire remains inside the rope shell. This done, the rope is ready to stand on its own.

Presentation "The Courtship" sketch provides the clown with an excellent chance to use the Hindustani Rope as an incidental, symbolic special effect. The basic premise of the sketch is that a male clown becomes taken with a rather buxom female clown. The male clown tries to impress her with presents and personal charm. However, he is a rank novice at this game, and each of his attempts to attract her end in failure.

This sketch is a dumb show; no words are spoken. Therefore, great care must be taken in the choice of the background music. "Bicycle Built for Two" or an instrumental medley of similar songs may be used for this routine. As always, "The Fifty-Ninth Street Bridge Song" or "The Pink Panther Theme" will work nicely behind the action.

As the sketch begins, the male clown enters with a length of rope. He seems to believe that something is wrong with the rope because he is examining it carefully. Both ends of the rope are held a few inches apart at about shoulder height. First, the clown drops one end (the hollow end). Then he grasps the rope at the center (allowing the solder to slide gently to the other end of the shell). He releases the other end (just vacated by the solder wire) and lets it fall limply. After a very short moment of contemplation, he raises the end again (this time the end that contains the solder) and holds the rope at arm's length. His other hand grasps the rope lightly but firmly just off center of the shell. (The clown is now holding a section of the rope that conceals the piece of solder wire.)

While he is examining the rope, the female clown, bumping and grinding to beat the band, enters and walks past him. When he notices her, the male clown is so taken by the grotesque vision the female clown creates that he momentarily forgets himself. He lets go of the end of the rope he has been holding, and the rope remains rigid in the air.

The female clown looks him over. She does not seem particularly intrigued by what she sees, and with a toss of the head and a slow grind, she begins to walk away from him. As she does this, the rope slowly goes limp. (The clown gradually allows the solder to fall to the other end.)

Without recourse to conventional histrionics, the male clown has displayed his feelings about the female clown. The rope becomes the externalization of his innermost thoughts. Once its job is done, the rope may be disposed of by winding it around the hand, starting at the hollow end, and sticking it in a pocket. The solder wire is flexible enough so that it will coil with the rope when twisted around the hand.

Suggestions on handling Never allow the piece of solder wire to drop too quickly through the hollow shell of rope. If it does, the rope will jerk when the wire hits the tied end. A piece of coat hanger may be substituted for the solder wire, but if it is, the rope will not be able to be coiled at the end of the presentation. The performer will only be able to prove the rope limp by repeating the maneuvers made at the beginning of the effect.

PAPER TEAR

Effect A newspaper is ripped to shreds and instantly restored right before the eyes of an amazed audience.

Ingredients Two identical newspapers, rubber cement, and wire.

Construction Fold the top two sheets of both papers, as illustrated in Figure 39. The first and last two pages are folded back to meet at the center fold of the sheets. Then the sheets are folded in half lengthwise.

Next, fold one quarter of the long rectangle formed by each paper from the bottom to the center. Fold the top half of each paper down and one-quarter of the top half back up so that it resembles Figure 40, from the side.

Turn each of the packets formed so that the corners of the pages face upward, as in Figure 41. Bend back the first two pages to form a triangle. These pages are labeled one (1) in the drawings and correspond to the last two pages of the paper. Beneath them is the center fold of the paper, labeled two (2). Bend the center fold back so that its corner touches the base of the triangle formed by one

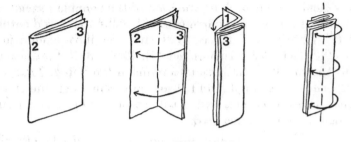

Figure 39

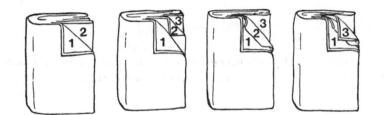

Figure 40

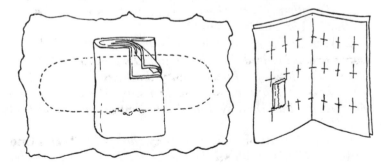

Figure 41

Figure 42

(1). Now bend two (2) back at the base of the triangle formed by one (1) so that the two free pages extend beyond the folded corner of two (2). Finally, bend three (3) so that the pages extend just slightly over the folded corner of two (2). Three (3) in the drawing refers to the corner of the first two pages of the paper. Thus, by gripping one (1) in one hand and three (3) in the other, the clown need only drop the packet, and it will unfold by itself in a flash. This is how the paper is restored.

The clip that holds the untorn packet in place and retains the torn pieces of paper is constructed by gluing the wire between two pieces of paper. The pieces of paper that surround the wire should be slightly wider than the packet and long enough to wrap around the folded paper. Tear the edges of these pieces so that they will later blend in with the torn paper. The wire should be about 18 inches long and, with its ends twisted together, shaped to resemble the dotted line in Figure 42.

Glue one packet to the center of the clip, as in the illustration, and fold the paper-encased wire around it. Turn the clip over and glue the other packet to the back. When the glue has dried, grip the folded corners of the exposed packet and let it drop. Close the paper, and the trick is ready to perform.

Performance The paper tear is ideally suited for "The Whip Cracker" sketch. Newspapers are already used, so the introduction of the gimmicked paper will go unnoticed. After the Whip Cracker has done away with several sheets of newsprint, he will be ready for the ultimate challenge:

> WHIP CRACKER: I will now split not one but two sheets of newsprint. *(As he says this, the Dummy picks up the gim-micked paper and opens it in front of him as he has done with all the other paper sheets.)* And to make this feat more difficult, I will do it blindfolded.
>
> *(The Whip Cracker pulls a pair of panty hose over his head. He gropes around to find the whip, which he placed on the ground while "blindfolding" himself. Standing, he peeks under the panty hose to make certain he is facing the right direction. Meanwhile, the Dummy has been getting more and more nervous.)*
>
> WHIP CRACKER: Ready? *(The Dummy shakes his head.)* One . . . two . . . (Unable to stand the strain, the Dummy rips the paper*

*in half. On hearing the tearing sound, the Whip Cracker stops
and peeks from under his blindfold to make sure everything is
kosher. He then begins once more.)* One ... two ... *(The
Dummy tears the paper again. The Whip Cracker pulls off the
panty hose and glares at the Dummy. Smiling, the Dummy
rips the paper again and again until he holds a bunch of torn
rectangular fragments. As the Whip Cracker speaks, the
Dummy bends the clip open and back to hold the torn paper.)*
Well, I hope you're pleased with yourself. *(The Dummy nods.)*
You've ruined my exhibition. You tore up the last of the
paper. Are you satisfied? *(The Dummy nods vigorously,
smiling broadly.)* Well, since you tore up the paper, *you* can
put it back together. *(The Dummy looks shocked.)* That's
right, you can put it back together right now! *(Shrugging, the
Dummy drops the packet, and the paper is restored.)*

The remainder of the sketch can be played out as usual. The
audience is so taken aback by the sudden restoration of the paper
that usually the clowns must stop the action for a few beats to let
the audience realize what has taken place. If done well, the paper
tear may even bring the audience to its feet. Certainly it will get as
much applause as it will laughter.

Note: For the ambitious clown, a superior paper tear is available.
"The Gene Anderson Paper Tear" will permit him to prove that
the paper is ungimmicked before he rips it to shreds.

THE PENNY TRICK

Originally called "The Seven Penny Trick," this effect of Terry
Lynn's has been published in Arthur Buckley's *Principles and
Deceptions* and in J. B. Bobo's *Modern Coin Magic,* but most
magicians seem to be unaware of its existence. Perhaps the reason
that this effect failed to interest the magic community is that as
described in these two volumes, the trick ended too soon. The
variation of this effect that follows carries the trick to its logical
conclusion. Please note that here the effect is not presented as a
trick but as a complication in the hectic world of the clown.

Effect Seven pennies are counted one at a time into the hand of a volunteer for safekeeping. One at a time, the pennies seem to penetrate the volunteer's hand and fall to the floor.

Ingredients Seven pennies, three hands (use two people if necessary), and a lot of guts.

Presentation A clown enters holding seven pennies. "I'd like to show you a trick, but to do it I have to have my pockets empty. So, would one of you help me out by holding my change. How about you? (The clown points to a member of the audience.) "Can I trust you with my money? It's only seven cents, but it's all I have with me. All you have to do is hold these pennies while I do the trick. Can you do that for me?" He waits for the audience member to respond before continuing. "Hold out your hand like this." He demonstrates by stretching out his hand, palm upward. "Now let me make sure I have as many pennies as I think I have."

Counting from one to seven, the clown places the pennies in the spectator's hand. The manner in which the coins are given to the spectator is very important to the success of the effect. Each coin is taken from the clown's left hand by his right and given to the spectator with the sole exception of the last coin. When the clown reaches the last coin, he tilts his left hand and allows the final coin to fall into the spectator's open palm. THE CLOWN'S RIGHT HAND NEVER TOUCHES THE LAST COIN. This maneuver is the setup for the deception and must be carried out consistently throughout the performance of the effect.

When the spectator is holding all the coins, the clown pauses and says, "Oh, I forgot to tell you something. Count the pennies into my hand, and I'll show you exactly how I want you to hold them." The volunteer begins to count the coins into the clown's hand. "You see, I don't want you to lose any of the pennies, so when the last penny is put in your hand, close your hand as quickly as you can." As the last coin enters the clown's hand, he makes a tight fist. "All right. Let's try it again." Again, the clown counts the coins into the spectator's hand. However, this time, he adds a sneaky move that the spectator knows nothing about. When he reaches the sixth coin, the clown clicks the coin against the others in the spectator's palm but does not release it. It remains hidden between the first two fingers and the thumb of the clown's right hand, which immediately goes under the spectator's hand. At the same time, the clown's left hand tilts and drops the last coin into the spectator's waiting palm (Fig. 43). When the

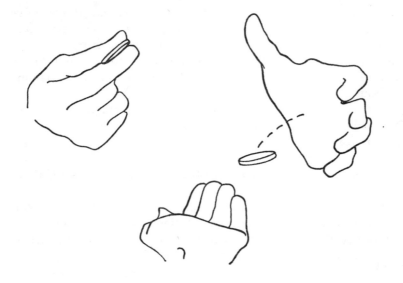

Figure 43

spectator makes a fist, the clown acknowledges the speed with which the fist was made and then drops the sixth coin, which clanks loudly on the floor.

The clown looks at the penny on the floor and says, "I think you lost one. Count the pennies back into my hand." Of course, the spectator only has six pennies, and the clown says, "Let's try again." The clown counts the coins into the spectator's hand, this time withholding the fifth coin. The procedure is repeated. At the next count, the clown withholds the fourth coin and so forth until the spectator is down to two coins. In frustration, the clown gives the spectator his two cents and adds, "If I were you, I'd get that hand fixed."

PRESLICED BANANA

Effect A banana is cut several times with an invisible knife. Apparently, the knife is dull because the banana at no time shows any signs of having been cut. But when the banana is peeled, it is discovered that the banana is segmented. It has been cut invisibly.

Ingredients One banana and one long sewing needle.

Construction Push the needle into the banana at the ridge formed by two sections of the peel. Wiggle the needle back and forth in a straight line. Repeat as many times as desired. The needle will neatly slice the banana and leave only a small dot on the peel. From a distance, no one will ever know that the banana has been gimmicked.

Presentation Since this effect requires no manipulation, the only problem left to the performer is how to use it. The presliced banana can be used in a variety of sketches. "The Whip Cracker" sketch is the one that comes most readily to mind. The banana is an excellent item to give the whip cracker's assistant to hold in his mouth.

A variation of the "Whip Cracker" sketch may also be performed using the presliced banana. A clown can give a demonstration of his ability at knife throwing. The knives he uses are so sharp that they cannot be seen with the naked eye.

The presliced banana is an excellent effect with which to experiment. It is good for walk arounds, sketches, and incidental bits. Try working it into some of the standard clown routines described earlier in the book. The banana might be just the thing to give an old routine appeal.

PROFESSOR CHEERS

Effect After performing a rope gag, the clown discovers a piece of rope dangling from his sleeve. He begins pulling it until the other end sticks on his left foot. He pulls this end and finds a third end of the rope snagged at his right ankle. When this end is pulled, the rope finally comes free, with the clown's shorts dangling at the end.

Ingredients A needle, a spool of thread, a small bag, a pair of shorts, and fifty feet of rope.

Construction Measure off a length of the rope against the right leg. Cut this length a few inches longer than the leg. Knot one end and sew the other end into a loop. Likewise, cut an additional few inches of the rope and attach it to the shorts so that a loop is formed.

Thread one end of the long rope through the loop on the short rope and then through the loop on the shorts. Pull the rope through the loops so that it matches the length of the shorter rope.

Figure 44

Knot both ends, making sure that the knots are large enough so they will not pass through the loops.

Sew the bag inside the jacket in the center of the back. Carefully coil the rope in the bag so that it will not tangle when pulled out. The end of the rope at the bag runs down the right sleeve. The other end runs to the left ankle. Down the right leg runs the short rope. By tucking the shorts into a belt worn beneath the costume, they will be kept in place until the clown wishes them to pop out. The final assembly appears as in Figure 44.

Performance This effect is the perfect way to end the coat penetration described earlier in the chapter. The clown has just tricked his audience at the end of that effect. What better time to hit them with another trick than when they are down.

The Clown thanks the volunteers and sends them back to their seats. As he bunches the rope he has just used into a ball, he snags the end of the rope that is running down his sleeve. The existence of this rope is hidden from the audience by the bunched-up rope he still holds in his hands.

CLOWN: See? Isn't that a great practical joke? And the nice thing about it is that you don't need any other ropes or gimmicks to play the joke on somebody. All you need are two ropes like these. *(He tosses the ropes aside and prepares to go on to something else. Suddenly, he notices the extra rope hanging down from his sleeve.)* Oh, look. Hey! I don't know what this is doing here. Like I said, you don't need any other ropes to do what I just did. Let me get rid of this.

(He begins to pull the rope out his sleeve and lets it coil around his ankles. When it reaches its full length, he will feel the end at his left ankle move. This movement is his signal to stop pulling for real and to simply mime the action. His left leg swings up to the side every time he apparently pulls the rope. Stooping, he raises his pants leg. There, caught on his ankle, is the other end of the rope. Pulling on this end, he drags the 50-foot-long rope back up his sleeve and down his left pants leg. When it reaches its end, his right leg rises. The Clown examines the right leg and finds a third end. He pulls on this, making sure that the loop and knot that connect the ropes remain concealed from the audience. Again the rope sticks. With a gargantuan effort, the Clown pulls the rope, and the shorts pop out. The Clown holds them up for all to see. Then he realizes what he has on his hands. He stuffs the shorts behind his back and sidles off the stage in embarrassment.)

The only difficulty the clown will ever have with this trick is when the ropes become tangled. If this should happen, the clown should play out the routine. Even shortened, the shorts will get a laugh.

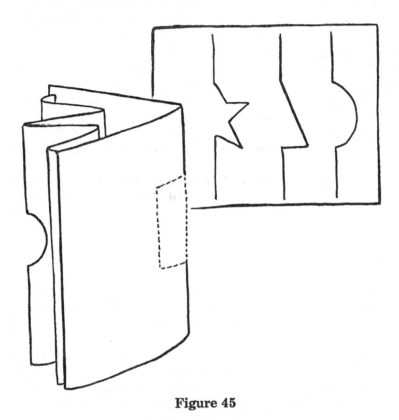

Figure 45

SOMETHING AMISS

Effect   A clown tries to cut a square in a piece of newspaper, but no matter how carefully he measures, traces, or cuts, the square always turns out to be something else: a circle, a triangle, or a star.

Ingredients   Two identical sheets of newspaper, a pair of scissors, and rubber cement.

Construction   Fold one sheet of paper, as depicted in the illustration, and cement it to the other sheet. Cut a circle in the center of the folded sheet and the trick is ready. A triangle or a star can be produced by preparing other papers in the same way.

Presentation   Announcing a contest, the clown gets two volunteers from the audience. He is going to find out who can cut the straightest. Each volunteer is given a sheet of paper and told to cut a square out of the center. The clown finishes first and asks each volunteer to hold up his handiwork separately. Finally, it is the clown's turn to display his prowess. He opens the paper with the inside facing the audience. The paper that has a square cut on the outside now shows a circle. "Mistrial," the clown announces. They try again. This time the clown ends up with a triangle. Well, at least the sides are straight. They go at it once more, and the clown ends up seeing stars. He awards each volunteer a balloon (if they are youngsters) or thanks them and hurriedly moves on to the next bit of business.

One final bit of advice: The clown must open his paper quickly. Otherwise, the audience will be treated to a good view of the gimmick.

THUMB TIE

Effect The performer's thumbs are securely tied together so that he cannot possibly separate his hands. He is prepared to resign himself to the immobility imposed on him, but he cannot. He becomes entangled with any object or person he encounters on the stage. Chairs, lampshades, and other performers inexplicably seem to pass between his bound hands to become linked on his arms. Finally, weighed down by everything that has become linked to his arms, he leaves the performing area in pandemonium.

Ingredients Two pipe cleaners and two thumbs.

Construction The preparation for this effect takes place in full view of the audience. The moves necessary to construct the thumb tie are not difficult to learn but should be practiced several times before the trick is presented. A mirror is essential to check the angles of presentation. In most cases, the audience will be too far away from the performer to see exactly what he is doing, but the extra care in preparation will ensure that the audience will never catch on to the secret of the effect.

First, the performer places the two pipe cleaners together to form a cross. For the purposes of this explanation, the pipe cleaner that forms the trunk of the cross will be referred to as A and the pipe cleaner that forms the bar of the cross will be referred to as B (Fig. 46).

To form the cross, the performer holds A in a vertical position.

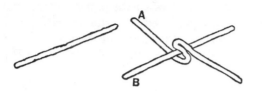 

Figure 46

He then places B horizontally on top of A, between himself and the vertical pipe cleaner. The pipe cleaners should intersect at their centers so that the cross resembles a plus sign.

This accomplished, the performer takes the top end of A and bends it toward his body and down, folding it over B. He then pinches A at the bend between his left thumb and left forefinger. This will increase the sharpness of the bend and ensure that B stays firmly in place at the bend.

Now the performer is at the crucial point in the construction of the thumb tie. He releases the top end of A, which he has just bent, and takes the bottom end of the same pipe cleaner. He bends the bottom end of A upward and away from his body. The pipe cleaners are again pinched together at the bend and are once more in the shape of a cross.

If these actions are performed smoothly, the audience will believe that the performer has twisted A completely around B, linking them together at their centers. In actuality, he has linked them, but only temporarily. A is merely hooked to B, and the two can easily be separated anytime the performer desires.

At this point, the pipe cleaners must be placed on the performer's thumbs. If this is done incorrectly, the pipe cleaners will actually link, and the performer's hands will really be bound together. To avoid this, the performer should always remember which side of the cross was facing him when the pipe cleaners were linked together. His right thumb is placed over the intersection of the pipe cleaners on that side. A is then twisted securely around the right thumb. The left thumb is placed under the right, and B is securely twisted around it.

The performer should now be able to unhook his thumbs or hook them back together at will. When rehooked, the pipe cleaners will appear to be as solidly twisted together as they were when they were first placed on the performer's thumbs. With a small amount of practice, the performer will be able to hook and unhook his thumbs so that his audiences will never know that his hands are not linked together at all.

Presentation This effect is perfect for a transition routine that takes place between two major sketches. A clown enters and begins to address the audience. While he is talking, a second clown with a great amount of noise comes in with a chair.

CLOWN ONE: Ladies and gentlemen. I would now like to inject a serious note into our program. *(Hears Clown Two and tries to ignore him)* You have laughed with us for a good portion of this evening, and for that I thank you. However, clowns are not always buffoons. *(Loud noise from Clown Two)* What are you trying to do?

CLOWN TWO: I'm not in this part of the show, and I just thought that it would be a good time to watch. I've always wanted to see the show.

CLOWN ONE: You want to watch the show? *(To the audience)* Excuse me for a moment. *(To Clown Two)* You can't watch the show. You're in the show.

CLOWN TWO: Not in this part.

CLOWN ONE: But it isn't done! If you're in a show, you never watch it. Why do you want to watch this part of the show, anyway?

CLOWN TWO: Well, you see—*(He coughs nervously.)*—I've always admired the way you handle an audience, and I thought I could learn a few things from watching you act in this part of the show. But if you want me to go ... *(He begins to collect himself to leave.)*

CLOWN ONE: Wait a minute. You *admire* the way I do things?

CLOWN TWO: Yes, I've always looked up to you.

CLOWN ONE *(Obviously swelling with pride):* You've always

looked up to me. Well, I tell you what. If you promise not to bother me while I'm out here, you can stay. Just sit there quietly and observe the old master.

CLOWN TWO: Oh, I can do that. I'll be as quiet as a mouse.

CLOWN ONE: Good. Now . . .

CLOWN TWO: You won't hear a word out of me.

CLOWN ONE: Fine. As I was saying . . .

CLOWN TWO: I'll just sit here quietly.

CLOWN ONE: Excellent. Tonight . . .

CLOWN TWO: I won't say a word.

CLOWN ONE: Will you shut up? *(Clown Two is silent. He begins to twiddle his thumbs. Clown One is about to begin his speech again when he notices Clown Two's thumbs.)* What are you doing now?

CLOWN TWO: Nothing. Just sitting.

CLOWN ONE: Your thumbs.

CLOWN TWO: Yes, I've had them for a long time.

CLOWN ONE: Will you stop that?

CLOWN TWO: Stop what?

CLOWN ONE: Do you want to stay out here?

CLOWN TWO: Yes, I told you I wanted to see you perform.

CLOWN ONE: Then stop—twiddling—your thumbs!

CLOWN TWO: Oh, I'm sorry.

CLOWN ONE: Look, since you want to stay out here, I'm going to help you out.

CLOWN TWO: Right.

CLOWN ONE: I'm going to help you sit quietly.

CLOWN TWO: How?

CLOWN ONE: With these. *(Takes the pipe cleaners out of his pocket)* I'll just twist these together—*(Twists the pipe cleaners together so that the link is formed)*—and put them on your thumbs. *(Binds the other clown's thumbs)* There. Now you should be no problem at all. Can you see all right from where you are sitting?

CLOWN TWO: To tell you the truth, I am having a slight problem seeing the whole stage from here.

CLOWN ONE: Then, why don't you move over there. *(Points to a corner of the stage. Clown Two picks up the chair and moves it to the corner. Throughout the rest of the speech, he becomes entangled with it.)* Now, as I was saying, the clown is not simply a buffoon but a very serious, dignified character who has for centuries mocked the petty vanities of man. *(Clown Two separates his hands and slips one of them through the back of the chair. He is now linked to the chair and cannot possible sit in it. He climbs over the chair and under it, trying to extricate himself from his plight.)* A clown does not always indulge himself in simple-witted exercises. Every now and then, he attempts to make a serious statement. *(Begins to notice Clown Two)* That is why I feel that part of this program should be reserved for a ... *(Watches Clown Two for a moment)* What are you doing?

CLOWN TWO: I'm stuck.

CLOWN ONE: Let me help you.

(Clown One acts as a cover for Clown Two to link and unlink his hands. First he removes one arm from his coat. Then he links himself through Clown One's suspenders or belt. The two begin to hobble across the stage picking up other objects as they go. The dialogue at this point should be ad-libbed. Other clowns may be brought on stage to be linked to the other two. Finally, the clowns struggle off the stage, dragging a number of objects with them, and a new routine is begun.)

THE UTILITY BAG

Effect An object, such as a handkerchief, is placed in a paper bag for safekeeping. The bag is ripped in half, and the object is gone. There is nothing in the bag but confetti.

Ingredients Two brown paper bags of the "lunch bag" variety, scissors, rubber cement, a multicolored scarf, and one cup of confetti.

Construction Cut one of the paper bags completely in half, the long way. Remove the bottom of the bag and angle the lower portion of the sides by cutting along the crease. Apply a thin strip of rubber cement along the three edges just cut. DO NOT PUT ANY RUBBER CEMENT ON THE TOP EDGE OF THE BAG. Slide the cemented section into the second bag (Fig. 47), being careful to align the edges of the bags. The edges need not match exactly. Press the glue-covered edges of the segmented bag to the bottom and sides of the second paper bag. Allow the glue to dry. The bag should look like any other paper bag, the only difference being that this paper bag has a secret pocket that can be used to

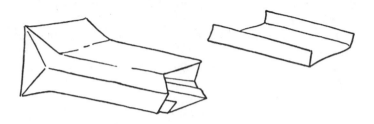

Figure 47

conceal a variety of objects. Just put the confetti in the bag and begin.

Presentation Two clowns. The utility bag is readily adaptable to the "Whip Cracker" sketch since its common appearance precludes any deception on the part of the performers. Its effect can be rendered even more baffling by recruiting the assistance of a member of the audience.

After his opening demonstration, the Whip Cracker steps to the front of the stage.

WHIP CRACKER: Ladies and gentlemen, you have just witnessed a display of the consummate skill with which I wield this whip. I see that you are duly impressed. *(The audience is not.)* For my next demonstration of this ancient art, I shall attempt to rend this handkerchief placed in this common paper sack. *(Displays the colorful scarf and places it in the secret pocket of the utility bag.)*

CLOWN ASSISTANT: You're going to what?

WHIP CRACKER: I'm going to rip the hanky inside the paper bag.

CLOWN ASSISTANT: Oh, I see.

WHIP CRACKER: Here. Hold this. *(Hands Clown Assistant the utility bag)*

CLOWN ASSISTANT *(Looks at the bag for a moment, then realizes that the Whip Cracker intends to crack the whip while he is holding the bag)*: Oh, no! Here is where I draw the line.

WHIP CRACKER: What's the matter?

CLOWN ASSISTANT: What's the matter? You don't know what you're doing. That's what's the matter. I'm not going to stand up here and let you take potshots at me with that thing.

WHIP CRACKER: It's perfectly safe.

CLOWN ASSISTANT: Then let one of them do it. *(He points at the audience.)*

WHIP CRACKER: All right. Could I have a volunteer from the audience?

(He chooses a member of the audience and has him stand, holding the bag, on the stool just vacated by the Clown Assistant. Carefully, he measures the distance from the stool. Then, with lightning speed, he turns and snaps the whip. With any luck, the audience member will flinch. Apparently, he missed his mark. Nothing has happened. He strides confidently to the stool, takes the paper bag, and rips it in half. The confetti flies from the sack in a rainbow shower. The trick is done.)

Suggestions on handling   To place the scarf in the paper bag, first drop it casually over the mouth of the sack. Then, with a straightened hand, push the scarf gently into the secret pocket. A little practice in front of a mirror should make this move look natural. Practicing magic effects before a mirror is a good way to check for stilted movements. At no time should the clown appear to be manipulating the objects he uses in performance.

THE WANDERING SHOE

Effect   The performer freely shows both sides of a cloth. The cloth is spread out on the floor, but instead of spreading smoothly, a lump appears in its center. The performer whisks away the cloth to reveal a shoe. It is obviously not the object he intended to produce. He looks at his feet and discovers that the shoe is one that he had been wearing a moment before.

Ingredients   A large cloth or handkerchief and a pair of shoes.

Presentation   To perform this effect, the clown must at some point during the show secretly untie one of his shoes. This can be done while picking something off the floor or while standing behind one of the properties used in the show. It can even be done before the show if the clown's shoes fit well enough to remain on his feet untied.

This accomplished, the clown is ready to display the cloth or handkerchief. He takes the cloth by the corners and turns it slowly showing both sides. He may even twist it and wring it through his hands.

The clown must then place the cloth on the floor in the following manner. As he bends to spread the cloth, he places the toe of his left shoe against the heel of his right. When the edge of the cloth comes into contact with the floor, he steps back, slipping his foot out of the right shoe. Done properly, this will look as if the clown is simply spreading the cloth smoothly on the floor. The maneuver resembles the way a beach blanket is spread to avoid wrinkles on its surface. The toe of the left shoe placed against the heel of the right will allow the foot to slide easily from the shoe and then conceal itself behind the left heel.

The clown looks at the cloth spread before him and points out that apparently something has appeared beneath it. He removes the cloth to reveal his shoe. Strangely enough, the audience never seems to notice that the clown has a bare foot until the clown points it out by looking at his own foot. The clown shows surprise and hurriedly replaces his wandering shoe.

This effect is a direct parody of the magician's art. It is the perfect trick to be presented at a show in which a magician appears on the same bill.

COMEDY AND STORE-BOUGHT MAGIC

Magic equipment bought from magic shops always manages to look like magic equipment. The clown using it will look like a clown doing a magic trick. To avoid this, the clown should alter the appearance of the production box so that it resembles a common household object. By doing so, he can ensure that his audiences will not suspect that they are being tricked until the trick is accomplished, thus achieving the maximum surprise. Unfortunately, clowns are performers and therefore lazy. Few clowns take the time to disguise their apparatus. Their audiences inevitably expect some sort of deception because the clown is holding a garishly painted contraption that could not possibly be anything but a piece of magic equipment.

Fortunately, a number of magical effects now on the market require little or no alteration to be used before an audience. Of the 16 effects listed below, only one requires drastic changes before it may be used before an audience. Five require some practice prior to performance, and the rest can be used almost as soon as they are removed from their boxes.

A word of caution should be included at this point. Every magic trick requires some amount of practice before presentation. As with slapstick comedy, all of the clown's movements must be precise and forceful, or his comedy will become muddled, and his audiences will fail to grasp the humor in his sketches. The clown should never cease to rehearse the routines and bits of business that make his audiences laugh. The comic mind is never at rest. The clown must always look for and rehearse those moments from the tapestry of human behavior that lend his comedy the immediacy that will capture and hold the imagination of his audience. Hopefully, the list of effects that follows will help the clown revitalize the old routines.

Foo Can   Three versions of this effect are currently in existence. The most common version consists of a brass or copper can with a partition inside. With it, a performer can show a can empty when, in fact, it contains a small amount of water. The brass or copper can has one drawback: It does not look like an ordinary can. Instead, it resembles a can of the decorator variety whose origin is India or some other Far Eastern nation.

The other two versions of the foo can are shaped like oversized soup cans and as a result do not appear to be pieces of magical apparatus. (The only difference between these two versions of the can is that one has a compartment to conceal a spring snake that can be released at the clown's discretion.) They are, however, usually painted with bright colors that announce loudly to an audience, "This is not an ordinary can." The clown can remedy this by repainting the can or by pasting the label from another can over the garish surface of the rigged one.

The foo can can be used by the clown to duplicate a bit of business that is usually seen only in movies or on television. The clown uses the can to transport water from the sink to a cup. When he tries to fill the cup, nothing comes out of the can. Nothing comes out, that is, until he takes the cup away from the can. Then water streams forth. As soon as the cup is replaced beneath the can, the water stops. This can be repeated several times, depending on the amount of water in the foo can. To accomplish this special effect, the clown only has to rotate his hand forward or backward a fraction of an inch.

Canes   Five types of canes are currently on the market. Each can accomplish a specific effect. One cane can seemingly appear from nowhere. Another can vanish. A third can change color. Number four can transform itself into a beautiful bouquet. The fifth and most recent model can dance. Any of them can be adapted to a clown routine.

The appearing cane can be pulled from an incredibly small box or from the clown's pocket. It permits the clown to be stylish at the drop of a hat and is an excellent incidental bit of business. As a living cartoon character, the clown should be able to do the improbable every now and again.

The vanishing cane can give the clown a springboard into a lengthy sketch. One clown gives a second clown his very expensive cane to hold. No sooner does the second clown have the cane in his hands than he stumbles. The cane dissolves into ribbons, and the fight is on. The day may be saved by using the appearing cane, or the disappearance of the cane might lead to "The Clown Chase."

As an incidental bit, the color-changing cane may be used by the clown who wants to color coordinate his wardrobe. Decked out in red or white, the clown may decide that a black cane is unsuitable, so he flicks his wrist and makes everything match. Similarly, the cane-to-bouquet can be used by the clown who no longer has need of his cane.

Finally, the dancing cane is perfect for the clown who is satirizing the drinking man. As he staggers and reels across the stage, his cane can appear to be as tipsy as its master. It lurches away from him and back again. It forever evades the clown's grasp, but it never touches the floor. The dancing cane requires the most practice to use of all the canes, but it is fun to play with and well worth any effort put into learning its secret.

Coins Many coin effects can be used by clowns for walk around. Inflation has made small change a laugh riot. Available to the clown are large coins three inches in diameter and microminiature coins like the Nixon penny. These coins are sold with routines that can be used almost verbatim by the clown.

Devil's Napkin This effect can be used by the tramp clown for a little bit of lighthearted insanity. The tramp enters with the devil's napkin tied to a pole. He mimes hunger and opens the napkin to reveal it empty. Sadly, he turns to go when he spots an egg on the ground. Carefully, he puts the egg on a nearby crate. Then, folding the empty napkin, he reaches into it and withdraws a knife, fork, salt shaker, pepper shaker, and anything else that might be necessary for his meal. Finally, tucking the napkin into his collar, he absentmindedly sits on the egg. All of his preparations were for nothing.

The devil's napkin is an easy trick to learn and can be found at any magic shop. It can be purchased in a variety of colors. If the color of the napkin matches the clown's wardrobe, all the better. Any item on stage that seems out of place will attract the audience's attention and suspicion.

Flik-flik The coloring book or stamp album effect makes an excellent walk-around stunt. Flik-flik by Emerson and West is the ultimate achievement of this effect. Basically, the clown flicks through the pages of a book several times. Each time he does, the contents of the book change. The first time the pages of the book may be filled with drawings. The second time, the pages might be blank. Flik-flik contains six different changes plus a wonderful story if the clown uses an English accent. However, the story can be easily altered to fit any nationality, and the effect can be performed with very little practice.

Foo News Operating on the same principle as the foo can, Foo News offers the extra advantage of not looking like a magic trick. Unfortunately, the version stocked by most magic shops is constructed from a Japanese newspaper, which destroys its credibility as an item picked up off the street. The clown would do well to buy the trick, break it down, and make his own from a local paper.

In performance, the clown pours some liquid into the paper. The liquid then vanishes or changes. Whatever happens to it, the clown must be able to justify his actions. He needs a reason for pouring the liquid into the paper. If the foo mechanism is already loaded with water, the clown, befuddled on a morning after, may accidentally read the coffeepot and pour the news. As a prop, the Foo News is just absurd enough to add to the clown's cartoon quality.

Funnel The comedy funnel has been used by magicians for many years. It is a contraption that looks like a funnel but doesn't work like one. Without putting anything into it, any liquid can be made to drain out of it. This violation of the natural order of things makes this effect a welcome addition to the world of the clown. While one clown is pouring some water into a container on one side of the stage, the liquid drains out of the funnel held by another clown on the other side of the stage.

Lota Bowl The lota has often been used by magicians as a running gag. A metal vase is shown empty. Mysteriously, it becomes filled with water, which is poured out. Later, it again becomes full. No matter how many times it is emptied, it continues to fill itself, much to the amazement of the performer and his audience. This effect can be used by the clown to milk an invisible cow. The clown selects a volunteer from the audience and teaches the volunteer how to milk the cow by grabbing its tail and pumping it up and down. Each time the volunteer pumps the imaginary tail of the invisible cow, the lota is emptied, having apparently been filled with milk. To make the deception more realistic, OOM, an oily substance that, when mixed with water, resembles milk, can be used to fill the bowl. OOM can be purchased at most magic shops.

Milk Pitcher This piece of apparatus permits the clown to pour milk from a filled pitcher into a paper cone or a borrowed hat. When the receptacle is turned over or crushed, the milk seems to have vanished. In fact, the milk never left the pitcher in the first place. This piece of specially constructed apparatus can be used by the clown in connection with the comedy funnel. One clown can appear to be pouring milk into a real funnel and have it come out of the trick funnel that another clown is holding.

Passe-Passe Bottles This effect consists of a bottle, a glass, and two cylinders that cover both objects. After the bottle and glass are shown, they are covered and somehow manage to change places. This is a perfect quandary for the inebriate clown. No matter which cylinder he picks up, he always gets the glass, while the bottle eludes him. A variation of this effect with multiplying bottles increases the madness of the situation.

Snake Box The snake box is an openly slapstick effect. It consists of an empty box that discharges a spring snake when anyone but the clown opens it. Since, this time, the trick is played on an audience member, the clown should be sure to choose someone who does not have a weak heart.

Square Circle In this effect, a box and cylinder are shown. Then, one at a time, the performer removes countless objects from the box. It is a standard piece of magic equipment and, as such, looks like a piece of magic equipment.

For the clown to make use of this effect, he must first alter its appearance. By repainting it gray and adding a false combination dial to the front of the box, it will resemble a safe. The addition of a hinged flap on the top of the box will aid the logic of the handling of the trick in performance.

A clown enters with a large wad of money. He opens the safe, holding up first the box and then the cylinder to see if they are secure. The money is then placed in the safe. To the audience, it seems as if the money is the only thing inside the box and cylinder. This done, the clown leaves. As soon as he is gone, a clown burglar enters and zeros in on the safe. He tries the combination but cannot break it. Not wanting to spend all night on the safe, the burglar brings out a massive stick of dynamite. (See the "Firecracker" sketch.) The safe is blown open, but the clown burglar finds anything but money. His thumb is caught in a giant rat trap; he discovers yesterday's laundry and comes face to whatever with a spring skunk. He flees the stage in confusion, chased by the skunk.

Tea Kettle   This is a simple effect that involves a tea kettle and food coloring. Each time the liquid in the kettle is poured into a glass, it is different. One time the liquid in the kettle is tea; another time, milk is poured. The clown is confused by the inconsistency of the container. Finally, after many glasses of many different liquids surround the clown, he looks into the kettle. He finds the kettle full of multicolored flowers and streamers and not a drop of water or any other liquid. The tea kettle is one of the many items in the clown's world that give him trouble by not acting as expected. This piece of apparatus can be a helpful tool for the inept clown butler or inefficient clown waiter. To perform this effect the clown needs to know how to pour liquid from a kettle into a glass and, as with all the other effects in this chapter, how to clown around.

18

The Actor
and the Fool

Comedy, according to Athene Seyler, is founded on truth. In fact, it is the truth unvarnished. Perhaps this is why comedy is sometimes considered tragedy's poorer cousin. It lacks the aesthetic ambiguity so often found in art. Tricking someone with a flower on a straw is more straightforward than the most symbolic scene in *King Lear,* but both deal with the subject of pride. And both are effective in their separate ways.

Like the tragedian, the clown employs the use of logic, movement, makeup, costumes, and characterization. Both must be sincere. But the clown must also be devious. Both have objectives. But the clown's objectives are oftentimes not what they at first appear to be. In effect, the tragedian reflects reality, while the clown must stand outside himself and reflect a distorted reality. This permits the clown the luxury of laughter.

The clown, in many ways, has a more difficult job than his dramatic counterpart, for to do his job, he must not try to do it. Nothing is less humorous than someone trying to be funny. Therefore, the clown must not try consciously to amuse his audience. Instead, he must believe in the reality of the absurd situations in which he finds himself. The "cat" that he holds is obviously a skunk, but he must believe for the moment that it is a cat. Otherwise, his audience will not try to convince him of his error. He will no longer be a clown but a sham.

To carry off his deceptions, he must constantly remind himself who he is, where he is, and what he wants. Then he must go after what he wants with sweeping absurdities until he arrives at his goal or misses it completely. This he must do effortlessly. Once in motion, he can not stop to give himself time to think. He must only do what must be done.

Stanislavski, the father of the method school of acting, realized this facet of the clowning art. He acknowledged the clown as a grotesque symbol of humanity and realized that the clown is not always funny. Sometimes the clown has something to say, and when he does, he says it. If people laugh at his serious moments, they do so only because he is a clown. Later, they will consider what he has said, and he will have made them think.

A number of techniques of acting can be used by the clown to prepare his sketches and routines for presentation. The list that follows can be invaluable in helping him find the humor in what he is doing:

Talk through the story of a sketch. This will establish the high points of the piece in his mind. Since most clown sketches are sketchy to begin with, the clown will have to improvise the details of the plot.

Establish the punch line. If the clown forgets the direction the sketch is supposed to take, he will fill the opening of the piece with extraneous bits and obscure the joke. Everything he does in the sketch must build to the punch line; otherwise, the clown will have defeated his purpose.

Establish the line of the action. With this set down, he can begin to embellish the piece, adding action to flesh out the story.

Block out the action. The clown must make sure that none of the performers in the sketch step on each others toes or lines and that the action flows from one performer to another. The timing of the bits can be set at this point by counting through and coordinating the movements.

Check the angles. This is to ensure that the audience can see all of the action. The clown who is carrying the action at each point of the plot must be in view.

Choose the tempo of the piece. Some sketches play faster, and some are better done slow. The clown must decide what speed best fits the sketch he is performing.

Set the tempo. This can be done by adding music to the sketch and running through it. The speed of the performance should be matched to the tempo of the music. This will also improve timing.

Set all the props and run through it in costume. Up to this point, the clown has simply been going through the motions, finding out where the objects he is to handle end up each time and getting a feel for the movement of the piece. Now he plays the sketch to see if the equipment he uses fits easily into the action. This applies only to equipment that must be set, like the rocket, camera, or fire alarm and engine.

Do it! Finally, the clown should not have to think about any of the preparations he has made. He should simply get up and play. If some parts of the sketch do not work, he must go back and run through them again immediately.

The important thing for the clown to always keep in mind is that when he performs a sketch, he is playing. He must, throughout his gesticulating and grimacing, whether he acts like a machine or a ballet dancer, remain childlike. He always should express the joy of discovery that can be found in a child with a new toy. Even if he is in the last degree undignified, he expresses life.

Appendix I

The following article on how to choose and handle audience members on stage was written by Tom Ogden, an innovative performer who has entertained audiences from New York City to Seattle. He is the coauthor of A Volunteer from the Audience. *Since Mr. Ogden is a magician, his remarks are slanted toward the presentation of magic, but they are equally applicable to the clown's performance. The article is included here by the author's permission.*

"For my next trick, I need the help of a volunteer from the audience." Instantly, dozens of hands shoot up ... or none. One spectator is chosen, or coerced, to come onto the stage. Why that one? Why an assistant from the audience at all?

The reasons for using volunteers are many and varied. First of all, a volunteer acts as a representative of the audience in the examination of props and attests to the fairness of everything on stage. As a result, each audience member feels more directly involved in the performance.

In many instances, the volunteer is the source of comedy in the show. The surprised reactions or naively innocent but humorous answers and actions made by the spectator almost always add to the overall effect of a routine, thereby increasing the reception and enjoyment by the audience.

Of lesser importance, an assistant might be used to speed up the pace of the show by helping with the props that would be unwieldy for the magician to handle alone.

Volunteers, then, should be used as often as possible to enhance the act. Certainly some types of performance, such as mentalism, escape magic, or hypnosis, necessitate audience participation.

In determining how often volunteers should be used in a

performance, it is essential that the entertainer honestly admit to himself how comfortable he feels when working with strangers. No spectators on stage at all is better than a volunteer misused or mistreated.

Every possible reaction to a given situation, or patter line, should be considered in the decision of what volunteer to select, if any. Some performers avoid inviting volunteers to assist for fear of being upstaged. While there is a legitimate possibility that an assistant might "ham it up" for his friends, the probability is that the volunteer will be quite passive until told what to do.

On the negative side, it is important that the volunteers never be allowed to slow down a performance: not every prop, especially those that appear ordinary, need be examined. For example, a spectator does not have to cut a rope if it is more easily done by a performer. A parade of spectators on and off the stage just for short, nonessential bits not only looks silly but slows down the show as well. Any stage wait is an interruption in the flow of a show, distracting the audience from the performer. Each such interruption must be weighed against the value of bringing a volunteer onstage.

It is best not to use a volunteer in any routine in which the performer wants to show skill or display manipulative dexterity. A volunteer will not only take attention away from the performer but may even be given credit for somehow secretly assisting him. As an example, even legitimate pickpocket acts are suspect of using stooges. Note, too, that in most magicians' coin-production routines the entertainer almost always plucks a dozen or so coins from the air before he begins to produce coins from the volunteer's pockets.

A volunteer should be brought onto the stage only when he will be directly involved in a routine or will improve the effect in some way. The spectator must have a valid reason for being onstage and should never be merely a casual observer.

The audience member is a guest onstage, and he must be treated with the courtesy that a guest deserves. He has allowed himself to be put into awkward, possibly even foolish or precarious positions, and the performer must not take advantage of that generosity. When the volunteer has finished his bits, he should not be ignored. As an additional courtesy, he should never be used as the butt of a joke or the scapegoat for any mistakes.

Not only must a volunteer be treated well, but once he is on stage, he becomes part of the show. While the audience may laugh at the volunteer's antics or empathize with his predicaments, in the end, the performer is responsible for the volunteer's reactions on stage.

The entertainer is also responsible for the safety of the spectator from the time the volunteer is pinpointed until he returns to his seat at the end of the trick. At no time should a volunteer be placed into a position of clear or present danger.

The performer should assist the volunteer onto the stage and should make it clear where he wants him to stand and what he wants him to do. Most of all, the entertainer must make the volunteer feel at ease. After the routine is over, the performer should thank the assistant and help him off the stage.

Only in the rarest of instances should the performer ask the committee that booked him to arrange for volunteers in advance. Such assistants are always suspected of being stooges. Volunteers should be preselected only if it will aid in the smooth running of the show or if it would otherwise be difficult or impossible to get the assistants onstage. Some possible conditions that warrant prearrangement might be the following: a platform without stairs to allow the volunteers to get on stage easily; a stage far removed from the audience, such as in a grandstand situation; a club date where the house is darkened so that the spotlighted performer can not see into the audience; an audience whose members the performer knows are too shy to volunteer; conversely, one in which everyone wants to volunteer and would run onstage; an elderly or handicapped audience for whom coming onstage would be an inconvenience.

After many performances, an entertainer will be able to establish certain "types" of volunteers for each routine. While there are no hard and fast rules in the selection of audience volunteers, it is possible to set up certain guidelines and general principles:

1. Pick audience members who smile: If the spectator is smiling during other routines, chances are he would enjoy being part of the fun. This enjoyment usually indicates that he will be willing to please and cooperate with a performer.

2. Call on neat, attractive people: To reiterate, once the spectator is on stage, he becomes part of the act. It is to the performer's advantage to be surrounded by assistants who are handsome, clean, and fresh in appearance. This is not to say that a performer must select only "beauties," merely that the volunteer's

appearance should not bring offense to any of the other audience members.

3. Pick volunteers of the right age for the props or effects: Card tricks, for example, generally should not be done with children who might not know the names of cards or have been warned not to play cards by their parents. Conversely, adult audiences are not suitable for rhyming or Mother Goose patter.

4. Pick volunteers of the right sex for the props or effects: Men, as a general rule, look better to the audience handling cards and cigarettes. Women appear more graceful handling silks and flowers.

5. Begin the mental selection of volunteers as soon as the curtains part: Start the show with a solo bit or one in which definite reactions from a volunteer are not necessary. While performing this bit, scan the faces of the audience for future assistants. Know in advance exactly how many and what types of volunteers are needed for which effects and begin looking for them immediately.

Perhaps the most prevalent myth in entertainment is the existence of the "Perfect Audience." No matter how flawless an audience may seem, the discriminating performer realizes that it is impossible to connect with each individual in a crowd on a one to one basis.

A silent audience can be terrifying, particularly for an entertainer who judges his performance by the amount of response he receives. Different cultures and ages react more quietly than others. One audience may be mentally challenging the performer to entertain them, while another may expect a serious show and believe that silence is the proper form of appreciation. The audience might actually be in awe of the performance or the entertainer and therefore react more quietly.

A shift in material will sometimes warm up stone-faced spectators. Move the routines that get the best response in laughter or applause to an earlier spot in the show. Depending on the type of show, repetition of magic words, clapping, or singing along almost guarantees some sort of response from the audience.

Inane remarks such as "Is this an audience or a jury?" "I know you're out there; I can hear you breathing," and "It was nothing; I can tell by the applause," while clever to the performer, are not to the people in the seats. In fact, such remarks might possibly discourage responses by increasing audience hostility.

A noisy audience is a far more common problem. Children, especially, have a tendency to immediately talk to their neighbors as soon as an idea occurs to them. Every act needs silent moments to break up the general noise level of the show, whether between tricks, between laughs, or during truly suspenseful moments. These quiet moments become rest periods for the audience and help prevent their becoming tired or overpowered early in the show.

One of the best ways to quiet an audience is simply to stand still and wait until they silence themselves, much in the manner of a principal who waits at the microphone at the beginning of an assembly program before speaking. Another old trick to avoid having to ask the audience to "Please quiet down" is to speak in a low voice or not use the microphone; soon the audience will stop talking in order to hear what the performer is saying.

The greatest problem in any audience is the heckler. Isolated catcalls are common and even to be expected in some magicians' acts. After all, magic often tends to be a challenge to "figure it out." One type of effect, the so-called "sucker trick," actually depends on loud response to be successful. The seeming rowdiness must be controlled to the performer's advantage.

Heckling might range from the often-heard "I've seen it before" and "I know how it's done" to personal attacks on the performer. In most cases, when a child yells, "I've seen it before," he is not saying that he does not want to see the trick again. He is merely telling the performer that he is familiar with the routine, possibly that it is one of his favorites. The shouts can be handled with gentle comments such as "I've seen it before, too." If the child becomes persistent, the magician might say, "All right, close your eyes and don't watch," or he might start to put the trick away. This ploy usually results in the rest of the audience crying out that they want to see the trick.

"I know how it's done" is best answered with "Ssh, don't tell; it will be our secret," thereby making the child feel special, a knowing assistant. Replying with a bubbly "So do I" also stops this heckle line.

Verbal attacks on the performer and his ability are much harder to deal with. Entire books have been written on "heckler stoppers," one liners to embarrass and thereby quiet the loud-mouthed spectator.

Unfortunately, heckler stoppers seldom, if ever, succeed. Instead, they tend to goad the attention seeker to greater putdowns until the show becomes a verbal battle of wits. The audience and the show are the losers in such a battle since the performer must lower himself and the act to the heckler's level.

As a general rule, heckling should be ignored whenever possible. Usually, the heckler will tire of drawing no reaction or will be silenced by the rest of the audience. If the heckling continues and must be acknowledged, the heckler should be quieted gently, perhaps by asking him to allow the rest of the audience to enjoy the show. After all, the heckler is usually only seeking attention and will stop once that notice has been received. Under no circumstances should the heckler be brought onstage to try to quiet him. He would not liven up the act. The end result could only be chaos and a spoiled performance.

As an added note, if a volunteer turns out to be a terror, is uncooperative, or "hams it up" once he is on stage, do not try to outdo his antics. Finish the routine quickly, ignoring the assistant's interruptions as well as you can and rush him back to his seat. Only under the most extreme circumstances should a volunteer be sent back to his seat before the completion of an effect: This reflects badly on the performer's ability to work with the audience.

Once the decision is made to use audience volunteers, the entertainer's ability to handle them is of paramount importance. If this is done well, the volunteer, in effect, brings the audience in direct contact with the entertainer. Each spectator can feel that he is the person helping onstage. The ability to select and utilize volunteers takes patience and practice to develop properly, but once acquired, it can add a new and human dimension to any act.

Appendix II: Directory

The clown, novice and veteran, will find the following collection of addresses helpful. The few that have been included in the text are reprinted here for easy reference.

CLUBS

Clowns of America
717 Beverly Road
Baltimore, Maryland 21222

International Brotherhood of Magicians
28 North Main Street
Kenton, Ohio 43326

The Shriners' clown club is open only to members of that group. Members of this club can often be found volunteering their time to perform for charitable institutions. Anyone interested in contacting this group can receive information through their local Shrine.

EQUIPMENT

Flosso Hornmann Magic Company
304 West 34th Street
New York, New York 10001

Illusion House
2617 Herr Street
Harrisburg, Pennsylvania 17103

Louis Tannen, Incorporated
1540 Broadway
New York, New York 10017

PERIODICALS

Amusement Business
1 Astor Plaza
New York, New York 10036

Calliope
717 Beverly Road
Baltimore, Maryland 21222

Genii
Box 36068
Los Angeles, California 90036

The Magic Magazine
801 Second Avenue
New York, New York 10036

The New Tops
Abbott's Magic Manufacturing Company
Colon, Michigan 49040

PUPPET PEOPLE

Poko Puppets
c/o Larry Englar
12 Everit Street
Brooklyn, New York 11201

Puppet Productions, Incorporated
Post Office Box 82008
San Diego, California 92138

SCHOOLS

New York School of Circus Arts
36 Lispenard Street
New York, New York 10013

Clown College
Ringling Brothers and Barnum & Bailey Circus
Post Office Box 1528
Venice, Florida 33595

TRAINED DOGS

Paul Hoskinson
Post Office Box 113
Seville, Ohio 44273

ANY LAST-MINUTE QUESTIONS

Toby Sanders
R.D. 1
Abbottstown, Pennsylvania 17301

Glossary

ad-lib *(n.)*   A spur-of-the-moment improvisation.
ad-lib *(v.)*   To improvise.
alley *(n.)*   Short for clown alley.
amateur *(n.)*   Someone who performs solely for the fun of it.
bit *(n.)*   1. An individual gag within a sketch. 2. Short for *bit of business.*
character *(n.)*   The performer's identity as perceived by the audience.
clown *(v.)*   To perform as a clown.
clown alley *(n.)*   A group of clowns.
clowning *(n.)*   The act of performing as a clown.
comedy *(n.)*   That which is funny.
gimmick *(v.)*   To add a hidden property to any ordinary object.
harlequinade *(n.)*   A grand chase at the end of a sketch that makes use of every character in the piece.
humor *(n.)*   The lighthearted way of dealing with the world.
milk *(v.)*   To put the audience in a position that demands a desired response.
out *(n.)*   An alternative used by a performer to *get him out of* any undesired situation that confronts him while on stage.
professional *(n.)*   A performer who receives more than 50 percent of his income from entertaining.
role *(n.)*   The part assigned to a performer's character within a sketch.
routine *(n.)*   A collection of related sketches into an integrated whole.
semiprofessional *(n.)*   Someone who receives less than 50 percent of his income from performing.
set *(n.)*   The scenery or backdrop used by the performer.

set *(v.)* To make ready.

sketch *(n.)* A short humorous play that sometimes uses a collection of related bits.

slapstick *(n.)* 1. The most physical kind of comedy. 2. A special stick that produces a loud noise in imitation of someone being hit.

stock *(adj.)* Standard.

style *(v.)* 1. To acknowledge the audience. (One or both arms are raised to the side above shoulder height to accept the applause.) 2. To point to another performer with a flourish in deference to his skill.

switch *(v.)* To adapt another person's material with the intention of making it one's own.

take *(n.)* A physical aside that designates either comprehension or confusion.

walk around *(n.)* A portion of the show during which the clowns go out almost into the audience to perform; the time reserved for the clowns to display their individual abilities.

wit *(n.)* Verbal humor that pokes fun at the paradoxical similarities and dissimilarities of objects and ideas.

Bibliography

Adamson, Joe. *Tex Avery: King of Cartoons.* New York: Popular Library, 1975.

Allen, Fred. *Fred Allen's Letters.* Edited by Joe McCarthy. New York: Pocket Books, Inc., 1966.

Allen, Steve. *Bigger Than a Breadbox.* New York: Paperback Library, 1968.

Allen, Woody. *Getting Even.* New York: Warner Books, 1972.

———. *Without Feathers.* New York: Warner Books, 1972.

Andrews, Bart. *Lucy and Ricky and Fred and Ethel.* New York: E. P. Dutton and Co. Inc., 1976.

Anobile, Richard J., ed. *A Flask of Fields.* New York: Crown Publishers, 1972.

———. *Godfrey Daniels.* New York: Crown Publishers, 1975.

———. *Hooray for Captain Spaulding.* New York: Avon Books, 1975.

———. *Who's on First?* New York: Avon Books, 1972.

———. *Why a Duck?* New York: Darien House, Inc., 1971.

Aristotle. *Rhetoric and Poetics.* Translated by Martin Ostwald. New York: Random House, 1954.

Barnum, P. T. *The Life of P. T. Barnum.* New York: Redfield Publishers, 1855.

Benchley, Nathaniel, ed. *The Benchley Roundup.* New York: Dell Publishing Co., 1954.

Bergson, Henri. *The Creative Mind.* New York: Citadel Press, 1946.

Bergson, Henri, and Meredith, George. *Comedy.* New York: Doubleday and Co., 1956.

Bettelheim, Bruno. *The Uses of Enchantment: The Meaning and Importance of Fairy Tales.* New York: Random House, 1975.

Bishop, Morris, ed. *Treasury of British Humor.* New York: Coward-McCann, Inc., 1942.

Bodkin, B. A., ed. *A Treasury of American Anecdotes.* New York: Crown Publishers, 1957.

Boles, Don. *Midway Magic.* Atlanta, Ga.: Pinchpenny Press, 1963.

———. *The Midway Showman.* Atlanta, Ga.: Pinchpenny Press, 1967.

Boleslavsky, Richard. *Acting: The First Six Lessons.* New York: Theatre Arts Books, 1975.

Boll, Heinrich. *The Clown.* New York: Avon Books, 1965.

Bradbury, Ray. *Zen and the Art of Writing.* Santa Barbara, Calif.: Capri Press, 1973.

Briarton, Grendel. *The Compleat Feghoot.* Baltimore, Md.: Mirage Press, 1975.

Camus, Albert. *The Myth of Sisyphus and Other Essays.* New York: Random House, 1955.

Carlo. *The Juggling Book.* New York: Random House, 1974.

Castenada, Carlos. *Tales of Power.* New York: Pocket Books, 1976.

Cavett, Dick (with Porterfield, Christopher). *Cavett.* New York: Bantam Books, 1974.

Cerf, Bennett, ed. *An Encyclopedia of Modern American Humor.* New York: Doubleday and Co., Inc., 1954.

Chaplin, Charles. *My Autobiography.* New York: Pocket Books, 1966.

Checkov, Michael. *To the Actor.* New York: Harper and Row, Publishers, 1953.

Claflin, Edward. *Street Magic.* New York: Doubleday and Co., Inc., 1977.

Copi, Irving M. *Introduction to Logic.* New York: The Macmillan Publishing Co., 1968.

Crockett, David. *Colonel Crockett's Exploits and Adventures in Texas.* New York: Nafis and Cornish, 1836.

Daniels, Les. *Comix.* New York: Bonanza Books, 1971.

Deleon, Walter, and Martin, Francis. *Tillie and Gus.* New York: Simon and Schuster, 1973.

Disher, M. Willson. *Clowns and Pantomimes.* New York: Benjamin Blom, Inc., 1968.

Duchartre, Pierre Louis. *The Italian Comedy.* New York: Dover Publications, Inc., 1966.

Eastman, Max. *Enjoyment of Laughter.* New York: Simon and Schuster, 1936.

Egri, Lajos. *The Art of Creative Writing.* New York: Citadel Press, Inc., 1965.

——. *The Art of Dramatic Writing.* New York: Simon and Schuster, 1960.

Fields, W. C. *W. C. Fields: His Intended Autobiography.* New York: Warner Paperback Library, 1974.

Finch, Christopher. *The Art of Walt Disney.* New York: Harry N. Abrams, Inc., 1973.

Firestone, Ross, ed. *Breaking It Up.* New York: Bantam Books, 1975.

Fitzkee, Dariel. *Showmanship for Magicians.* Oakland, Calif.: Magic Ltd., 1945.

Freud, Sigmund. *Jokes and Their Relation to the Unconscious.* Edited and translated by James Strachey. New York: W. W. Norton and Co., Inc., 1960.

——. *On Creativity and the Unconscious.* Edited by Benjamin Nelson. New York: Harper and Row, Publishers, 1958.

Gasset, Ortega y. *Meditations on Quixote.* New York: W. W. Norton and Co., Inc., 1963.

Ghiselin, Brewster, ed. *The Creative Process.* New York: The New American Library, Inc., 1952.

Gilbert, Douglas. *American Vaudeville.* New York: Dover Publications, Inc., 1968.

Goldberg, Rube. *Rube Goldberg vs. the Machine Age.* Edited by Clark Kinnard. New York: Hastings House, Publishers, 1968.

Hagen, Uta, and Frankel, Haskel. *Respect for Acting.* New York: Macmillan Publishing Co., 1973.

Hawes, Bill. *The Puppet Book.* San Francisco, Calif.: Beta Books, 1977.

Hay, Henry. *The Amateur Magician's Handbook.* New York: The New American Library, 1972.

——. *Learn Magic.* New York: Dover Publications, Inc., 1975.

Haycraft, Howard, ed. *The Art of the Mystery Story.* New York: Grosset and Dunlap, 1947.

Herrigel, Eugen. *Zen in the Art of Archery.* New York: Vintage Books, 1973.

Hethman, Robert H., ed. *Strasberg at the Actors Studio.* New York: Viking Press, 1965.

Hope, Bob. *Have Tux, Will Travel.* New York: Pocket Books, 1955.

Huber, Jack. *Through an Eastern Window.* New York: Bantam Books, 1968.

Hurrt, Margaret, trans. *The Complete Grimm's Fairy Tales*. New York: Random House, 1972.

Huxley, Laura Archera. *Between Heaven and Earth*. New York: Avon Books, 1975.

Ionesco, Eugene. *Notes and Counter Notes*. New York: Grove Press, 1964.

Jacobs, Joseph. *Celtic Fairy Tales*. New York: World Publishing Co., 1971.

Jeeves, Mahatma Kane (Fields, W. C.). *The Bank Dick*. New York: Simon and Schuster, 1973.

Kalmar, Bert, and Ruby, Harry. *Duck Soup*. New York: Simon and Schuster, 1972.

Kaufman, George S., and Ryskind, Morrie. *A Night at the Opera*. New York: Viking Press, 1972.

Kaye, Marvin. *The Stein and Day Handbook of Magic*. New York: Stein and Day Publishers, 1975.

Ketchum, Richard M. *Will Rogers*. New York: Simon and Schuster, 1973.

Koestler, Arthur. *The Act of Creation*. New York: Dell Publishing Co., Inc., 1964.

———. *Insight and Outlook*. Lincoln, Neb.: The University of Nebraska Press, 1949.

Kopp, Sheldon B. *If You Meet Buddha on the Road, Kill Him*. New York: Bantam Books, 1976.

Kunzog, John C. *The One Horse Show*. Jamestown, N.Y.: John C. Kunzog, 1962.

———. *Tanbark and Tinsel*. Jamestown, N.Y.: John C. Kunzog, 1970.

Lahr, John. *Notes on a Cowardly Lion*. New York: Ballantine Books, 1970.

Laurie, Joe, Jr. *Vaudeville: From the Honky-tonks to the Palace*. New York: Henry Holt and Co., 1953.

Lax, Eric. *On Being Funny: Woody Allen and Comedy*. New York: Manor Books, Inc., 1977.

Leacock, Stephen. *Humor: Its Theory and Technique*. New York: Dodd, Mead and Co., 1935.

Lewis, Robert. *Method—or Madness*. New York: Samuel French, Inc., 1958.

Marx, Harpo, and Barker, Richard. *Harpo Speaks!* New York: Freeway Press, Inc., 1974.

Maskelyne, Nevil. *Maskelyne on the Performance of Magic*. New York: Dover Publications, Inc., 1976.

May, Rollo. *The Courage to Create*. New York: W. W. Norton and Co., Inc., 1975.

McCabe, John. *The Comedy World of Stan Laurel*. London: Robson Books, 1975.

———. *Mr. Laurel and Mr. Hardy*. New York: The New American Library, 1966.

McCabe, John, and Kilgore, Al. *Laurel and Hardy*. New York: Ballantine Books, 1975.

McCay, Windsor. *Dreams of a Rarebit Fiend*. New York: Dover Publications, Inc., 1973.

———. *Little Nemo*. New York: Nostalgia Press, Inc., 1972.

McGarry, Mary. *Great Folktales of Old Ireland*. New York: Bell Publishing Co., 1972.

McVicar, Wes. *Clown Act Omnibus*. New York: Association Press, 1960.

Miller, Henry. *The Smile at the Foot of the Ladder*. New York: New Directions Publishing Co., 1966.

Nelms, Henning. *Magic and Showmanship*. New York: Dover Publications, Inc., 1969.

Neville, John T., and Chaplin, Prescott. *Never Give a Sucker an Even Break*. New York: Simon and Schuster, 1973.

Newcomb, Horace. *TV: The Most Popular Art*. New York: Anchor Books, 1974.

Nimoy, Leonard. *I Am Not Spock*. Millbrae, Calif.: Celestial Arts, 1975.

Nye, Russel B. *The Unembarrassed Muse: The Popular Arts in America*. New York: The Dial Press, 1970.

Orben, Robert. *Comedy Technique*. New York: Louis Tannen, 1951.

Perelman, S. J. and Johnston, Will B. *Monkey Business*. New York: Simon and Schuster, 1972.

Perrine, Laurence. *Story and Structure*. New York: Harcourt, Brace and World, Inc., 1966.

Pirosh, Robert, Seaton, George, and Oppenheimer, George. *A Day at the Races*. New York: Viking Press, 1964.

Plato. *Phaedrus*. Translated by W. C. Helmhold and W. G. Rabinowitz. New York: Bobbs-Merrill Co., Inc., 1975.

Polti, Georges. *The Thirty-six Dramatic Situations*. Boston: The Writer Inc., 1973.

Prather, Hugh. *Notes to Myself: My Struggle to Become a Person*. New York: Bantam Books, 1976.

Richter, Hans. *Dada: Art and Anti-art.* London: Thames and Hudson, 1970.

Rogers, Will. *The Autobiography of Will Rogers.* Edited by Donald Day. New York: Avon Books, 1975.

Rourke, Constance. *American Humor: A Study of the National Character.* New York: Doubleday and Co., Inc., 1953.

Senelick, Laurence. *A Cavalcade of Clowns.* San Francisco, Calif.: Bellerophon Books, 1977.

Sheehy, Gail. *Passages.* New York: E. P. Dutton and Co., Inc., 1974.

Sheridan, Martin. *Comics and Their Creators.* New York: Luna Press, 1971.

Sontag, Susan. *Against Interpretation.* New York: Dell Publishing Co., Inc., 1969.

Sorell, Walter. *Facets of Comedy.* New York: Grosset and Dunlap, 1972.

Stadelman, Paul. *Ventriloquism Plus Television Ticklers.* Chicago, Ill.: Magic Inc., 1966.

———. *For Ventriloquists Only.* Chicago, Ill.: Magic Inc., 1966.

Stanislavski, Constantin. *An Actor Prepares.* New York: Theatre Arts Books, 1967.

———. *Building a Character.* New York: Theatre Arts Books, 1971.

———. *Creating a Role.* New York: Theatre Arts Books, 1968.

———. *My Life in Art.* New York: Theatre Arts Books, 1952.

———. *Stanislavski's Legacy.* Edited by E. R. Hapgood. New York: Theatre Arts Books, 1968.

———. *Stanislavski on the Art of the Stage.* Edited by David Magarshack. New York: Hill and Wang, 1961.

Sutherland, James. *The Oxford Book of Literary Anecdotes.* New York: Pocket Books, 1976.

Sutton, Felix. *The Big Show.* New York: Doubleday and Co., Inc., 1971.

———.*The Book of Clowns.* New York: Grosset and Dunlap, 1968.

Tolstoy, Leo. *What is Art.* New York: Bobbs-Merrill Co., Inc., 1960.

Towsen, John. *Clowns.* New York: Hawthorne Press, 1976.

Trudeau, G. B. *The Doonesbury Chronicles.* New York: Holt, Rinehart and Winston, 1975.

Twain, Mark. *The Autobiography of Mark Twain.* Edited by Charles Nieder. New York: Harper and Row, Inc., 1966.

Vernon, P. E. *Creativity.* Baltimore, Md.: Penguin Books, Inc., 1975.

Wertham, Fredric, M. D. *Seduction of the Innocent.* New York: Holt, Rinehart and Winston, 1954.

Weston, Jessie L. *From Ritual to Romance.* New York: Doubleday and Co., Inc., 1957.

White, E. B., and White, K. S. *A Sub-treasury of American Humor.* New York: Coward-McCann, Inc., 1941.

Wilde, Larry. *The Great Comedians.* New York: Citadel Press, 1973.

———. *How the Great Comedy Writers Create Laughter.* Chicago, Ill.: Nelson-Hall, 1976.

Wiley, Jack. *Basic Circus Skills.* Harrisburg, Pa.: Stackpole Books, 1974.

Willette, Allen. *These Top Cartoonists Tell How They Create America's Favorite Comics.* Fort Lauderdale, Fla.: Allied Publications, Inc., 1964.

Wylie, Max. *Writing for Television.* Chicago, Ill.: Henry Regnery Co., 1970.

Index